ENIGM

Published by Landmark Books Pte Ltd

ISBN 978-981-18-8806-9

Printed by Oxford Graphic Printers Pte Ltd

ENIGMAS

TAY SEOW HUAH, MY FATHER,
SINGAPORE'S PIONEER SPY CHIEF

Simon Tay

·LANDMΔRK· BOOKS·

To

My son, Luke Tay Jun Yong,
and my nephews, Guan Yang Yue,
Guan Yang Sheng and Guan Yang Ze,
grandsons who never knew
their grandfather.

Magni Nominis Umbra

CONTENTS

Foreword 11

Introduction: Biography, Memory & Imagination 15

1 The *Laju* Incident 27

2 Childhood & Family 82

3 Young Man Going Fast 117

4 The Rising Path 150

5 Spy Chief 179

6 "Progress for Our Nation" 227

7 Senior Civil Servant 255

8 Endings 286

9 Coda: Conversations, Memory & Imagination 322

Chronology of Key Events 348

Selected Bibliography 354

FOREWORD

WHEN SIMON FIRST TOLD ME he was writing a book on his father, I thought he was very brave. However, in order not to discourage him, I did not convey my feelings to him. I believed that his father, like other important pioneer generation public servants, deserved to have a book published about him.

It would have been so easy for Simon to slip into filial sentimentality and become over-defensive or over-protective about his father. On the other hand, he could have tried to compensate for his feelings, sentiments or emotions by cutting out personal anecdotes and focusing on the historical context. This would have resulted in a less interesting read. Having read the entire final draft of the book, I am happy to say that Simon has made an excellent job of balancing emotions with objectivity. In describing his father's strengths and achievements, Simon has not failed to mention Seow Huah's flaws and vulnerabilities.

I was keen to read about Seow Huah because he was my first boss when I joined the public service in 1970. My privilege of working under him was, however, short-lived. After only about a year, he went off overseas on a course and thereafter was promoted to Permanent Secretary (Home Affairs). But I stayed on in the Security and Intelligence Division (SID), which he started, for 24 years. My knowledge of Seow Huah was primarily second-hand, from those who knew him better, like Dr Goh Keng Swee, S R Nathan and my SID colleagues who had worked more closely and longer with him.

Simon's book gives a thorough coverage of Seow Huah's achievements. I can vouch for several assessments he makes, because they were consistent with what I heard about Seow Huah. First, Seow Huah's superior intellect and leadership ability. Then PM Lee Kuan Yew and Dr Goh clearly valued his analysis of geopolitical events and trusted his judgement. Second, his steady and calm attitude, especially during a crisis. This must have been the reason why Lee Kuan Yew entrusted the handling and coordination of the *Laju* Incident to Seow Huah. Simon was correct to bring out more prominently his father's key role in that crisis. He may not have led the Singapore hostage group to Kuwait, but he was the one who had to ensure that Singapore had a coherent strategy. He had to deal with the complicated and complex task of leading the whole Singapore team in negotiating with the attackers, managing the media and difficult foreign stakeholders like the Japanese, and anticipating and reacting to sudden changes, as well as keeping our political leaders properly briefed. Third, Seow Huah's ability to start an organisation from scratch and with limited resources, learning quickly from foreign friends like the Israelis, and bring it to a stage where it could take off and grow. Without Seow Huah, Singapore would not have been able to understand the intentions and capabilities of our antagonists in its early years as a nation. We owe him a great debt for his work in safeguarding Singapore's security and starting our external intelligence service – our first line of defence.

I find comments by other people about Seow Huah less compelling. It is true that among all the Directors of SID we have had, Seow Huah was the one who comes closest to the popular misconception of a spy chief, viz. James Bond. He wore dark glasses, he owned and drove fast cars, and he was handsome and attractive to women. But he, and other SID officers, never shot and killed his foes in the course of their work. Simon says that his father preferred John Le Carré to Ian Fleming. But I would say that even Le Carré oversimplified the motivations of spy chiefs and tended to unfairly depict their worst traits and weaknesses. Seow Huah was neither James Bond nor George Smiley.

Seow Huah died too young (at 47). If he had survived another two or three decades, Singapore would have benefitted much more from the contributions of this outstanding pioneer public servant and patriot.

Eddie Teo
Former Director of the Security and Intelligence Division, and Internal Security Department, Singapore

INTRODUCTION

BIOGRAPHY, MEMORY & IMAGINATION

THERE IS WISDOM in the advice that we consider our obituaries. This is what is said in the encyclopedic Singapore National Library Board e-resources about Tay Seow Huah who died in September 1980, aged 47:

"Prior to his retirement in 1976, he was… a senior civil servant who served at various times as Director of Special Branch, Director of Security and Intelligence Division, Permanent Secretary (Home Affairs) and Permanent Secretary (Defence). He was awarded the prestigious Meritorious Service Award in 1967 and Eisenhower Fellowship in 1971. He also headed the government team that dealt with the *Laju* hijacking in 1974."

This man was my father. On 23 April 2020, on what would have been his 87th birthday, I did a social media post with four photos from the latter half of the 1960s. One of him at his desk in 1965 as Director of Special Branch; of his security pass badge numbered 0001, probably as the first director of the Singapore's Security and Intelligence Division; of him at a packed press conference as he dealt with the terrorist attack known as the *Laju* Incident; and of him on a trip abroad, at a formal reception, shaking hands with a man who looks like a very eminent Thai. In response to that anniversary post, some who knew him suggested then that I should write a biography. I had considered such an undertaking, and more than once. There are reasons to do so.

The generation that Tay Seow Huah belonged to is now

acclaimed as the "pioneers" of Singapore. Their contributions and sacrifices are recognised by specific government schemes and special assistance. The number of biographies and memoirs from that generation grow, by and about the top government leaders and leading businessmen. The government plans for a Founders' Memorial. Writing about my father could add to the record of those pioneers. Like many of that generation, he made a personal choice to commit to Singapore and to give much of his work and life to public service.

He was involved with events that are of historical record for the newly independent Singapore and for its security. Of these, the most prominent event was the *Laju* Incident – when international terrorist networks bombed the oil refinery on Pulau Bukom island and then tried to escape. This had been headline news at the time, not only in the Singapore but across much of the world. Yet, it is now forgotten among most of the current generation. So, too, are other storms of that era – the threat of Communism, merger with and separation from Malaysia, Konfrontasi by Indonesia, the Cold War and the US war in Vietnam – that set the critical conditions for early Singapore and his work in security and intelligence.

The current generation can have the convenience of confining these circumstances to a distant history. This is because the pioneers were largely successful; able to respond to these multiple and complex challenges, and keep our country secure, stable and set on a path to move ahead. Things have settled. The same cannot be said of other countries who became independent at around the same time; they seem captive to turbulence. Yet, even if the present for Singapore is stable, there may still be experiences that could be of use in addressing forces of change which are unfolding – globally, regionally and within our country – today and into the future. The specific issues may differ but the need remains to keep the spirit of resolve and response.

There are also personal reasons to write about Tay Seow Huah, my father. We all owe debts to our parents, but we may struggle to truly understand them. I was only 19 when my father died, doing my National Service and not even certain what I would study at university. In the 40-plus years since, some of what I have tried to do in my own life has drawn inspiration from my father, while others are perhaps things we might have disagreed upon. For my own son, Luke, born in late 1997, he never knew his grandfather who had died many years before. There have been some anecdotes shared over a dining table but little more.

I have therefore ventured to write the life of Tay Seow Huah for these reasons, and along these themes: as Spy Chief, Pioneer and Father. So why did I ever hesitate?

Time, Secrets, Memories

There are general challenges to biography and there are special ones relating to one about Tay Seow Huah. These, in sum, relate to time, secrets and the limits of memory.

Consider again these words in this book's subtitle: Spy Chief, Pioneer, Father. Each one reveals a specific role played by Tay Seow Huah and each also represents an obstacle to knowing him. A Spy Chief works with secrets and his work is kept secret. A Pioneer lived in conditions that have now changed and are quite beyond the understanding of the succeeding generations. A Father is so close a relative that a son may struggle to be sufficiently objective, and is thus well-advised to respect his privacy.

This is especially because, in a biography, the effort must be not only to describe but to explain; not just what happened but why. It is difficult to take account of motives and factors even with people who are alive and with whom we can ask to explain; what more when it is 40-plus years since his death, and many others of his generation who knew him well have also passed.

In these decades, moreover, Singapore has developed rapidly. While this is largely for the better, the success and speed of change cover over our beginnings and foundations of what was; like a grand skyscraper built – as many are in Singapore – on what was previously a much smaller and humbler building or vacant land or even sea. The present often has no memory of what was before and the past is a different country. The Singapore of the 1960s and 1970s, the time of Tay Seow Huah's public service, was a very different nation.

There is an additional and central issue to writing his biography that stems from the nature of his public service: his work was focused on security, defence and intelligence and the fundamental nature of this sector is secretive. While my father could be quite garrulous in a social setting, in matters of work he was discreet. Shortly before he died, he was interviewed by Singapore's Oral History Unit, then a relatively new undertaking. He had to be encouraged to speak for posterity and assured that access to the recordings would be limited. Yet, listening to the recordings, there are areas where he seems to hedge and say less than all there is. Moreover, because of his early and quite sudden death, only a few recordings were made and these hardly covered the start of his career.

I bumped into this issue of secrecy in 2015, when the Security and Intelligence Division of the government was making preparations to mark its 50th anniversary in the next year. A commemorative book was planned for the occasion (appropriately in limited edition and for restricted circulation only). My father had served as the founding Director for Security and Intelligence of the then Ministry of Interior and Defence, from 1966-1970, and so his successor approached me to write an essay about him. The period of his service was a long time ago, when our country was young and I was a child.

I asked if they might help by making available archival information and help me to touch base with his contemporaries and those who served with him. Most, if not all, had retired but more than a few were still alive. They agreed and later reverted with some complimentary recollections about my father as a person and a boss, but nothing about what he or the security and intelligence agencies actually did in those years. This underscores the culture of confidentiality within the organisation. Not only is the current work held secret, which must be the case. Habits keep closed what happened more than

50 years ago.

Another factor of difficulty arose in writing about the personal life of Tay Seow Huah – or Sonnie as he was known to family and closer friends. Much is based on anecdotes of family tales and old gossip; things that cannot be properly called "history", as that term evokes a certain fact-checked veracity. I have spoken with some of his siblings who remain, and also contemporaries who knew him.

Recollections have grown uncertain with age and the passing of so much time. There are gaps and contradictions. What they tell me is sometimes inconsistent – not only between what one relative or friend said compared to another, but even between what the same person said some time ago when we first spoke and what he said subsequently. What they say is true, for them, to the best of their recollections, at the point in time of telling. But the stories we recount are subject to our selection and emphases of the time and the contexts.

The same is true of things I myself remember from my childhood, heard around the house: impossible to verify and not fully understood, as I was young then, or the memory has faded with the years. I have tried to capture these memories and, even as I have aimed for accuracy, am reminded of the literary concept of the "unreliable narrator".

In response to these challenges of time, secrecy and memory, what is offered as such is not entirely and strictly a biography and history. I have ventured to write this book with a different aim and diverse approaches that might, I hope, match the fact that while I am a lawyer and professor, trained to observe facts, I am also his son, and a writer. Perhaps, rather than biography, this may be better described as a personal memoir and creative non-fiction.

The research and writing suggest to me that there are real limits to what we may think we know of a person – even when that person is your father, and of a place – even in Singapore your home, and in time – even when these are decades in which you were alive, although a youth. For this reason, the title I have selected is *Enigmas*.

Structure, Approaches and Scope

This is a work of different parts and there are shifts in focus and method.

The book begins with the public service of Tay Seow Huah and specifically, the *Laju* Incident in 1974. This incident was in the headlines not only in Singapore but internationally, with implications for the global economy amidst the oil shocks and spate of terrorist attacks in that era. For Tay, it was a highpoint in the public recognition of his work in helping ensure the security of Singapore, when so much else of what he was involved with remained secret. There is a considerable amount of information about the *Laju* Incident that is available from different sources. I have sought to record these objectively to deal not just with differences of fact but also with how the events might be interpreted. This begins in the middle of things (what storytellers call *in medias res* structure). I have chosen to write this in the present tense to try to capture a sense of the immediacy and impact of the *Laju* Incident.

Chapters 2 and 3 then narrate Sonnie's beginnings and his personal life: his childhood during WWII in the north Malayan town of Taiping as well as his early adult years, when he came to Singapore to study at the then University of Malaya in Bukit Timah. His time in Singapore, including his courtship of a Peranakan girl from Katong – Cheong Keong Hin or, as he and other close friends would call her, Cecelia, is also related, as are his university days. Much of this draws from family stories as well as conversations with family members and those who knew him. There are contradictory accounts and gaps in his activities in this period, as well as a number of revelations. But what is more certain is that he was shaped by his times and circumstances: in the horrors and losses of war, the difficulties in post-Malaya and then in the rush towards the end of colonial rule.

In Chapters 4 and 5, Tay's early career in the civil service is described. During these years leading up to independence, he interacted closely with many of the characters who were critical to Singapore in that era. These include the political leaders, PM Lee Kuan Yew and Dr Goh Keng Swee, as well as George Bogaars and S R Nathan, who were among his closest colleagues in civil service in those years. He served at the Special Branch as its first director for an independent Singapore and then transformed that institution left by the British. A new Security and Intelligence Division was created, with the Internal Security Department, under the then unified Ministry of Interior and Defence. In writing about his public service, I have relied primarily on documents on the public record since Singapore does not routinely declassify older documents, as is the practice in some other countries. While I have tried to sort out the factual record, I have drawn dotted lines between them to try to guess at wider patterns. I have sought to adduce key issues which preoccupied Tay during the early years of Singapore, trace his development of a world view and set his thinking in the context of the nation's emerging security and foreign policy.

Chapter 6 then pauses to consider how his personal and family life interacted with the opportunities and the pressures of his public service. As Singapore stabilised and conditions improved, he hoped to see the improvements and progress as an individual. Tay lived his life voraciously and his energies applied not only to work but equally to his personal interests and pursuits. The relationship with his wife was, however, stressed in ways that would later result in estrangement. Their marriage is difficult to narrate and discuss truly and fairly as they are my parents; I have tried to be honest whilst still honouring them.

In Chapters 7 and 8, I return to his career and public service. During the *Laju* Incident, Tay was already serving as permanent secretary, the apogee for a civil servant and, in its aftermath, a high point in public recognition. However, he suffered a heart attack just months after. He survived and underwent a major and difficult surgery under a specialist in the USA. It was a scarring episode and his health and energy were impaired, never the same. He tried to cope but, soon after, he was retired on medical grounds. He struggled to find purpose in his new circumstances and, with time and a slow recovery, he found a degree of equanimity; things were looking up for him. However, further medical complications intervened that led to his death in 1980, at the age of 47 years old.

I close by offering some reflections and perspectives with a memoir that I wrote about him as my father, and then through the device of imagining myself in conversation with him. In this last part, a coda, fragments are captured from reports and writings that he left, as well as from my memory of how my father would talk. These conversations focus on three themes that run through and thread the different chapters. The first is of the security and stability of Singapore, a small country in a dynamic region and amidst shifting global order; primarily a political and strategic question. A second theme is of our progress as a people, as Singaporeans; primarily an enquiry about society and community. The third borders philosophy: to consider how we should live our lives.

People expecting a straight biography may protest. But although there are solid facts and dates within it, this book is not presented as a purely factual biography. I hope that this last section is not fabulation or fantastical conjecture, notwithstanding elements that go beyond the "plain facts", to get some of the essence of my father and my relationship with him. To assist the reader more keen on the facts per se, a time line of key events in Tay Seow Huah's life is presented.

If what I have written is to be placed within a wider history of our country and region, I suggest that it may at best be seen as a small jigsaw piece, in a much larger picture of many parts. Its edges connect to considerable themes of the return of the British after the Japanese Occupation of WWII and then their exit, and the beginning of post-colonial governance for Singapore and the years of merger and separation, leading to the first decade-plus of an independent Republic of Singapore. In particular, what I have written about my father – from research, memory and a degree of conjecture – relates to the security and politics of the first decade of our country, when there were imperatives to find stability and prosperity, amidst challenges generated from both within our society and from outside events and influences.

Acknowledgements and Dedication

What I have written is about one man's work and life in the context of the country and times. I do not intend that any credit ascribed to my father here should be read to minimise the contribution that others made. This relates to the considerable figures of our history, PM Lee Kuan Yew and Dr Goh Keng Swee and other figures who served as ministers and to whom Tay reported. There are also his colleagues, fellow pioneer-generation civil servants, especially George Bogaars and S R Nathan, who went on to serve as President of the Republic. Many of these figures have written their own memoirs and had biographies written of them, especially, of course, PM Lee. In this book, they are mentioned where their work and lives connected to Tay. But more, I wish to acknowledge the many colleagues who are mentioned only in passing or even left unnamed. I hope that what I write may be taken as one example of what this pioneer generation faced and how they responded, but I am unapologetic about keeping the focus on a single man.

In this regard, I recall, when my father died, the many who came to the memorial service. There included those who had served with him in different capacities and different ministries, institutions and committees. Even as they shared their commiserations and recollected interactions with my father and we thanked them for their time and thoughtfulness to come, neither I nor my family recognised many. That so vividly told me how many people had been in contact and in some way were involved in my father's life and also how so many gathered there collectively contributed to the life of the country. They were a remarkable generation that found a purpose in the making of Singapore. They are to be remembered and thanked, not only for the brilliance of a small handful but acknowledged for the contributions of so many others.

It is my hope that this memoir will be more than a family

project and a curiosity. I hope that what I have written may be of interest to some readers, including those who never knew my father or even heard of him before this. For even as I have written about one man who was my father, my hope is that different readers – from those interested in the politics and public life of the pioneer years to those more interested in lived or social histories – may find something of interest and use in their own lives today and into the future.

I also hope that my book acknowledges the limits we face in trying to understand a person from another time. He was Tay Seow Huah and Sonnie, and to me he was Dad. He was Spy Chief, Pioneer and Father. These names and titles reveal and also conceal. He was never a simple man, and lived an intense and often secret life, and those elements and complexities have increased the mysteries of character, times and circumstance, even as the stories are written and are told. What's more when the effort to understand and explain is made by his son, through the telescope of time past, respect and love, which distances even as we try to see clearly.

In the face of these challenges, I have found some comfort, a parallel. My father studied history and was careful with facts. Yet, in much of his work and life, he was always trying to gather and sift facts not only from public record but from what information people shared and the stories they told. In this, he must have faced many similar challenges to those I have faced in writing this: to discern fact from what was remembered or even fabricated intentionally, and to admit that the distinctions are slippery, even as you construct a narrative.

I wish to acknowledge and thank many people. Firstly, the friends and former colleagues and contemporaries of Tay, especially those who have made the effort to share some of their recollections with me. These include those whom I have come to know in the decades since my father passed on. They have been of great help. I wish to thank Eddie Teo for providing the Foreword of this book. He is the most appropriate person to do so. He was recruited into the intelligence services during my father's tenure, was later appointed Director, and spent his career in security, defence and intelligence.

Secondly, relatives who have shared stories with me whether specifically for this memoir or simply as stories told over a dining table about the "old days", in particular my father's brother, my uncle Jack Tay Seow Hor. Thirdly, I wish to also thank the National Archives of Singapore and *The Straits Times* for access to their archives and researchers who helped me extract from these materials. I especially acknowledge the historian Ang Cheng Guan, who first found the lecture that my father gave in 1971 that sets out in the public record much of his thinking of the trends and concerns facing Singapore in that period; I have used the material extensively in this book. Finally, I wish to thank those who read sections of the manuscript, especially Jin Hua, my wife, who read through it critically, and my publisher, Goh Eck Kheng, who has encouraged me with this project and helped me try to make it more than a personal enterprise.

I wanted to dedicate this book to my sister, Joanne Tay Siok Wan, the firstborn in our small family and the family archivist, with a memory far better than mine. She has helped me with this project from the start, to add, cajole, caution and suggest edits, and even when I have disagreed, I am grateful. In these many years since our father's passing, there was never a time I have not thought of him, and I know it is the same, if not more, for my sister. But I think it is most fitting that this book is dedicated to the next generation in our family: my son, Luke Tay Jun Yong, and my sister's children – Guan Yang Yue, Guan Yang Sheng and Guan Yang Ze. They are grandsons who never knew their grandfather, and I wish it were otherwise.

Chapter 1

THE *LAJU* INCIDENT

THE PORT OF SINGAPORE on the morning of Thursday 31 January 1974 is busy as always. The tide is rising, higher than usual, and there is fair weather with clear visibility. Ships just arriving are being piloted through the busy waters of the harbour to anchor. Newer container vessels proceed to berth at the recently opened specialised terminal at Tanjong Pagar while other ships, that came in overnight and already at anchor, are now being served by the lighter boats with goods taken off the larger ships and then conveyed to the port and warehouses. Crew going ashore too are ferried by a floatilla of assorted small craft to the jetty from where there are connections to the city by bus and gypsy taxis.

The jetty at the Jardine Steps, a simple structure of concrete slabs, wooden planks and a light-zinc roof, is busy. Boats tie up briefly here for some passengers to alight, after which others get on. They are mainly narrow and wooden-hulled, made up along the traditional lines of fishing sampans, although powered by loud outboard motors. From this jetty on the southern tip of the main island of Singapore, they come and go briskly, plying for customers for runs out to the ships or to the smaller islands to the south.

At around 10.15 am, four men hire a boat from near PSA Gate 9. They say they want to be taken out to a sandy reef nearby for fishing. This is a well-known spot within the busy harbour where the waters are shallow. The larger incoming ships conspicuously steer clear of the spot, lest they strike the

27

reef, and, conversely, it is warm and clear enough to provide decent catch, despite the oil refinery just nearby. A bargain for the trip is struck at $25 with the boatman, Yeo Chua Fatt.

The men clamber aboard, hefting long, big bags of fishing tackle. They set off, with the engine loud and the waves churning behind them. One of the men – an Asian with spectacles – comes forward and asks in English to change destination to Pulau Bukom or else the island next to it, Bukom Kechil (Small Bukom), where there is a beach. The oil refinery is a prohibited area, and the boatman refuses. The passengers react immediate and violently.

The first man grabs the boatman Yeo, and the second swings a blow, using the long metal rod that serves as an engine starter. They quickly tie him up and dump his slumped-over body in the stern of the boat. One man takes the wheel. They are prepared for the exigency that they might need to operate the boat but they do not know the harbour waters. That inexperience leads to error; they run aground on a coral reef. Improvising, they hail a passing boat and pay for their boat to be towed off the reef. The second boat obliges. As soon as the boat approaches the shore at Bukom, they jump off into the shallow waters and scramble onto the beach, and then over the sea wall. Only afterwards, when they have gone from sight, does the second boatman discover the unconscious Yeo.

Now on the island, the four men are heaving along the beach with their bags. It is hot and sweaty work. They orientate themselves. There remains just a short way to one of the perimeter gates from which the road leads inland to the refinery. While their plans have not gone off exactly right, the men are not inexperienced and remain confident that their outcome can still be achieved. Unzipping the bags, they take out their pistols. They recheck the plastic explosives and trigger devices that have been prepared.

The plan is to blow up the oil refinery at Pulau Bukom and shoot whoever tries to stop them. The refinery is owned by Shell, the Anglo-Dutch multinational, and is the largest in the entire region. The explosion will cripple production here and will disrupt oil supplies across the region. This will wound the USA and its military operations in Vietnam, which vitally depend on the oil processed at this plant. It will also escalate the oil price war, hitting Japan and other countries that rely on oil imports from the Middle East. A single act of violence on a small island off a small island at the tip of Asia will impact global events: this is what the men and the groups behind them anticipate.

Now the plan must be executed. The refinery is large and quite imposing, built so high on the low-lying island that its structures are the only thing you see from a distance, as if they emerge out of the water itself. Built up over decades, it has different sections and checkpoints, each with guards. Shell operates in many risky parts of the world, and have brought that expertise into the running of Pulau Bukom, although its Singapore operations have never before faced any threat. At the first gate entrance, the four men surprise and quickly overpower the single guard stationed there. Then they wait there for a vehicle passing through. They need transport; moving across the island by foot would take too long and they would be easily spotted and stopped. Having studied the layout of the island, they understand that this first fenced-off area is where the oil is only bunkered – the tank farm. For the maximum impact, they should penetrate deeper into the complex, into the refinery itself. Once there, the bombs can be deployed for maximum damage and bring the refinery operations to a halt.

They do not wait long. A small lorry driven by one of the many service providers working on the island passes by the gate checkpoint. The men run out and try to stop the truck. Yet, while surprised, the driver manages to weave out of the way. They open fire, but the driver speeds up and drives off. A second vehicle comes by and they try again. But, again, without success. By now the alarm is flagged. The police auxiliary who serve as the island's security force hurry to respond. The men have guns – two 0.32 Belgian-made pistols – but the auxiliary police unit deployed on the island has some 20 officers on duty. The men know they could easily and quickly be outnumbered.

They have to hurry.

The original plan of bombing the core of the refinery is no longer possible. Instead, they decide to deploy explosives at four of the large tankers that store the oil – picking numbers 202, 203, 206 and 211. Each of these contains approximately 5,000 tons of crude oil. They reckon this will create a large explosion and potentially cause a fire that will set off most of the tank farm and then spread across to the plant. It is still not impossible to disrupt and disable the refinery. They set the timers on the explosives on the tankers and scatter more so that that the spreading fires can then set these off too.

Now the men must quickly make their escape and, here too, they must improvise. They decide not to return to the beach and the boat. They head instead to the jetty that Shell run on the island. There, they find a vessel, with its crew on board and engine running, just getting ready to cast off. This is the *Laju*.

It is a ferry owned by the Straits Steamship company that plies between the refinery and mainland Singapore, serving to bring Shell workers and staff on and off Bukom, even children from families who live on the island and are going to school on the main island. Jumping aboard, the four men land on the roof of the ferry boat and then enter the wheelhouse, seizing control from the crew. They order the *Laju* members to cast off and set out and, when a crew member hesitates, one of the men fires a single round at his feet to show that they are willing to use deadly force. The helmsman – or *serang* – obeys them and sets course southwards, not to the main island and their normal route. They are set instead to exit Singapore's territorial waters and enter into the stretch of international seas, just before the first islands of Indonesia.

At 11.45 am, the first explosion at the tankers goes off. The blast is loud on the island and booms across the harbour waters. A second follows just as loud, and then others, with all but one of the explosives attached to the tankers going off. The first of the oil tankers bursts into flames and fire crackles in the air. Alarms sound.

Within minutes, the explosions have been reported. Not

only to the security guards and auxiliary police at the refinery, but also to the police on the main island. Responding, the Marine Police mobilise their vessels from their headquarters at the Kallang River mouth. Other government craft in the harbour – customs launches as well as marine command gunboats – are also activated. Shell is mobilising on the island and so the government craft focus on the *Laju*.

By 12.20, the government vessels spot the ferry near Sisters Island and begin to give chase. They are catching up. The men aboard realise the ferry cannot make it into international waters before they are overtaken. They change course, veering to head back towards the Singapore harbour and the city jetty. The police boats follow and rapidly gain and close ground. The *Laju* comes to a stop at the Eastern Anchorage of the harbour. By now there are almost twenty assorted government craft that encircle it. What next?

*

It has been a busy morning. In his office at Pearl's Hill, Tay Seow Huah has been responding to a number of matters. As the Permanent Secretary of the Ministry of Home Affairs, he is the top government official in charge of Singapore's internal security and order, including the entire Police Force. Even as the Singapore government teams on the ground have been urgently responding to the situation in Bukom and the harbour, the reports have been urgently relayed up the chain of command. As soon as he hears, Tay knows immediately that while there had been other priorities for the day, everything else on the agenda will need to be set aside.

He has dealt with tense and difficult situations before. For the past decade since Singapore became independent, the 41-year-old Tay has been a key figure in the security agencies. There had been many situations of high tension and intrigue especially in the first years of independence and, although the specifics now differed, he is calm, prepared. There had been a similar situation just two years earlier, when an airplane coming into Singapore – Olympic Airways flight 472 from Sydney – was thought to be hijacked. He had led Singapore's security agencies to scramble in response and, although this turned out to be a false alarm, lessons were carried forward. The events facing him this morning had not been anticipated, but Tay steadily makes a rapid and preliminary assessment.

The fires on Bukom are quickly put out and damage seems to be minimal. The *Laju* is presently contained within the cordon of government vessels; no one will be leaving the ferry. With the rapid responses of the different agencies, the situation is being dealt with. There can be a reasonable confidence that further danger can be prevented. Tay will need to inform the political leaders. But there are a number of unknowns he would prefer first to clarify: who the men are, why they attacked, and what they want.

The first bits of information are coming in from the officers at Bukom and also on the water, on board the boats. Radio communication is not smooth, and facts are still emerging. This will not be a case of shoot first and ask questions later; Tay determines that opening up communication with the attackers is the priority. The instruction relayed is that the police are to await further instructions. For the time being, the stance is to be, "no war, no peace".

The first efforts to contact the attackers directly is made from the lead Marine Police boat in the cordon. The young head of the Marine Police, Tee Tua Ba, is aboard the craft. Following Tay's instruction, he picks up the loud hailer and assures the men that they will be safe if they surrender. There is no response initially. Then a plastic bottle is tossed into the sea. As it floats out towards the Marine Police boat, it is scooped up and a handwritten note is found inside:

We are Japanese Red Army and Popular Front for the Liberation of Palestine.

Just Now, we exploded the Pulau Bukom's tank for the solidarity with Vietnamese revolutionary people. And for making the revolutional situation after considering the situation of today's oil crisis.

Now we want to negotiate with you. Call at once, Japanese Ambassador! Hostages are in our hand. And we have big explosives with us.

If you let us carried to the airport we promise you never kill them. But if you try to attack us, we explode ourselves. We want to escape to another country.

The reasons for the attack are now clear, and the affiliation of the attackers is claimed. The motivation for the attack on Bukom reach far beyond Singapore and the spotlight on that small ferry in the southern waters. The men say that their attack on the refinery is in retaliation against imperialism and was aimed at disrupting the oil supply from Singapore to South Vietnam, an act of solidarity with the revolutionary forces in Vietnam. They also want to bring attention to the plight of Palestine. They offer to leave without further violence but, although surrounded, the attackers do not give up. They have explosives and guns, and there are real concerns for the lives of the crew members on board, held hostage. The attackers identify themselves as members of the Japanese Red Army and also the Popular Front for the Liberation of Palestine; both organisations known to be ruthless. The immediate danger is contained. But the situation can easily evolve; even if there are no more actual blasts, the politics around the situation are potentially explosive.

It is timely for Tay to report to the political masters. His office places calls to the minister in charge of Home Affairs, Chua Sian Chin, who is just a year into the portfolio. He also directly informs Dr Goh Keng Swee, the Defence Minister, and the Prime Minister, Lee Kuan Yew. Tay is to go to the Istana to brief the political leaders on the situation and what should be done.

Before leaving, he moves quickly to assemble a team to deal with the situation. Tay knows the men who are suitable and reliable under his Ministry, in the Internal Security Department and in the Police Force. Ruby, his secretary, quickly and efficiently places the calls through to them, getting them out of whatever other meetings they are in so they can speak. He also knows colleagues in other agencies that are needed and reaches out to them too. One of them is S R Nathan, the Director of the Security and Intelligence Division of the Ministry of Defence, with whom he has worked closely before, and well. Tay calls Nathan and asks him to go immediately to the Marine Police headquarters, then at Kallang Basin. Tay himself heads to the Istana to brief the Prime Minister. Each of these calls is concise and decisive.

So is the briefing at the Istana. The Prime Minister, Lee Kuan Yew, 51, is an experienced political mind. As ever, he is sharp in setting the broad strategic directions to deal with the situation. Dr Goh Keng Swee, while appointed Deputy Prime Minister only the year before, has long been the astute policy thinker and implementing hand of the government, and this is his second stint in dealing with the defence portfolio. Both the politicians know Tay to be a seasoned troubleshooter. He has their trust. He is charged with a clear mandate to handle the problem and directly heads to the Operations Centre at the Marine Police HQ at Kallang to assume control of the situation.

The Operations Centre is buzzing, running well enough, considering the short and urgent notice to set things up. At 3 pm, a first surprise comes. The attackers make contact using the radio telephone on board the *Laju*. In fractured English they claim that one of their team is still on Pulau Bukom. Security officers and the military's bomb disposal unit are deployed, together with police dogs. A scramble ensues to search the island once more, quickly and thoroughly. More explosives are recovered from different areas near the oil bunkers – these are not attached to the refinery structures or activated like the others that had gone off, but these too might have gone off should the fires have spread. Eight unexploded packages in total. No further attacker is found, however.

So why the red herring? The best guess is that the attackers are testing how organised and ready the Singapore officials are.

Tay does not mind the games. There remains a buzz from the resulting wild goose chase, but there is some satisfaction. If this was a first sally, the Singaporean officials have acquitted themselves well enough. Yet he senses some uncertainty.

There is considerable anxiety about what lies ahead in the coming days, beyond the situation of the boats in the harbour. The packages found unexploded during the second sweep of the island say that the damage could have been much worse and point, quite literally, to other things that could yet blow up. It is not only the men on the *Laju* with their arms and explosives. The connections of the attackers to wider networks of terrorists – the Red Army and Palestinian groups – mean that new elements and other actors could intervene. Singapore will need to be prepared and, with so many parts of the government activated and deployed, there are questions about what precisely is to be done next and by whom.

Tay briefs the senior members in the operations team and sets procedures in place. There are many aspects of the situation that relate not only to the operation on the water, so considerable effort will be needed to coordinate responses across different parts of the government. Tay takes charge overall and will be based at the Ops Centre in Kallang. He will also liaise with the political leadership at the Istana, brief the press and coordinate with other parts of the government in dealing with the Japanese and other governments that are or might be involved. In each of these areas, he will be assisted. But it will be Tay who will have to manage the full range of operations, and manage them well. It is Tay, as recalled by President Nathan in his memoirs, who is "continually shuttling between the operations room at Marine Police headquarters, the Prime Minister's office, and the Japanese embassy. On top of all that, he had to brief the press of each day." This is not merely administrative but to ensure the overall strategy is coherent.

When he calls a stop to the briefing, Tay stands up at the desk and feels the tension build up in his broad shoulders. He stretches his arms akimbo and looks out across the room, through the windows and across the water. There would be moments when his heart would race but he knew he would have to remain calm and composed in response, and convey that sense of assurance to all involved in managing the ground operations.

From the Ops Centre, there is no sight of the *Laju* and the government boats. But it is all clear in his mind: the detailed map of the vessels and the islands and features nearest them and the demarcation with the open sea and international waters beyond Singapore's jurisdiction. There is another kind of larger and still evolving map in his mind – this of connections between the attackers and their networks, and the governments to be involved in seeking a resolution to the broader situation. This was key to the discussion at the Istana and Tay must keep sight of this, even as he navigates the detail of operations on the ground and responds quickly to the unexpected. He adjusts his dark-framed spectacles, opens a fresh packet of cigarettes, unfiltered Camels, and lights up. There is some hot coffee. Now and into the coming long days, there would be much to do that had never really been done before. The situation would not last for long but would be intense and complex, the circumstances and context fluid and still changing. All the team would be stressed in the days ahead but the pressure is particularly intense on him. These are critical days for not only Tay and the men gathered there, but for the country.

*

At about 5 pm, the *Laju* starts to move. It begins to circle the cordon established by the government boats, trying to find a gap and squeeze out. But the ferry is neither fast nor large enough to force or ram its way through. Perhaps they are just trying their luck. But the effort could also signal desperation and a lack of trust that the police will not attack them. The attackers on board, moreover, still have their weapons and explosives. A head-on response to the *Laju*'s movements must therefore be avoided, Tay instructs. The government boats hold the line standing off about 300 feet (92 m) away from the *Laju*. That is reckoned to be enough to prevent any escape but for the attackers not to fear that the police will act suddenly.

The tactic allows the ferry to keep running and expend its remaining fuel. In parallel, another effort is made to speak to the attackers through the radio-telephone quite extensively. This will run down its battery so they cannot communicate with anyone via radio. Operations aim to contain the situation, and cut off their radio contact, to cauterise the danger. By the end of the day, the battery signal of the *Laju* is weak and, by late that first night, the vessel will be out of fuel and be adrift.

While keeping their distance, surveillance is carried out. There are high-powered binoculars and cameras. But just as useful are the Marine Police officers on the scene, and the young Marine Police Commander, Tee. They are directed to observe movements on board the *Laju* and report on the number of attackers and the hostages. When food and drinks are demanded by the attackers, the police, as instructed, readily supply them. The effort from the operations team as a whole is to gather as much information as possible about what is happening on the *Laju*.

Two or three men are seen in the wheelhouse cabin. Consistent with the message the attackers sent earlier, some do look Japanese, while others were swarthier and could be Arabs. But it is not clear who are attackers and who might be hostages. The Shell company that operates the refinery is asked to provide information on the usual staff on the ferry service and the Singaporean helmsman, one Mohamad bin Nik, is identified. There may be more men in other parts of the ferry, below deck in the engine room, out of sight. Only at the end of the evening will they be able to confirm that there are four attackers on board, with five hostages.

While eyes are focused on the boats, there are other concerns. No one can rule out that the attackers might have accomplices elsewhere on the island of Singapore. The level of alert is raised and patrols are told to keep an eye out for abettors. Zones are covered and anything suspicious is reported and evaluated before being sent to Tay. Security at the airport is increased, both on those coming into the country and those trying to leave. All this is done, however, without fuss. There is every reason to avoid panic across the country.

Other factors will be rising, Tay anticipates. The elements of the situation are intrinsically international. The terrorists are Middle Eastern and Japanese and the organisations behind them and their networks are global. There is also the context of the fragile oil market and the fact that the attack was staged against a major multinational. Media attention comes not only from *The Straits Times*, the *New Nation* and the Chinese-language newspapers, but from worldwide media. *The New York Times* and BBC as well as *The Japan Times* and news agencies are covering the story and actively. Some are working through correspondents long based in Singapore and the region, or else local stringers. Others are flying in. The US-based CBS will bring in its well-known anchor, Ed Bradley, from Vietnam, and events in Singapore will potentially be relayed to the living rooms of every American home. All the media are hungry for information, bristling with questions. Yet there are limits of how much is known and, crucially, how much can be divulged. Unless handled well, the Singapore authorities might be shown up in the crisis. The first media briefing on that first night is a crucible.

Convened at 8 pm at the press office at City Hall, just some nine hours after the first explosions, the assembled media will expect facts about what happened, explanations for why, and an indication of what will come next. Tay delivers the government's statement, and the questions come fast and thick after. He responds calmly and directly but his manner is calibrated not to be bland and evasive. He will tell them all he can, and as soon as he can: this is the tone needed, and it must be set from the start.

Within that, he knows the full circumstances will be hard to discern and do not promise quick and clear resolution. There are many grey areas to be probed and negotiated. Singapore's status as a small and newly independent republic must also be safeguarded in this situation when a number of factors is outside its control, even as the government is asserting that it will be the key decision maker and main actor. This impacts how to approach the media. Should the Singapore government agencies stonewall and say too little, there may well be accusations of inaction and indecision, and even incompetence. But Tay knows that it is not only the public that will hear of Singaporean assessments of the situation but also the compatriots of the attackers. He cannot say nothing, but there is a thin and grey line that he must walk to avoid saying too much. The security agencies are not given to publicity, and answering to the media does not come naturally to them. That Tay understands this is one reason why he has been assigned to take charge of this aspect, in addition to overseeing all the ground operations and negotiations with the attackers. He will personally chair the media sessions held every evening, and serve as the spokesman for the government.

The ways that the situation is framed and communicated to the public and internationally are moreover a major part of the government strategy. There are perceptions to be put into play even from the first. This could affect the entire outcome, and increase the likelihood that Singapore can achieve the ideal outcome discussed at the Istana.

At the media briefing on that first night, Tay announces the Singapore government decision that the men will be offered safe passage out of Singapore. The stance is not to retake the ferry by force, unless the attackers use force and there is no other way to resolve the situation. Instead, Singapore will try to meet the demands that the terrorists have made for safe conduct. This is a key decision. It is made known to the terrorists through the line of communication that has been established, and is calculated to help put them at ease. It is also critical to signal intent to others, especially the networks behind the attack.

But it needs to be justified, made plausible. To the gathered media, Tay explains that no life has been lost, there is minimum damage to the oil tanks, and the safety of the hostages is at stake. *The Straits Times* cites government estimates that the explosions had inflicted only some $30,000 in damages to the tankers, with a further $15,000 loss in crude oil destroyed. The names of the five hostages are also announced – Low Man Seng, Mohammed bin Nik, Pelosi bin Tris, Omar bin Ahmad, and Ahmad bin Awang – with the assurance that, for now, they are safe and unharmed.

The media briefing is successful not only in conveying the information and clarifying key points, but in establishing trust. From the start, the media must understand that some things are still unknown and also that some things must be held confidential. Within that, they must be assured that Tay will share with them as much as he can.

There is much else that Tay does not reveal to the press in conveying the Singapore government's decision to grant safe passage. There has been an evaluation of possible responses. A hard and armed response to storm the ferry is considered but, upon evaluation, would pose problems. The obvious problem, if that might go badly, is the loss of lives and potential loss of confidence in Singapore and its security agencies. No one needs to mention the botched events at the 1972 Munich Games, just two years earlier, carried out by the Germans. A successful use of force could invite more troubles. The Japanese Red Army has a reputation for being ruthless. The Palestinian terrorist groups, backing the attackers, have been relentless and resourceful in their campaigns. More, the Palestinian cause has considerable sympathy among the Muslim countries of the region and among the Muslims in Singapore itself. If they killed or captured the four men, that "success" would only create other and perhaps more complicated problems. Either way, successful or not, going for the hard option might have heavy costs.

Tay well knows this. Back in 1965, MacDonald House, a building along busy Orchard Road, had been bombed as part of the clandestine Konfrontasi war that was pursued by the then Indonesian President Sukarno. There had been fatalities and more injured but, responding, the police were able to apprehend the two Indonesian marines. So, in this sense, there was a successful response operation. Yet that "success" led directly to the decision to put the Indonesians on trial and then to carry out the death penalty, that then resulted in an up-swelling of anti-Singaporean sentiments in Indonesia and the sacking of the embassy in Jakarta, followed by years of tense and often acrimonious relations. It had taken much effort to put those relations with Indonesia back in balance.

On the other hand, seeking a peaceful resolution must not lead the country to be perceived as a "soft target". That would only invite more attacks. While Singapore was physically distant from the Middle East politics that had driven the attackers, there are significant connections. Although it does not possess a single drop of oil, the country operates a hub not only for this refinery but for a wider oil economy. As the American involvement in Vietnam has increased, moreover, the engagement with Singapore has notably stepped up. There are also old connections with the Israelis who had assisted the country for years to build up its defence capabilities and this would have been known to the attackers and the networks they belonged to in citing the Palestine situation as one of the motivations. There might be elements in the region who were open to taking up the cause and acting violently against Singapore.

The situation would best be framed not as an attack directed at Singapore itself, but rather one occurring within it. The attack must be addressed as a matter of law-and-order, of public safety, rather than as politics. This is critical so that Singapore avoids being drawn deeper into the turbulence of Middle Eastern differences and perhaps being targeted again in future. It must also be clear that the Singapore government, as sovereign, is in sole charge of the handling of the situation. The Singapore government leaders and officials, including Tay, must demonstrate their effectiveness and competence. At the same time, Singapore must not be the party that is solely responsible for the resolution. Not all the elements for a solution are within the control of the Singapore government.

The first of such elements arises from the need to deal with the Japanese. This was inevitable, given that the message-in-a-bottle read, "Call at once, Japanese Ambassador!' With two of their nationals and the Red Army involved, Japan has a right to know. Moreover, there is the prospect that, if played correctly, Japan could be convinced to help deal with the situation in a way that could be positive to Singapore's interests.

*

The effort to engage the Japanese was set in motion from early on. At around 2 pm, after Tay had left the Istana, the Japanese Ambassador, Tokichiro Uomoto, is summoned for a discussion with the Prime Minister. The diplomat seems keen to be involved and offers full cooperation. His background seems solid enough. The nondescript 57-year-old has served in the Japanese Ministry of Foreign Affairs all his working life. By coincidence, he was director-general for the Middle East and Africa in the ministry, based in Tokyo, immediately prior to his appointment to Singapore. He would have knowledge about the elements that are involved in this attack. Throughout the afternoon, Japanese embassy staff seek to be more involved. Their requests to the Singaporean officials at the Operations Centre start politely enough but soon turn into outright demands for the ambassador to have direct access to the attackers and even be involved in negotiations.

But this access is closely controlled and monitored. Quite deliberately, it is only after the media briefing and statement by Tay on behalf of the Singapore government that the Japanese are duly allowed to visit the scene. Late that first night, Ambassador Uomoto is escorted onto a Marine Police vessel that enters the cordon. From the front deck, he is able to talk directly to one of the Japanese attackers. Accompanying the ambassador on board the Marine Police vessel, as specifically instructed, is Nathan. Tay knows Nathan understands Japanese from the WWII days. So, quietly, the Singapore side is placed to know what the Japanese will say directly between them.

The discussion does not go well. Following Tay's statement

that the attackers will be given the opportunity to leave safely, the attackers want the Japanese Ambassador to accompany them on the trip out from Singapore. The diplomat is in effect asked to substitute for the release of the Singaporean hostages aboard the *Laju*. At one point, the attackers even ask for the ambassador's lady secretary to accompany them so that they can double the assurance that their safety will be guaranteed. It is clear that the ambassador is not inclined to serve as hostage and, quite soon into the discussion, there is a sharp shift in tone. The attackers change their minds about wanting the Japanese embassy involved at all. Quite the reverse. The attackers threaten violence if the Japanese police are brought in. Ambassador Uomoto is escorted from the scene, unhappy not only at the way the discussion has gone, but also at the way his participation was at first delayed by the Singapore side.

In later media coverage, the Japanese Ambassador would be credited as one of the three men who had to deal directly with the men on the *Laju* – besides Tay in the Ops Centre and Tee Tua Ba at the helm of the Marine Police boat. But from the first contact and subsequently, Uomoto proves not to be a settled quantity. After his meeting with the attackers, he is quoted in the media as saying that he saw the men had "carbines", and that there were only three of them – details that were inaccurate. His keenness to be involved fades. The ambassador is badgered by the media and is terse in response, unsettled by both the demands of the attackers as well as the sometimes aggressive questioning from the international reporters. There were whisperings that he had been less than forthright and brave in dealing with the request that he personally accompany the attackers out of Singapore. More importantly, his refusal of the attackers' request has raised their suspicions that the offer for safe conduct out of Singapore might not be honoured.

After Ambassador Uomoto leaves, there is another twist in the story that many reporters are already rushing to write up and despatch to meet their deadlines. The attackers reiterate their request to leave the country. They want to be given safe passage out of Singapore to an unstated destination. Only later will they identify a Middle Eastern country. This is more or less aligned with Singapore's hopes: for the outcome to be peaceful and also to have the Japanese provide the logistics and air flight for the attackers to leave. Even while bringing in Ambassador Uomoto, caution has been exercised not to cede authority over the situation to the Japanese government. The same is true for all the other governments who call in to find out more about the situation and make various suggestions and offers to assist. Notwithstanding the Japanese and international elements, this is first and foremost an attack on Singaporean territory, for which the Singapore government alone must exercise the first responsibilities and its final right to respond.

This is the preferred outcome. This is – with the announcement at the media briefing on that very first night, and in managing the operations and controlling access to the *Laju* attackers – what Tay is trying to shape. Although Ambassador Uomoto had backed away, the Japanese must continue to be involved; they would have to be, given the nationality of two of the attackers. If not only Uomoto but the higher-ups in Tokyo try to unduly assert themselves, they would have to be held at a distance. If they drag their feet and refuse to help, on the other hand, they would have to be nudged and even dragged to that conclusion.

This is not going to be simply a policing operation against four men aboard a ferry. Tay knew this from the start and the first day hammers home the point.

Day 2: Friday, 1 February
It has been less than 24 hours since the men boarded the small boat at Jardine Steps. Not only has so much happened in their attack and attempt to escape, there have been further developments overnight, since the media briefing.

The attackers were at the front of the ferry, talking with Tee the Marine Police Commander and officers about provisions and the logistics of supplying their needs. During a momentary distraction, two of the men held hostage come up from the engine room to the rear deck and, from the stern of the *Laju*, slip into the cold water. The two men – Low Nam Seng and Amat bin Awang Cik – seize the moment and quietly swim away across to one of the government boats in the cordon, where they are assisted safely on board. Commotion breaks out among the attackers when they discover what has happened right under their noses. They are surprised and anxious that this was a machination to distract them, to reduce the number of hostages before storming them. Assurances are given, repeatedly, that they still hold other hostages. Angry words are exchanged. But no shots are fired.

After they are settled and dry, the two escaped men provide information about the situation on board the *Laju*. There are four attackers: two are Japanese while the other two appear to be Arabs, guessing from their looks and language. As for hostages, three other crew members remain on board. The information is welcome, potentially useful. The offer of safe conduct remains and the preferred outcome continues to be a peaceful outcome. But, if the situation should change for the worse, other options cannot be ruled out: to try to overpower the attackers or bring in snipers. Knowing as much as possible about the situation on board could prove critical in the event.

There is another development overnight that is important. This is in the headlines, literally.

Media coverage follows from the briefing given by Tay that first evening. In *The Straits Times* the next morning, the headline is "Safe Passage For Bukom Bombers". There is a large picture of the ferry. The scrawled note that the attackers first sent is transcribed, spelling out their reasons and their appeal to the Japanese. There is also, on the front page, a small but significant picture of the Japanese Ambassador.

When Tay sees the front page and quickly scans the report, he nods to himself. The intention in briefing the media is not only to simply inform the public. The effort is to shape opinions, with the prospect that those perspectives can then influence what different actors might do. In the reports, it is important that the men are described as bombers and hijackers, not terrorists. The latter term would be highly politicised; the old adage being that one man's terrorist is another's freedom fighter. After this first headline, there will be a conscious effort to emphasise the men as hijackers, rather than "bombers", despite the fact that bombing the Bukom refinery had been their objective. There are, now and again, slips. But most of the time, the terms that Tay employs at the media briefings – attackers, hijackers – gain acceptance and are dutifully and usefully repeated in the media. The newspaper in text and images constantly emphasise the *Laju* ferry rather than the Bukom oil refinery. This helps lessen attention to the actual and strategically important subject of the terrorist attack, and shifts the focus to the rather mundane means of their foiled escape plan. This is more than PR.

The attackers on board the *Laju* have asked for copies of the newspapers and this has been agreed to. So, it must be assumed that they will read what is said and this can impact their state of mind, which can in turn either lead to a successful solution or to disaster. The headlines will also be read by the networks behind the attackers.

It is therefore important that there is a message that four men are being treated fairly and under no immediate threat of being overwhelmed. This means that no second attack on Singapore is warranted. To the Americans and other foreign governments concerned about the security of Singapore and their investments in the country, the signal has to be that the events are driven by external motivations and not directed at Singapore itself. After the turbulence of the 1960s, Singapore is more stable and safe and has emphasised those qualities in reaching out to investors like Shell. Maintaining that reputation is central to the mission.

The reaction of the Singapore government agencies is also emphasised – speedy, steadfast and reasonable in approach. There is nothing said that points out that the guarantee of safe conduct is made solely by Singapore. The references to the Japanese and their ambassador then raise the expectation that the Japanese must be involved for a resolution to be reached. This is a first step to hem in the Japanese to help provide the solution, and to ensure that the solution is what Singapore wants. Despite the difficult exchange with the Japanese Ambassador the day before, the Singapore government reaches out to the government in Tokyo. As per the request of the attackers, they ask for the Japanese to provide an aircraft specially to take them away. The second day is off to a good start.

But there is little movement. Not from Tokyo, with either a brisk Yes or even a No. There is also little happening on the water. The ferry is running out of fuel and has dropped anchor within the cordon maintained by the Marine Police and boats from the navy – three new Jaguar class boats, including the *Sea Wolf*. The cluster of ships is outside the main lanes used for the harbour traffic and the busy schedule of the port continues, unimpeded. Tay does not mind this lull. Rushing forward can work against getting the best solution. The situation is stabilising, with operations controlling what they can.

From visual observations and what the two escaped crew have said, the officials establish beyond doubt that the four hijackers consist of two Arab-looking persons and two Japanese. Efforts to identify them are being made through all possible channels. On board the *Laju*, all persons on board – both the hijackers and the three remaining hostages – appear to be in good health. They are supplied food and drink, although some of the attackers are complaining of a little bit of sea sickness in the early afternoon.

However, through the Pulau Bukom radio link, they express impatience and concern with the apparent delay in exchanges with the Japanese embassy. The Singaporean officials try to facilitate.

At about 3 pm, a representative from the Japanese embassy is escorted to talk directly with them, a certain Mr Odaka, the Minister Counsellor. Accompanying him are police officials and Haji Rahman, who works with Radio Television Singapore (RTS) and speaks Arabic. Speaking to Rahman, one of the Arabs says that their mission is to destroy the Shell installations, and is not to harm Singaporeans or to trouble the Singapore government. They want to be sent to any part of Arabia which supports the Palestinian cause. They also prefer to go together with the two Japanese, as a unit. Rahman reckons they are Palestinian, although one of the men speaks with an Egyptian accent. They seem, in his opinion, sincere.

This is followed up with the Japanese Ambassador going out on a police boat to talk again to the men on the *Laju*. Afterwards, Ambassador Uomoto calls the Minister for Home Affairs, Mr Chua. This is just before the media conference, which has now been set to be held regularly at 5 pm each day at the City Hall press office. The response is not only late but negative: No, there will be no special plane from the Japanese government.

The Japanese do offer a commercial Japan Airlines plane. But this is provided two major conditions are met. First, the attackers must be disarmed by the Singapore government before they board the aircraft. Secondly, while the Japanese government would assume responsibility for the attackers of Japanese nationality, they would not do so for the Arabs. The Japanese also insist that a number of their police and security officials would come down from Tokyo to assess the situation first-hand. This is duly conveyed to the men on the *Laju*.

They are livid. They do not trust the Japanese to keep their word that they will be safe after they lay down their weapons. Repeated references are made to the 1972 Olympics massacre when the Palestinian Black September terrorist group seized 11 members of the Israeli contingent at the Games village in Munich. At first, the German authorities had negotiated and agreed to provide the terrorists safe passage to leave but these promises were mere subterfuge; the German police tried to ambush the terrorists. The Singapore government is well aware of that comparison and the outcome: a botched operation that ended with the deaths of all the Israeli athletes as well as five of the terrorists. Such an outcome – simultaneously angering the networks behind the attack and also showing up operational incompetence – must be avoided at all costs in Singapore.

The attackers agree to drop their requirement that the Japanese Ambassador accompany them out of Singapore. This is conveyed to the embassy. But the men remain adamant that they will not give up their arms until they reach safe haven. Nor will the two Japanese agree to split up from the two Arabs. The Japanese government seem insistent on the two conditions. With the terrorists rejecting the conditions, there is a standoff. Even as the cabinet in Tokyo decorously apologise, Japan Airlines refute that they are willing to provide any aircraft.

At the press conference that evening, after being told of these developments, the obvious question is raised. If the Singapore government guarantees safe conduct for the attackers, will it provide a plane?

While willing to consider the attackers' requests, Tay dismisses repeated suggestions from the media that Singapore should have a responsibility to do so. Any airline would be unable to fly the attackers unless they surrender their arms, he explains. Moreover, the attackers have specifically addressed their demands to Japan. He does not say it outrightly, but putting the emphasis on Tokyo is critical for Singapore to balance between angering those behind the terrorists and being taken as a soft target.

The media focus shifts to the Japanese. There are questions about the Japanese Ambassador Tokichiro Uomoto, whether he is intransigent as a matter of his government's policy or is personally unwilling to accompany the attackers. Tay makes it clear that neither he nor any Singaporean official is saying anything about the ambassador. He even goes further: "My impression of the Japanese Ambassador is that he is a brave man. He has been out to the ship, to the *Laju*, several times in the full glare of floodlights that was played on him." While there are problems that prevent a faster solution, "I do not attribute this to any lack of personal qualities on the part of the Japanese Ambassador."

These remarks are perhaps more than what could be supported by the actions up to that moment. But Tay knows there is nothing to be gained from public complaint. Perhaps, to the contrary, undeserved praise could nudge the Japanese and its ambassador. Further delays will not only frustrate the attackers but can lead them to fear that there is secret planning afoot to storm the *Laju*. Such suggestions are already emerging among the media and will erode any prospect of building trust. "No, it is not part of any strategy of deception," Tay says. "It is a genuine promise." He puts it as plainly and clearly as he can. Trust is in deficit, and will deliberately need to be built up. Open speculation is unhelpful.

While nothing seems to be moving ahead, no one should mistake the situation as being stable. The men on the *Laju* vividly remind anyone who thinks otherwise. They still have explosives on board and, that evening, they threaten to blow themselves and the hostages up if anyone tries to board the *Laju*. Operations are directed accordingly. No one comes out – the original point of the cordon is expanded. Now, no one goes in. Communications by the attackers are controlled and stable. The dialogue between the terrorists and the Marine Police is ongoing via loudhailers. Yet, the men on board are prevented from reaching others outside, directly or through the many media outlets following the situation, where they could publicise their cause and try to win sympathy. The media is not allowed to approach the attackers directly and when some hire private boats to get up close, the Marine Police step in and push them off to a distance.

Like the boats floating in the water, the situation at the end of the second day seems relatively calm. But dynamics will change as surely as the tide. Tay knows not to expect Tokyo to move quickly in the direction that Singapore wants. The question of Singapore's own responsibility, which Tay has quelled so far, can grow. Managing the perception and the psychology of the attackers is already a problem and, the longer it goes on, will become even more difficult. There are ongoing efforts to identify the men and learn as much as possible about them and anything about their character and likely responses. That kind of insight will be critical. Another need is to try to identify and monitor the networks behind the attack. The attack was unforeseen. But it would be remiss not to try to anticipate and guard against any next steps.

Days 3 and 4: Saturday, 2 February to Sunday, 3 February

Dawn comes across the harbour. In this hour between night and morning, the air is moist and the light, grey and soft, the water dark, almost cold. This is always an odd moment for Singapore, usually so hot and sweltering under strong, even harsh, sunlight. Tay has not slept much but he wakes early and feels refreshed, ready. The morning breeze near the water is bracing. To the eye, even through high-powered binoculars, nothing seems to have happened. The *Laju* is still bobbing on the waves. Around the ferry, at the agreed distance, the cordon is maintained by the Marine Police and other vessels.

Yet, behind the scene, things are developing. While the Japanese are stalling about the request that they provide a plane, they are moving on other things. In Tokyo, the police execute a raid on the office of a left-wing group that is reported to be connected to the *Laju* hijackers – that *The Japan Times* refer to as "guerrillas". The raid can be useful. It is important to identify the individuals and learn as much as possible about their past experiences in order to try to anticipate what they might do when the situation changes. But the raid raises alarm bells for them and their networks. When combined with the stalling tactics of the Japanese, such actions feed the suspicion that the Japanese have no intention to be bound by the promise of safe conduct made by the Singapore government.

There are media reports that Japanese police officials are to arrive in Singapore, and will take up key roles in the operations to handle the situation. This, Tay realises, is most unhelpful – counterproductive in managing the attackers and building up their trust with the Singaporean officials. To the media that day, he states that while the Japanese officials have arrived to form their own assessment, it is untrue that the Japanese will take up a substantial role in dealing with the situation. Tay says that it is "absolute rubbish" that they are supervising or even directly assisting. None of the Japanese officials is at the Marine Police Headquarters Operations Centre or in any Singapore government building. Singapore is in charge.

But even as he says this, he knows that stalemates cannot be left unresolved forever. Some things will need to be considered – even if these are less than ideal. It would be useful to think of Plan B, rather than to rely solely on the Japanese. Not least, these would give further evidence of Singapore's sincerity in trying to offer a peaceful resolution. It would also help fend off more questions about supplying a Singaporean plane.

It is proposed by the Singapore government to let the *Laju* ferry refuel and then be used by the hijackers to set sail to a safe haven of their choice. If they do so, they will be allowed to keep their weapons, which they seem adamant on doing. The *Laju* is capable of perhaps 500 nautical miles, carrying bunker on board, within what are called Home Trade Limits, and this could quite easily take them into international waters as they had planned. In fact, they could go into Indonesian or Malaysian waters or even try to get as far as the Southern Philippines or close to Communist North Vietnam, where they could be received by comrades in their networks.

There are sticking points with the suggestion. There is again a question of trust – the switchover of the crew and the process of refuelling could easily provide opportunities for a hard response from the Singapore security officers. There are also issues about what the response might be from Indonesia or Malaysia when the *Laju* enters their waters with the men armed with guns and explosives. Even as they put forward the offer, the Singapore officials make clear their preference for the Japanese to agree to provide the plane. It is not unexpected that the attackers will decline. But what is hoped is that the offer shows the flexibility and willingness on Singapore's part.

The men on the *Laju* consider but decline the offer. They return to their original demand: a plane from Japan. That remains their first preference. Even while the impasse continues, a plan is made on the assumption that Japan relents and provides a plane. A detailed strategy is needed to get the men off the ferry, release the hostages and give up their arms before being allowed onto the plane. It is clear to Tay that the plan must be agreed to by all sides, and, for the attackers, must be "one that includes guarantees that are satisfactory to them in the absence of their own firearms and in the absence of hostages". Planning on how to carry out something that neither the Japanese nor the men aboard the *Laju* have agreed to may seem a waste of effort, but the effort is made.

Something else is prepared, beginning on the third day and into the next. The Singapore government is reaching out to counterparts in the Middle East to ask if anyone might be willing to receive the attackers and provide an airplane for their safe passage. These alternatives are explored as the Japanese delay continues. The involvement of the Popular Front for the Liberation of Palestine is confirmed by a spokesman, Bassama Abu Sharif; the organisation had cooperated in the attack with two members of the Japanese Red Army guerilla movement. No offers come from Middle Eastern countries. The Singaporeans approach other airlines without success.

Meanwhile, the attackers on the *Laju* publicly communicate their demands to leave for any Arab country friendly to the Palestinian cause. For much of the time, they seem comfortable enough and feel that the Singapore government is trying to resolve matters. But things are not moving forward and they are getting tired from the tense situation and frustrated. Their mood rises and falls like the *Laju* on the waves.

They are not the only ones. Among the Singaporean officials too, there is strain. At times, they have to scramble when something new and unexpected happens. At other times, there are periods when nothing much is happening, during which boredom fogs vigilance, and their ability to keep projecting a positive and efficient "can-do" attitude to all – not just the men on the *Laju*, but to the media, the Japanese embassy, other governments and interested parties. The hours are long and tense, and the adrenalin of the first encounter is ebbing. Tay, responsible for operations, has to ensure the men remain ready and able to act. He sets the example. Even late into the night, he makes himself available to respond to the operations staff on developing situations or to the government public affairs team when key media questions are raised, and of course to the political leadership. Tay must deal with all this and cannot even count the short hours he has managed to snatch some sleep, before returning to the Operations Centre in the early morning, already briefed and in charge.

There is a need to manage the different backroom agencies and personalities involved in the handling of the situation. A system is set in place. The Marine Police Commander, Tee, is tasked to remain on the scene and serve as the direct contact with the attackers. The hope is that the affable and energetic commander can strike up a personal trust with the men. But the operations extend far beyond that. The Police Force is fully extended in running the operations on top of their normal duties, and auxiliary police units and even officers from the government-run corporate security, CISCO, are called up to assist with regular functions. In dealing with the *Laju* Incident itself, the Internal Security Department (ISD) is the backbone, with the men under Director Yoong Siew Wah involved throughout. Knowing the manifold challenges ahead, Tay asks Nathan to stay on, despite he being from the external intelligence agency, the Security and Intelligence Division (SID). Tay is not unmindful of some tension that might arise from these arrangements. But it must be that the men and agencies assembled remain determined to work together to secure the country even if there will be inevitable differences in view, as well as questions of coordination and responsibilities. He would have to keep all united in purpose and aligned with decisions taken ultimately by the Prime Minister.

While they are not in the media spotlight or operations directly, there is no doubt that the political leaders are fully seized of the situation. These include Dr Goh, in charge of Defence, and Mr Chua the Home Affairs Minister – but not just them; the Prime Minister especially is energised and generates some of the alternatives that attempt to nudge the situation forward. It is not in the public record what was discussed and decided, what precise instructions were given to Tay, and what decisions taken in the course of developments on the ground.

Lee Kuan Yew is the key political mind, vigorous and even often pugilistic. He needs to know the details but yet be able to rise above them to strategise to serve as the active chairman of the situation. He has trust in Tay to be in the front, not just with internal agencies for Singapore or with the attackers, but also to brief the media from all over the world. Tay is expected not only to consult the Istana, but to take the responsibility to make decisions that align the situation on the ground with the overarching strategies and interests. From the start, Tay sees that there will be many steps, half-steps and false paths in negotiations with the attackers. More than a few possible solutions will be offered by one side or the other during the long-drawn and often difficult negotiations. There will be underlying issues of distrust that cannot be dissolved but there must be every effort to keep lines open and secure cooperation, wherever possible.

The wider geopolitics are the key focus for PM Lee. These include the relationship of the situation to the US presence in the region, which he sees as essential and yet possibly dangerous with the outcome of the Vietnam War. There are also concerns about Singapore's ability to provide a stable and secure base for foreign multinationals, which many other governments still shun and suspect of political interference. Another factor is the reality of the limited resources Singapore can bring to the situation, and the real need to bring in the Japanese to take a share of the responsibility. This has to be done without giving the impression that Singapore is helpless and out of its depth. All these imperatives are conveyed to Tay and – whatever options are pursued, what he and the operations do, and how they proceed – everything has to reflect them.

Days 5 and 6: Monday, 4 February to Tuesday, 5 February
The new work week begins and there is some anticipation that the resolutions must come. Yet there is still no response from Tokyo. They continue to hold to the two conditions that the attackers refuse: disarm and split the Japanese from the two Arabs. Even attempts to agree on a plan for a handover – if there is any agreement on conditions – cannot be detailed. Frustration grows.

Dealing with Japan is proving difficult. Tokyo is far ahead of Singapore or any other country in Asia in wealth and many other indicators of development. Many countries of the region are not only poor but still far from stable, both because of domestic troubles and from the pressure of the Vietnam War. From the late 1960s and into the 1970s, Japan has traded and invested in the region as a key player alongside the USA. The Japanese are assertive, even superior, in dealing with other Asian nations, including Singapore.

Violent anti-Japanese protests had broken out in Bangkok and Jakarta, capitals in which they had considerable investments. These riots were held in opposition to visits by the powerful Japanese Premier Kakuei Tanaka, and represented an affront to their sense of pride. These occurred in January 1974, just weeks before the *Laju* Incident. The government in Tokyo was still trying to piece together why the riots had happened on what was supposed to be a routine tour of the region, and how best to respond. Eventually, the Japanese would recalibrate and shift to new ways of managing their relationships, in what would be called the Fukuda Doctrine.

But as the *Laju* Incident unfolds, Tokyo seems to be less than helpful, obdurate in its demands, perhaps still roiled by the anti-Japanese sentiment of the riots. The intelligence gathered from Tokyo and from sources around the embassy in Singapore suggests that it is more than indecision and caution; there is a narrow calculation about how much they should do to assist in the situation. While Japanese are stalling on the preferred outcome, the Singapore government is in need of not only a Plan B, but some kind of Plan C.

It is announced that Singapore would allow the attackers to leave the *Laju* and their hostages to take refuge in any diplomatic embassy of their choice. The attackers respond positively and ask to be taken in by the North Koreans. Upon this request, Prime Minister Lee Kuan Yew personally sends a message to President Kim Il Sung and later speaks by telephone to the reclusive leader. But Pyongyang declines to accept them.

A representative of the Al-Fatah Palestinian organsation

based in Malaysia publicly offers to help in the negotiations. But more foreign intervention is not something that the Singaporean authorities are willing to accept. Indeed, there is reason to keep them at a distance. While the Al-Fatah are not the most extreme organisation involved in the Palestine controversies, suspicions have been raised in intelligence reports about its office in Kuala Lumpur. This is not only generally about their political advocacy but that they may have been one of the conduits in the preparations for the attack in Singapore.

None of these proposals reaches fruition. Each involves considerable effort, requiring not only inputs from Tay and other officials, but ultimately the political leadership at the highest level. Tay and the government operations team have to engage the attackers in a painstaking back and forth dialogue to explain and then detail the different proposals, in a way that can continue to build up trust rather than develop acrimony. To the onlookers of the media, not much may seem to be happening, but the negotiations on the different proposals are time-consuming and tense.

At one point, the men threaten to blow up themselves and the remaining hostages unless there is progress. Efforts are expended to explain the delay and plead for patience and calm. They relent, eventually.

Reporters come not only from the Singaporean media but from international newspapers and news agencies. Some of the press are bored for many hours in the day when nothing is visibly happening and they cannot get any access to the attackers. The media sessions expend that pent-up energy. At the nightly briefings by the Singapore government, they ask many questions and it is up to Tay to answer on the spot.

His work goes on after the media briefings and into the night. There are briefings at the Istana, to update the leadership and then to hear of new initiatives suggested. Thereafter, Tay regroups with the key members of the operations team and informs them of instructions for the next day.

There are new developments from the ground. Through various diplomatic and intelligence channels, information about the networks and the men is coming in. This takes some time because, focused on the region, Singapore's intelligence agencies do not have the same capacity in the Middle East to track these international terrorist networks. There is, as such, a need to reach out to intelligence agencies of friendly governments – a more time-consuming, indirect means. A photograph is distributed to the media of the Japanese man who is identified as the leader of the group. The media is also informed that, from his accent, one of the Arabs is thought to be Egyptian.

The Japanese attackers are with the Sekigun, or Red Army, an ultra-leftist organisation in Japan. This claim, from the first communication they made, is confirmed. They are said to belong to the group that hijacked a plane from Japan to North Korea in 1970; the same group are believed to have trained the Japanese guerrillas who attacked Tel Aviv airport in May 1972, and who seized and blew up a plane in Libya in August 1973. Over the years, the group has been reported to have connections with Palestinian, Cuban and Uruguayan guerrillas, and with the Black Panthers in the United States. In Japan itself, the Red Army had led a wave of robberies and bombings, especially in 1971, and even plotted the assassination of the then Japanese Premier, Eisaku Sato. In response, the Japanese police's efforts to root out the group were increased, with a measure of success. By 1974, when the *Laju* Incident occurred, many of its leaders had been arrested and some 70 members were in prison. Even after the *Laju* Incident, they were a threat: seizing the French embassy in the Hague later in 1974 and the AIA Building in Kuala Lumpur the next year, taking more than 50 persons hostage.

The two Japanese attackers on the *Laju* have been on the wanted list of the Japanese police even before they struck in Singapore. The man known as Hiroshi Kimura (alias Kazuo Tanaka), with a brooding intellectual look, is fluent in English and Arabic and has been personally dedicated to terrorism in support of the cause of Palestine. According to the sources available, he was involved in the attack at the Lod (or Ben

Gurion) Airport in Tel Aviv in 1972 when Japanese attackers opened fire in the airport terminal with their sub-machine guns and set off their grenades, killing 26 people and injuring nearly 80.

Information about the other three attackers is less detailed. The other Japanese man, Akira Sato (alias Hideo Yokoi), is also known as a terrorist by the Japanese and international agencies. The two Arabs involved in the attack are identified as seasoned members of the Popular Front for the Liberation of Palestine. One man is thought to be Saleh Salim (alias Yahaya Ayyob) and, though somewhat reserved in manner, is senior on the team. The taller and bigger man, Husain Mohammed Saad, seems louder, almost boastful, and might be more volatile, less measured. But, if anything, it is Salim who seems the largest threat. The Front to which they pledge loyalty in this period is notorious for armed attacks and aircraft hijackings. In its statements claiming responsibility for the Bukom bombing, its spokesmen said that the operation was prompted by "the aggressive role" of Shell and other oil companies against the Arab people in general and the Palestinian people in particular. There was also mention, specifically, of the Singapore government.

What is learnt about the attackers has implications for the three remaining hostages. No threats to harm them have been made explicitly. But, given the ruthlessness of the attackers in their past attacks, this cannot be ruled out. There seems little chance of escape, as two others did on the first night. The three hostages left behind must now be under constant watch.

While the execution of the attack on the Pulau Bukom refinery had been botched, the preparations for the raid had been quite extensive. The plans were originally hatched and outlined with considerable detail for months, abroad in Beirut. The four attackers had then slipped into Singapore unnoticed and spent weeks in the country putting together the logistics and final planning. One of them, Akira Sato, had made several recce trips to Singapore, even visited Bukom, and rented their Taman Serasi safe house. In the run-up to the attack on 31

January, the two Arabs had arrived on 23 January, spending some eight days in preparation, and had time to relax in the Botanic Gardens. It is believed that some of the materials for the explosives were ordered while they were in Singapore, all without suspicion.

A car was identified, parked for days at Labrador Park. Inside the car, keys were found that led to the Taman Serasi flat. It was proposed to force entry into the apartment.

Clearly, there were risks: there could be booby-traps or compatriots of the attackers might be holed up inside, and a shoot-out could ensue. As with many of the other aspects of the Laju Incident, Tay understood that the risk had to be measured, and then taken. The operation carried out by ISD officers was successful. The apartment was unoccupied. Inside, more plastic explosives were found. Even more, there were documents that very usefully confirmed and added to what was known about the attackers and their plans.

They had planned alternative escape routes. One involved driving away into Malaysia before taking an Aeroflot plane from Kuala Lumpur airport to New Delhi. The tickets had been booked and paid for in advance. They had rented a car from Avis in Singapore for this purpose. The car boot was all packed with their equipment, including more ammunition and explosives. This plan to leave from Kuala Lumpur confirms the suspicion about why the Al-Fatah organisation there wished to help in the negotiations.

Were there other associates who assisted them in Singapore? In one media session, Tay is asked this: how the attackers – known terrorists – were able to enter Singapore and then move around, making their final preparations, for a week. He answers: "Gentlemen, let me make it quite clear: that answers of an operational nature, which are still somewhat delicate, I am not prepared to answer."

The involvement of Red Army underscores Japan's involvement. As difficult as it is proving, Tokyo is part of the problem and has to be part of the solution. Complications continue with discussions at the highest levels of government. The role of Japan's Ambassador to Singapore, Uomoto, is often in the spotlight, with mixed views emerging. Some feel that he is anxious to be involved and could be pivotal to a solution; on the very first day, he was summoned for discussions directly with PM Lee, and he did interact directly with the attackers on the *Laju*. But his refusal to serve as hostage in lieu of the Singaporeans, as demanded by them, contributed to the stand-off and delays, and Tay said this was "one of the problems" in finding a solution to the situation. Whatever the personal predilections of the ambassador, or the policy priorities for Tokyo, working with Uomoto and the Japanese in the situation is not an option but a necessity.

Singapore and Tay are not up against just the four in-dividuals aboard a ferry. These men are the spearhead of sprawling networks of ruthless and experienced groups. In the days of stand-off in negotiations around the *Laju*, there are already reports of sabotage against Shell facilities elsewhere, in Saigon. This is carried out not on the scale of ambition as the bombing at Pulau Bukom but claimed by the same organisations. Another terrorist group carries out a hijacking at sea off Karachi, with the direct aim of releasing their comrades who are under arrest in Athens, but they also express solidarity with their "brothers" on the *Laju*. Violence is necessary to draw attention to their cause, and Singapore is merely one more backdrop for their operations.

Tay knows that he has to consider the bigger picture. The situation must be seen in a wider frame, linking to things in the currents beyond the horizon. There is more than sufficient reason to expect that the following actions and possible resolution would arise not from anything done here, but from actions elsewhere.

Day 7: Wednesday, 6 February, 6 pm
The currents are shifting, literally. The *Laju*, while anchored, has over the days been pulled into the eastern entrance, to a part of the harbour that sees heavy traffic of larger ships – the Keppel Straits. As they shift, the ferry and the cordon of Marine Police,

navy and other government vessels will pose some obstruction to the busy shipping in the port waters. More, there are stronger currents running here, and an increased risk that the ferry's anchor might not hold. If it doesn't, the ferry can easily be pushed onto the rocks.

The Singapore officials explain the situation to the men aboard the *Laju* slowly and patiently, and offer to tow them to a safer location. At first, there is nodding and agreement. But when the tow line is actually handed over, they refuse to tie up. The officers in the front try to explain and convince them again. But, after some going back and forth, the instruction is to not force the issue. Another solution is offered and accepted: a second anchor is set to prevent further drift.

All this is mundane. Information and decisions and counter proposals being relayed take up a lot of time. Tay can leave much of this to the team but the situation exemplifies how there remains a deficit of trust from the attackers. Such distrust needs to be addressed before any resolution – even if finally agreed in principle – can be made to work practically.

Once the additional anchor for the *Laju* is agreed to, Tay leaves the Operations Centre for the ministry briefly before heading to the media briefing. It remains lively but with the lack of new developments and progress, there is some frustration and conjecture from the journalists. Each of them is anxious to have something dramatic happen and then to be first to report it, and is therefore disappointed that so little is going on. The international media, content with updates, usefully re-emphasise the wait for Japan's response. The Singaporean media are, by now, reporting about the boatmen and the hostages who got away – human interest stories around the events. From the media briefing, Tay goes home to rest, have something to eat and see his family briefly, before going out again to the Istana.

The house where Tay lives is a government-owned colonial bungalow, a black-and-white, set in large grounds on a small hill near the centre of the island called Mount Pleasant. Entering the long driveway to the house, it seems a world of quiet, far away from the harbour and the tensions and comings-and-goings of the situation there. Yet, the house provided by the government to him as a senior civil servant is very close to the Police Academy and an Internal Security Department-operated facility at Onraet Road. It is also just a short drive up the wide Bukit Timah Road to enter the Istana from its side entrance on Cavenagh Road, nearest the PM's office in the Annexe. Inside the house, there is a wide staircase where there is a phone with an electronic scrambler so that he can make or receive confidential calls. He is at home this evening, but still very much in contact and ready to respond. That readiness is not just in the current circumstances; it has been Tay's life over the last decade.

Later that night, the call comes through. There has been a major development; something that, from the moment he learns of it, Tay knows will drive the situation forward from the impasse of these last days.

On 6 February, armed men storm the Japanese embassy in Kuwait. The attack starts before noon in Kuwait, 6 pm in Singapore. The minimal protection at the gates of the embassy is quickly overwhelmed. Within the hour, the Japanese ambassador is taken captive, together with some 16 other embassy staff. The attack is swift and unexpected. It is the first such attack on Kuwaiti soil and somewhat surprising since the royal family has openly supported the Palestinian cause. Once in command, the perpetrators identify themselves in leaflets thrown from a window of the embassy: they are members of the Popular Front for the Liberation of Palestine. Their demands are made clear on the leaflets: "We demand that the Japanese Government send a Japanese airplane to Singapore immediately in order to carry our four heroes to Kuwait."

They release three of their hostages, Arab women who had served in clerical roles in the embassy. They threaten to begin executions of the remaining hostages one by one unless the Japanese capitulate to their demands. The attackers telephone the Japanese foreign ministry at around 9.35 pm Tokyo time.

The Japanese government, almost immediately, agrees.

When he learns of this development, Tay rings his senior officers to have them reconfirm the events through contacts and gather their reactions. He then prepares to go to the Istana to discuss the developments with the political leaders. The high drama had not occurred on the *Laju* which had been cordoned and cauterized. Nor had Singapore been the target, thankfully. In part, this may be because of the low profile Singapore has maintained and the care not to cause offence to the attackers and their networks. Another reason is the quiet but real rise in the level of alert at the borders and across the island to guard against a second attack to force the situation. Intelligence agencies had also been on high alert to scan the horizon because the pressure of the situation would build up and lead to a response somewhere. Tay is glad that Singapore has not been hit a second time.

But there is no celebration that evening. Nor will be there much time for sleep. Things are in motion and the Singaporeans must, even after the long, drawn-out week, keep moving as events now take on their own momentum, and prepare for what is to be done next.

Day 8: Thursday, 7 February

The offer from the Japanese is relayed to Singapore and this is relayed to the attackers on the *Laju*. However, care is taken not to tell them of the capture of the Japanese embassy in Kuwait. The Japanese have capitulated and given in to what the attackers have always wanted. Yet, the level of trust with the Japanese government is so low that the attackers initially refuse. The Singapore side has anticipated that this might be their response. The reply is immediate and strict: if the attackers refuse, Singapore will make no further efforts. Singapore officials will instead step away and allow the Japanese government to deal with the men on the *Laju* directly.

Tay instructs Tee, and Tee relays the position. A deadline is set to push for them to decide. After so much delay, and the attackers setting the deadlines, there is some satisfaction in this. The resolution to allow the men to fly out on a Japanese airline is what Singapore has wanted all along. As expected and hoped for, finally the men agree.

One last matter remains: to provide assurance for the flight out to the attackers. This has been a another sticking point and no detailed plan has been agreed on. From one perspective, allowing the attackers to board the airplane with arms and explosives would be foolhardy. Yet, from their perspective, the dangers of betrayal are real. Hostages could be a compromise arrangement, it is realised. But who?

It cannot be the three remaining hostages on the *Laju*. It has been a primary responsibility throughout the negotiations for the Singapore operations to secure the safe release of these innocent citizens; they cannot now be sent aboard the airplanes to the Middle East. The proposal is therefore that these hostages would have to be released and that, in exchange, a group of Singapore officials would accompany the flight to Kuwait.

On 7 February, the four attackers come off the *Laju* still armed. They are escorted to Paya Lebar Airport. The hostages are freed. It is decided that the request for the attackers to surrender their arms and explosives is to be made by Tee. He had been the man in direct contact with them from the start and had built up some measure of rapport. When they hesitate, Tee offers to let them keep a revolver with one bullet that could be held to his head as security. Tay had anticipated their hesitance and this dramatic gesture was also something that Tay had anticipated and asked Tee to be prepared to make, if need be. The attackers agree to this last step and give up all their weapons.

Tay personally meets the attackers the night before their departure, face-to-face, after the long and seemingly unending hours of negotiations. What was said in that meeting is not all on public record. But Tay was clear in telling them that the promise of safe passage is genuine. He also stated a proviso: that upon arrival in Kuwait, the situation will depend on the authorities there.

At 1.25 am on 8 February, some eight days since the first bomb went off on Bukom, the plane departs.

On board with the hijackers are 13 Singapore government representatives acting as guarantors, two Japanese government officials and 12 JAL crew members. The Singapore delegation comprises eight government officials, drawn from those who had been involved in the operations, as well as four Singapore Armed Forces commandos. The leader amongst those aboard the flight is Nathan. The Head of the Internal Security Department, Yoong Siew Wah, serves as deputy leader of the delegation. Others on the manifest are Tee, Seah Wai Toh, Andrew Tan, S Raja Gopal, Saraj Din, Tan Kim Peng, Gwee Peng Hong, Teo Ah Bah, Tan Lye Kwee, Haji Abu Bakar and Haji Rahman. Arrangements had been made in detail on the seating, with the Singaporean delegation serving to buffer the attackers from the Japanese officials on board. The Singaporeans will later be commended for their roles, and rightly so.

It is not a matter of public record why Tay was not among the hostages. It is said by some that he did volunteer but this request was declined by the political leadership. There was concern for his safety as he was overall in charge of the negotiations and also the media briefings. He may have upset the terrorists in the prolonged negotiations and different offers. Or, in briefing the media every night, he could have said something that could have upset the backers of the attack who might be waiting in Kuwait for the plane. In comparison, except for Tee, Nathan and the others had not dealt with the attackers or spoken publicly on the situation. Tee Tua Ba was later to recall that, as he was boarding the airplane, Tay buzzed him on his walkie-talkie to personally convey a message from the political leadership that Tee's was "a job well done" – as Tee recounted to me when I researched this book. While not on that flight physically, Tay cared not only for the outcome but the people involved in the operations he had directed. While every measure had been taken to minimise the risks, he knew there remained risks that had to be run. The flight is not without tension nor is their safe arrival home sure. But the Singaporean delegation are able to adjust and cope in this final stretch without misstep. Once in Kuwait, the matter is handed over to the Kuwaiti and Japanese governments.

In a media briefing after the landing, Tay shares a detail about one thing the attackers said when they met. Did the men regret the attack? Tay's immediate and off-the-cuff reply is recorded in the archived transcripts of these media briefings.

"The only regret was that they did not come to Singapore simply as tourists. They found Singapore a tourist paradise. I am putting in a plug for the STPB now. And one of them said that he would in fact like to come back… and we asked him to let us know in advance." There is laughter across the room, loud after all the tense and exhausting hours.

Assessments

Some five decades have passed since. In these years, while generally stable, Singapore has had to deal with other terrorists; in the public domain are incidents such as the 1991 hijacking of a Singapore Airlines plane SQ117 and a plot in 2001 to bomb a train station where US armed forces personnel transit to their stations in the north of the island. Broader challenges have also confronted the country, emerging from diverse sources like the Asian financial crisis, SARS and the Covid-19 pandemic. Yet, through this time, Singapore has made considerable progress. Consider economic growth. The Singapore economy in 1974, the year of the *Laju* Incident, was about $5.2 billion measured in annual GDP. In the year before the pandemic, 2019, it was measured at almost $375 billion, more than 70 times larger.

Against this background, the *Laju* Incident is not widely known. Singapore schools do not include it as part of the compulsory social studies curriculum – which does cover other incidents such as the race riots of 1964. The many headlines generated in Singapore and abroad have faded. Yet, the *Laju* Incident is not wholly unknown. It is mentioned in a number of websites and can be searched in the National Archives of Singapore. Even so, only a brief summary is offered in most cases. This seems a result of a culture of secrecy. The general policy of the Singapore government, unlike many democracies, is not to automatically declassify government materials, even decades after. This penchant to keep things classified and away from public eye covers even many mundane matters. It applies even more for the *Laju* Incident and other events that were once sensitive in the security realm under defence and intelligence agencies for whom secrets are their trademark. As such, most references to the *Laju* Incident on government websites only provide bare bones.

In a number of the accounts of the *Laju* Incident, the primary spotlight is given to S R Nathan. This is warranted in part since he did play a major role in operations, especially when he was selected to serve as the leader of the delegation aboard the plane. The focus on Nathan is understandable in that the then SID director went on, many decades afterward, to serve as the President of the country. The first time he stood for election for that office, moreover, there was specific mention to his part in the *Laju* Incident as one of the key markers of his lifelong contributions to the country. But the attention given to the role that Nathan played and the flight means that there is accordingly not much said about the negotiations that led to the resolution of the situation, and to the roles that others played.

One corrective to those omissions comes, ironically, from the memoirs by President Nathan himself. The memoirs, at 672 pages (including index), detail his life from childhood to the start of his term as President, and his account of the *Laju* Incident runs some twenty-four pages, from pages 397 to 421. More emphasis is given to the flight, given the leadership role he played in that part of the events. But the account has useful detail on the days leading up to the flight too. He recognises the central roles that Tay played, and that it was Tay who pointedly included him in the operations team.

The account in the President's memoirs is also helpful in sorting out many of the contemporary sources of reports in different newspapers and media. These are multiple and often full of minutiae, some of which is sometimes conflicting. For instance, some contemporary newspapers reported that the two *Laju* crew who were held hostage were pushed off the boat by the attackers, whereas other and later reports state – correctly – that they had escaped by slipping out from the engine room into the water. Another example are articles that quote the Japanese Ambassador, Uomoto, saying that when he met the men, he saw their "carbines". From this, some reports and later website summaries record that the attackers had submachine guns. The less dramatic but accurate assessment is that the attackers had, in addition to the explosives, only two automatic pistols.

The narrative offered in this book is consistent with the memoirs of the late President. I have also taken account of another source about the *Laju* Incident. While secrecy is maintained, selective government agencies do make efforts to help citizens be more aware of the dangers and sensitivities that face Singapore. One of the main efforts to do this is headed by the Heritage Centre of the Internal Security Department, under the Ministry of Home Affairs. The centre at Onraet Road has an exhibition that explains different episodes that threatened the security and stability of Singapore, and the *Laju* Incident is one of them. Even as this centre provides more detail than other sources, it is not to be assumed that there is not more information; there is in almost all cases a difference from what is chosen selectively for a presentation, and having full access to all documents. There is, for example, not much attention given to the undercurrents of the politics and the strategic aims of the Singapore government in handling the situation. The *Laju* Incident, being a public event, can be seen and described, but insights beneath and beyond the reported facts remain to be deduced. In my account, I have drawn assumptions on Tay's thinking and actions, and some other points; these are best guesses that stand to be corrected if and when the official documents are declassified. Until then, an extent of enigma remains.

Given this, how best can we see the *Laju* Incident in context? It was a crisis that involved not only Tay and the Singapore operations and their political leaders, the terrorists and their networks, the Japanese and Kuwaiti governments – it grabbed attention. There were headlines in the newspapers and an anxiety and curiosity among the public. The media attention fed that with reports of the minutest detail. Looking back time after, we may ask "why"? What was the fuss?

The 1974 *Laju* Incident was named after a mere ferry and was played out in the southern waters of Singapore. Yet, this was much more than a localised crisis; it was a significant event on a much larger canvas. First and foremost, it was an attempt to bomb the oil refinery at Pulau Bukom. Singapore, by then, was already the world's third-largest oil refining centre and the terrorists sought to disrupt global oil supplies. The attempted strike on the Shell facility on Pulau Bukom was not an isolated incident but connected to wider events in a troubled period in the region and wider world. This was the era of oil shocks and Singapore was supplying oil across the region. With the USA in Vietnam, the refined petroleum and oil products from this refinery supported the entire US military operations in Indochina. The terrorist attack on the Pulau Bukom refinery had not only economic and strategic importance but consequences on the geopolitics. Had the attackers successfully destroyed the refinery in 1974, there might have been a shortage of oil in the region for years.

The facility was also critically important to Singapore at that stage of its development. Pulau Bukom had already become the biggest centre for oil storage, blending, packing and bunkering in Southeast Asia. The refinery was the part that added the highest value and took Singapore beyond the role of trader – a long-established strength – and into the new ambition of being a manufacturing base. This commitment was made early, with the first refinery opened in 1961; large at $30 million and holding high political signature, as it was opened by then Finance Minister Goh Keng Swee. There were as many as 5,000 residents on Bukom in the early 1960s, the majority of whom were Shell employees and their families. Amenities on the island included housing, two markets, chapels, a mosque, a community association, four clubs, an open-air cinema, two schools and a clinic. Four more refineries were added over the next decades, which raised processing capacity from 1 million tonnes of crude oil a year in 1961 to reach, by 1980, 25 million tonnes.

It was not only Shell that was beginning to invest more into Singapore in this period. The country's industrial programme was beginning to take off, moving from low-wage and labour-intensive work and up the value chain. The refinery was a star investment that had started in 1961 and had continued to expand and be upgraded. If the refinery had been devastated in the attack, or if Singapore was taken to be a soft target, this might well have set back overall development. Not only Shell but many other multinational corporations might have been much more concerned whether Singapore could prove itself to be a secure and stable base in the dynamic but volatile region.

This is especially because the incident was Singapore's first real encounter with international terrorism, and it had happened within the first decade of its independence. Its security agencies had only been recently indigenised and reorganised, and was still learning from ties with a number of other countries. This was a severe first test as the waves of terrorist attacks across the world in that decade were growing. If this first incident had been wrongly handled, Singapore might have been cast as a belligerent or else a soft target, with implications for the future. Subsequently, Singapore made another effort to head off recurrences. Its diplomacy began to respond on the question of Palestine – the cause cited by the attackers. This was in spite of its long-standing ties with Israel, and always squared with a consistent stance against terrorism, no matter the reasons.

Singapore would engage the recognised authorities in Palestine, and call consistently for peaceful coexistence and a two-state solution. This position was in accordance with recognised principles of international law, resulting in votes at the United Nations against Israel and the USA. This diplomacy developed in the wake of the *Laju* Incident and has evolved to serve as a foundation in responding to later controversies and crises, including the 2023 Hamas attack on Israel and the subsequent bombing of the Gaza.

In the end, the critical step was taken outside Singapore, when the Japanese embassy in Kuwait was seized. This forced the Japanese to accede. An English-language newspaper in Kuwait, *The Times*, was later to criticise the Japanese stance in the *Laju* Incident. Its view was that the Japanese government "prevaricated on the issue of providing a plane to the Singapore hijackers for four long days" (before immediately agreeing once the Japanese embassy was held hostage). The conclusion of the Kuwaiti newspaper was that, "this attitude shows that the Japanese government is not really worried over commando actions if they involve other countries but sits up and acts automatically only if Japanese citizens are involved. This is a selfish attitude."

In Singapore, nothing was said by the government. From the 1970s, Japan was, increasingly, an important foreign investor in Southeast Asia but the relationship, raw from the WWII experiences, was still to be smoothed. It was only from 1978, with the Fukuda Doctrine, that Japan's relations with Singapore and the region were reset and to the positive.

How did Singapore acquit itself? In a subsequent interview reprinted in *The Straits Times* of 9 February 1974, Prime Minister Lee Kuan Yew summed up his views: "The fact that Singapore was not involved does not guarantee the Republic's safety. But the fact that Singaporeans can and do look after themselves will minimise chances of another Bukom-*Laju* emergency. Singapore was caught by surprise this time, but it has shown it is no pushover." The incident, said Lee, demonstrated how impossible it was for Singapore to "isolate ourselves from conflicts in which we are really spectators. We will minimise the reasons for any group to pick any quarrel with us". Rather than trying to overpower the men once the *Laju* was circled, Singapore had taken the prudent approach so as to avoid reprisal attacks. Nevertheless, Singapore was determined not to let it happen again, and determined to strengthen its abilities to respond if it did.

The internal debrief assessed things that could be improved.

One of the gaps was clearly the lack of sufficient protection for the refinery itself which, although owned privately, was a vital installation. In the aftermath of the *Laju* Incident, these were beefed up, not only on Pulau Bukom but for a long list of other facilities. With new technology and increased international cooperation, there would be efforts to increase surveillance at the borders and of those entering Singapore, and to gather information that might help prevent future attacks. The *Laju* Incident also exposed improvements that were needed in the response capability. The next effort would be to develop "a sufficient reserve of trained officers who could be relied on to supplement regular officers during a security crisis". Anti-hijacking forces and dedicated negotiators were not available as options to manage the crisis at the time of the *Laju* Incident.

There was a fuller response that went beyond increasing security capabilities with guards and specialised agencies for response. This was to build up the ability to gather and use intelligence – not only from our region but from across the world. In tandem with this, efforts were redoubled to build trusted networks with other intelligence agencies, so as to be able to share information with them, quid pro quo. Diplomacy would also play its role, to strengthen ties with the Middle East and try to be even-handed about critical issues like Palestine.

Within the Singapore government itself, there was a question about coordination and roles – whether the Director of Internal Security from the Ministry of Home Affairs (MHA) or the Director of Intelligence from the Ministry of Defence (MINDEF) should lead the crisis management, or – at a higher level – should it be a permanent secretary and, if so, from which ministry.

Tay had been in the security agencies from the days of the combined Ministry of Interior and Defence and was well able to deal with the different agencies and coordinate between them in the days of this crisis. He personally had the standing and networks to do so. He also had the capability. The police officers who worked with him during the *Laju* Incident were to recall later in *Police Life*, an internal publication of the Police and

Ministry of Home Affairs: "Mr Tay was a man who remained calm and composed even in the most tense of situations... recall the confidence with which he conducted ground operations and his astute handling of the Press conferences at which he briefed both local and foreign correspondents on developments in the incident. To many professional police officers, Mr Tay's grasp of ground operations was remarkable – even amazing."

In his autobiography, written when he was the incumbent President, Nathan was, as always, careful and precise about the details about the roles Tay and others (himself included), played. Nathan specifically recounts how he was first informed and involved: "An urgent call came in from Tay Seow Huah, permanent secretary at the Ministry of Home Affairs. He asked me to come right away to the Marine Police headquarters at Kallang Basin." Nathan records standing in for Tay initially while the latter was at the Istana. Towards the end of the first day, he recounts: "Tay Seow Huah returned to the Marine Police headquarters and resumed control of the operation. However, he asked me to stay on."

There is the question about the role that Nathan played vis-à-vis the officers of the ISD and their then Director, Yoong Siew Wah. The old ISD veteran was clearly important as he accompanied the attackers on that flight, serving as deputy leader of the delegation. The ISD men under him were the backbone of the entire operation. But there was a question about the responsibilities between Nathan and Yoong and their respective agencies. This can again be seen in the autobiography of the late Nathan, where he touches twice on the issue.

At the SID, Nathan was in charge of looking at Singapore's external security under the Ministry of Defence. As Nathan himself later was to note, "the logical person... would have been the deputy secretary of Home Affairs, or the police commissioner, or the director of internal security." But, as he wrote: "There was no time to ask 'why me?'" At that time, Tay offered no elaboration and Nathan did not hesitate to do as asked. Tay had been the founding SID Director, preceding Nathan, at a time when, under the Ministry of Interior and

Defence, both internal and external security were conjoined. When Tay was Permanent Secretary at Home Affairs in 1971, he was sent to the USA for an extended period under a prestigious fellowship named in honour of President Eisenhower, and Nathan served in his stead. Going even further back, the two worked together in the early years of their careers on matters critical to the port of Singapore. There was a long-established rapport between the two men. Tay knew and trusted that Nathan would be of great help.

On leading the delegation on the plane, Nathan recalled, "… there was a tough dispute within our ranks about leadership of the team officials. Tay Seow Huah had told me earlier that Yoong Siew Wah as director of internal security, felt strongly that he should have been in charge." This appears to have deepened with time, when subsequent media coverage of the *Laju* Incident seemed to play up Nathan's role, at some cost to acknowledgement of what the ISD had done. But during the days of the operation, the two agencies did cooperate under Tay's overall charge and, in many ways, the response of the agencies and the team as a whole redeemed what would otherwise have been a heavy body blow to efforts to secure Singapore.

But for the future, such a key role could not be dependent only on individual strengths; subsequently, an Executive Group (EG) was set up "to handle hijacking and hostage taking". The structure identified the leadership for handling such situations, appointing the Permanent Secretary of the Ministry of Home Affairs as chairman of the EG. Comprising senior officers from the security forces and various ministries (including communications and diplomatic agencies), the EG was the first interagency coordination platform across the Singapore Public Service. Largely, this followed and formalised the precedent that Tay had extemporised in the response to the *Laju* Incident. Then, taking charge overall, he had brought together many of these same elements, drawing on those people he knew and trusted to help in the situation, and his pioneering experience in the security agencies of Singapore.

The development of the Singapore system after the *Laju* Incident can be seen in the way that Singapore responded to the next terrorist attack: on 26 March 1991, when Singapore Airlines Flight SQ117 was hijacked soon after takeoff from Kuala Lumpur. There were 114 passengers and 11 crew taken hostage, and, despite it being just a 50-minute flight, the Singapore security agencies led by the EG were ready and deployed at the airport. After making contact and assessing the situation in the course of the night, they stormed the airplane and took it by force – an instruction that was decisively implemented by a Special Operations Force with specialised training and equipment for such situations. The aircraft was retaken without loss of life of any hostage or any damage to the aircraft. Back in the 1974 *Laju* Incident, the use of force was an option that was considered but put to one side. By 1991, the Singapore government response system had been strengthened.

At the pinnacle of that system was still the political leadership. The PM at the time of the SQ117 hijack was Goh Chok Tong, who had then just succeeded Mr Lee in that post. In the book, *Standing Tall: The Goh Chok Tong Years*, it is written that after being briefed by the Home Affairs Minister, PM Goh went to sleep, and slept well. Singapore's second-generation leader knew he could depend on the system that had been built up with effort and planning. In the *Laju* Incident, the pioneer generation – of leaders, civil servants, and the security agencies – did not have that assurance. Instead, under close scrutiny of the top political leadership as well as intense international attention, the pioneers dealing with the *Laju* Incident managed with what resources they could muster and what solutions they could improvise. For Tay, in particular, the hard and tense times of the *Laju* Incident were to take a toll.

In the Public Eye
In the immediate wake of the *Laju* Incident, Tay emerged with a degree of recognition in the public and media. He was the one who had led all the government briefings to the press – both Singaporean and foreign – in that intense period. Media

is sometimes seen as mere sound bites that are ephemeral but, in fact, a broader and longer-term characterisation can be created of an individual and the institution or country that he presents. This is especially in times of crises, under pressure and in the public eye. What impression did Tay make in the *Laju* Incident?

A summary of the events was published subsequently by *The Straits Times* in a special book commemorating its role in Singapore's history, which characterised the event as a "first brush with terrorism". Leslie Fong, who was later to become the overall editor of the newspaper, was then a 24-year-old reporter tasked to cover the incident, blow-by-blow, and he gave the scene some colour. He reported a mix of boredom and drama at the site. "There was nothing you could actually see from a distance. Other reporters tried to hire bumboats to go out but were turned back by police."

In contrast, the tension played out the nightly press briefings when the international press was fierce, demanding answers and the "right to know" how the government would handle itself. "Mr Tay would not bat an eyelid," said Mr Fong.

"He would say, 'You know what I choose to tell you…. You are in my country, you play by my rules. And if you cross the line, I will not hesitate to deport you.'

You could see his mastery of the details. He opened my eyes to how a self-confident civil servant in a developing country could conduct himself with dignity and confidence."

The media briefings were important not only for Tay personally but for what and whom he represented: the security agencies and, even more, Singapore. He and his team would have had to craft the media releases and control the information released. His ability to handle the questions was important to show mastery of the details, and he had the self-confidence to stand up in the international spotlight. Singapore was then just in its first decade. So were the country's institutions for defence, security and intelligence. In most estimates, like Fong's, Tay did well for Singapore and her security agencies.

Some attention stuck to him personally. Tay was tall and

broad-shouldered, with a strong physical presence, handsome. He spoke well, with clarity and confidence, and would sometimes respond off the cuff beyond the text, and even with some wit. He drove sports cars and was known to enjoy the finer things of life. In the world of the Sixties and Seventies, still enamoured of James Bond and Cold War thrillers, Tay looked the part of a spy chief. In the following weeks, there were several media mentions, all largely admiring. He was described as "a brilliant administrator and tough trouble-shooter". Some seemed perhaps a little star struck. One write up in *This Singapore*, a magazine to mark the tenth anniversary of Singapore's independance, described him thus: "Tay is good-looking... a keen tennis player and skindiver... and likes to drive sports cars. A romantic secret agent type, perhaps?"

It was unusual for a senior civil servant to be featured in this way, then and still today. Permanent secretaries hold an enormous sway over the policies and state actions in Singapore, yet few are publicly known and only the political leadership is in the news. In the contemporaneous media reports of the *Laju* Incident, Tay was featured more than the then Minister for Home Affairs. Among the government team, while others played important roles assigned to them, he was the one in the spotlight. From the tension and uncertainty of the *Laju* Incident, he emerged from the aftermath not only with a successful outcome but with an increased degree of public recognition.

He was glad of the result and proud of the different men and agencies involved, most of whom he had known for many years. Whatever else Tay had done before, or did after (or might have done), these critical days would be one high point in the public recognition of his work. Certainly, this has been the case in the records of others who were involved during the *Laju* Incident and went on to distinguish themselves in various ways afterwards. For Nathan, his service in *Laju* was cited when he was nominated to stand for the presidency of the Republic, and featured prominently when citations recounted his decades-long contributions to Singapore as a senior civil servant, permanent secretary, and ambassador. So it was too for Tee Tua Ba, the young Commander of the Marine Police, who would go on to eventually become Police Commissioner and serve as an ambassador. For Tay himself, although there were other things he did in his career, the *Laju* Incident would prove to be a pinnacle in many ways.

*

I was just 13 when the *Laju* Incident happened. In our household, we had the habit to keep in touch with the news and we followed the events, step by step. Doubly so, given my father's involvement: we watched him on the TV in our family room upstairs, and whoever spotted his name or photograph in the newspapers would let the others know around the table at breakfast or dinner. I was proud that my father was helping our country at this critical time but the media attention and publicity also felt odd.

We hardly saw him in those days. Most mornings, he would be gone before us, and we were in the morning session for school and would leave by 7 am or earlier. In the evenings, he missed or was late for most dinners, and yet he made the point of trying to come back between the media briefings and heading off to the Istana. In some ways, we were used to this. We had always known he was involved in security matters, and working beyond office hours was routine. But the days during the *Laju* Incident were especially intense. When he did come back for dinner, late, even if we were finished with our meal, we would sit down with him – unless he wanted to be alone. Sometimes, he would say a few things about the events of the day. At other times, he would be quiet and just eat. Or, as a father, as normally he would, he would ask my sister, Joanne, and me about our day in school.

Throughout the period, when the situation was far from settled, we had a pride in seeing my father involved in this critical, headline matter and my sister and I were never in doubt that he would manage. Even when our mother told us that he would be very tired and tense, we never once thought he might fail. Such is the faith of young children in their parents, and therefore our blindness to the pressures and anxieties they face.

My father was discreet but there were things we inevitably heard in the home, around the dining table, or through my mother, before the rest of the public. On that first day, when the situation was breaking and before the first newspaper headline or radio announcement, he had called home to tell my mother broadly about the attack, say not to expect him for dinner.

On one of those days, I remember my father complaining about how a story in the newspaper had claimed some of the Singaporean crew had been released by the attackers. He felt urgently the need to correct that to emphasise how two had escaped. I also remember asking him if the attackers were really armed with machine guns (which was reported based on what the Japanese ambassador said). He said that the information gleaned suggested otherwise.

When it was announced that S R Nathan would lead the Singapore government delegation to accompany the attackers on the flight, I asked my father why he wasn't going. To my memory, he explained he had wanted to go, but that the assessment was that – having been the chief negotiator and although it had been resolved – there was a real risk of reprisal when they reached their destination. Some weeks after the incident, he opened up his briefcase to show me a picture of the guns and the explosives that had been surrendered by the attackers. Those were the only times I felt any of the risk and pressure he faced. This is how my father – whatever concerns he faced – tried to shield us, his children.

When it was over, he got a lot of attention following all the publicity. He could not have been but a little pleased at the acknowledgement. He took the accolades, moreover, as being for all of those who had served. Personally, there was more than a fair share of ribbing from close friends and relatives, many jokes to keep my father modest. It was his intention to keep his life private. Being in the public eye was not fully comfortable.

While he was not unknown, his long years in security had meant that his work was most often unreported, not within the public domain.

It was more than happenstance and the humdrum job rotation that he was Permanent Secretary for Home Affairs during the *Laju* Incident. He had been prepared for those critical days by his preceding years; the fuller context set from the very start of his career as a civil servant and the first years of an independent Singapore. For my father personally, many of the factors that drove him through those years require a look even further back, to his beginnings.

Chapter 2

CHILDHOOD & FAMILY

THERE ARE MANY TERRORS in times of war and Malaya was not spared in WWII. Nor were Tay Seow Huah and his parents. When the war began, Sonnie (pronounced "sunny") – as he was known to his family – was just a child. By the end of those years, having suffered the loss of his father, he was still only an adolescent but already the man of the house. That growth was painful even after the war, as the son of a poor widow. There were deprivations in those times, inevitably separation from his family and years of scraping by, with too little money, food and assurance and security about what might lie ahead. The worst of fears were successfully traversed and there would be instances of happiness. Sonnie not only survived but excelled. Yet, there were scars – literal and permanent. There were deeper hungers that were to propel him to leave the family home and Malaya, and would continue to drive him onwards during his adult years, at headlong speed.

Sonnie's father was Tay Hooi Eng, born in 1905 as the second-youngest of seven siblings. His own father was in business – trading timber and rubber – but Tay Hooi Eng was employed by the British colonial administration in Penang. The Empire was then at its height and British Malaya was one of its more successful and profitable possessions; the tin mines and rubber from estates across the peninsula were major and valuable inputs into the industrial engine that was England. Within this vast colonial Empire, Sonnie's father held what was a minor administrative post, more or less a clerk. He was posted to work outstation – as the British called the remote offices, located far away from their main administrative centres in larger towns and cities like Penang and Singapore.

Sonnie's mother was Goon Goot Meng, the daughter of a goldsmith. She and Tay had met in Nibong Tebal, a village that lies some 60 km south of Penang. The young lady's sister had married and moved there, where she had come to know Tay's elder brother. Through this connection, it was arranged for Tay Hooi Eng and Goon Goot Meng to meet. They quickly engaged and married when he was 19 and she was 20. They began their life together in Nibong Tebal but the young wife travelled back to be with her family in Penang when it was time for her to deliver the children. Their first child was a girl born in 1931, Seow Lin. Two years on, in 1933, came their first son, Seow Huah, my father. Then in quick succession came the next two, Seow Aun (Mannie) and Seow Inn (Shelley).

Tay Hooi Eng was then posted out to the far north, near the border with the provinces of the Kingdom of Siam (as Thailand was called then). He was tasked to help in sorting out where and how to demarcate the border. This was not easy. The Kingdom of Siam was the only one in Southeast Asia not to be colonised by European powers and had been the key influence over the semi-independent entities of Songkla, Yala and Narathiwarat – southern states that served to buffer them from British Malaya. A treaty had been agreed back in 1909 but as the British began to exert influence on the border area, the Siamese were being very watchful against any intrusion.

It did not matter that the border was a wild terrain that ran for the longest stretch across mountain ranges, with another stretch along the deep and most remote part of the valley created by the Golok River – areas so remote that there was really no one who was effectively in charge. Nor did it matter that the line drawn with precision on paper in an office was, in reality, so very fluid, with people going back and forth with little regard to the formalities and niceties of any treaty. Even today, there are some twenty crossing points between the two countries, and many reports of "grey" trafficking in goods and even people. Back then, the border was near-impossible to administer.

It was hard work and living conditions were poor. Tay was stationed in a border town known as Kroh in Thai, and Keruh in Malay, and which is known as Pengkalan Hulu today. It was on the Eastern boundary of the state of Kedah under the British and had once been part of the princely kingdom of Reman, under the state of Petani. The shifting identities of Kroh and the peripheral development of the town exemplified the wider conditions in the border area at that time. Housing allocated was a typical rural wooden house, built on stakes in a jungle clearing to help prevent animals from coming in. But the one given to Tay was especially run-down: the stairs creaking underfoot and there, in the middle of what should have been the living room, was a large and gaping hole through the floor. It was not fixed before Tay and his family arrived, and would not be during the entire time they lived there. Instead, a big metal cooking pot was placed over the hole, with a large heavy stone placed on top to secure it. This literal stopgap measure was to keep the young children from falling through. It also helped to prevent snakes from slithering up from the long grass that grew under the house. The work was hard and tedious, the conditions difficult for a single man and insufferable for a family.

After enduring this, the Tays were glad to be posted to Taiping. This was a tin-mining town, small but prosperous compared to Kroh, and civilised too. It was connected by railway to Port Weld and from there to Penang. The town had risen with the tin mining, and once had been the state capital, with a number of British administrative functions and buildings. The quarters allocated to the Tay family were not large or grand but notably better; safe and comfortable enough for all the family to be gathered. It was at this time that three more children were born: Seow Hor (Jack), Seow Peik (Peggy) and Seow Hai (David). This made seven children in all. The youngest in the family was just two years old when the Japanese invaded, and Sonnie only nine.

Wartime Horrors and Hungers

On 8 December 1941, Japanese forces landed in the north of the peninsula. The Siamese had been adept to reach a compromise and would not protest or fight, provided that the Japanese would only transit through their kingdom to get into British-held Malaya. On their war path southwards, the Japanese streamed across the border that Tay had tried to demarcate and administer. The island of Penang was taken on 15 December 1941, and the Japanese continued into Taiping, bombing the market ahead of the troops who advanced on bicycles. Only a small band of British and Allied soldiers stayed behind to try to defend the town and these were quickly defeated. Those killed were later buried in the cemetery along the road leading to the town's waterfalls at the foot of Maxwell Hill.

It was then that Tay Hooi Eng made a critical decision. As the Japanese advanced, his wife evacuated with the children to join his brother and family at Nibong Tebal. Tay stayed behind. He was under instructions to assist the British to destroy files as well as a stock of currency to prevent these from falling into the hands of the Japanese. Only after that duty had been discharged would he leave to join the family. There was much concern if his young wife and the many children would be able to get to Nibong Tebal on their own, but they did. When he too made the journey from Taiping, successfully joining them one day later, their most immediate anxieties seemed over.

But the Japanese arrived shortly after. Someone in the small town informed the Japanese what Tay had done before leaving his post. Late one night in the first weeks of 1942, they came for him at the house. No one could stop them. Not the relatives and adults, and certainly not the young children and nine-year-old Sonnie. Tay Hooi Eng was taken away by the Japanese, never to return.

The record shows that in WWII, the Japanese practised many forms of torture and killing, even skinning those they captured and wished to question. There were also incidents when those rounded up – especially Chinese – would simply be shot en masse, in a large pit that they themselves had dug.

One of my aunts said, many years later, that he was doused in kerosene and set on fire. An uncle believes Hooi Eng was bayoneted and after dying was set aflame.

As a child, I had always imagined that it had been water torture, a practice for which the Japanese were notorious. A story I was to write later, entitled "A History of Tea", traced a family history somewhat like the Tays, attributed to a fictional family with the surname of Teh. (Although the Chinese character for Teh is different from that for "tea", there are many puns that can and have been made about the surname.) In this short fiction, there is a grandfather who was taken away by the Japanese for helping the British hide and escape and, as he was a merchant who sold tea, the Japanese bloated him with provisions and tea, instead of the normal water, and then "danced on his swollen abdomen [until] the food and drink choked him from the inside." Such were the horrible possibilities of that time: it can seize the imagination and poison it with a curious morbidity. Whatever way he was killed, after the first days of shock and uncertainty, any remaining hope that he might be returned gave way to a sense of finality: the young civil servant, husband and father of seven children, Tay Hooi Eng, was gone.

The loss was compounded by a sense of terrible injustice. He had not been an active combatant or trying to be any kind of hero. He only carried out a duty and caused no harm to anyone. In the wake of this event, the family was bereft not only by sorrow but insecurity. The immediate insecurity was that Japanese were known not only to punish the individual but sometimes his entire family. Moreover, the informant was someone in the village who knew him and, in some ways, this betrayal was the worst. They had left Taiping to come to Nibong Tebal because they had family there, and this was where Tay had first met his wife, and these familial ties and familiarity with the town had given them some sense of assurance when the war broke. How false that proved.

His wife and young children who were in the house when he was abruptly taken were traumatised. There was no way to even say goodbye properly and they were never to know what exactly happened to their father or where he was buried: that harsh reality stung and remained a deep wound after the war ended. It would run through the family and into future decades, a scar not only on the widow but all the children. Eventually, when the British returned, the administrators were to hand over a certificate to commend the late Tay Hooi Eng for help given to British forces to evade capture. But this altered nothing.

Not long after, the widow decided to leave Nibong Tebal. The siblings and extended family of her dead husband were not disposed to help her and the children, certainly not to the extent that she hoped. She returned to her own family in Penang, the place she knew best, where she had studied and grown up. Yet, there too, help and support were insufficient.

The pre-war prosperity of Malaya and Penang was gone. While the fighting had been brief and largely one-sided, the economy did not rebound during the Japanese Occupation. Mere basics were in short supply. These conditions imposed limits on generosity and care even within families and, for the widow, there were so many young children to feed. There was sympathy, but they could not live on that. She would have to find a way to earn her keep, and for her children too. A course of action was decided upon that would normally have been unthinkable: she would leave the island of Penang and move to a farm on the mainland. There was a logic to this plan. She could feed the family by working the farm. They would at least have enough to eat.

But she and the children were townsfolk, and town life was all they knew. The general aspiration of Chinese migrants had always been to go from being coolies and farmers to become merchants and then professionals and office workers, and reversing course to take up farming was against that current; not only a desperate act but one that neither she nor the children were prepared for. They did not know rural areas or how to farm. Their attempt at life on the farm did not survive long. Within a year, she returned to Penang with the girls and younger boys. But the widow decided that Sonnie and the second eldest son, Mannie, would remain with a relative of hers to continue on the farm. Sonnie was coming to 10 years of age and his brother was nine; being boys, they would have to help work the land. There was little other choice; there were just so many that her family in Penang were willing to accommodate.

This was a time of deprivations. No one had much; even back in Penang, people were just surviving. But, on the farm, there was even less. Sonnie would remember working endlessly and being scolded non-stop by the farmer-uncle who had no patience with this little boy from the town. He would remember being dirt poor and helping to sell *kueh* near the market and how his own stomach so ached with hunger that he wanted to snatch the cakes and run somewhere to devour them, even if that would end in a beating from his uncle. Yet, these daily hungers were not the worst of these hard times. The young boy would catch yellow fever and be so ill they thought that he would die. Hearing the bad news and fearing the worst, his mother sent across a parcel of tiger meat for him, a traditional and expensive remedy. The boy recovered but slowly. During his severe illness at that hardscrabble farm away from almost everyone and everything that might have given him assurance, the young Sonnie must have felt his abandonment and insecurity especially keenly. Notwithstanding, he had got through.

He recovered and resumed work but was then to be scarred, literally and permanently. One day, he was helping to clear thorny bushes from the land nearest the house when one of the thorns pierced his finger badly. The thorn was extracted, the wound was roughly washed and just left; his uncle said that it was really nothing. By the time Sonnie was taken to a doctor, the infection had spread and the bone in that part had to be removed. The infection subsided and finger remained, but it was odd and ugly, flat and spatulate. There was no proper finger nail either, just hardened and yellowed skin. Sonnie would grew into a man who was tall for his generation and who gave an immediate impression of strength and manliness. The finger was on his left hand so did not interfere much. But for the rest of his life, that digit would be a reminder of the deprivations and uncertainties of these years; an intimate and daily marker.

Much later in the 1960s, when he was settled and successful and his house would be open for a party with many guests, he remade his scar into a parlour trick. While the parents ate, and after the drinks were poured, he would come over with a big smile to where the children played to amuse them and himself. It was common enough: you tuck one thumb behind a crooked finger so it seems to be the tip of that finger. Then you slide it along so the finger appears to have been severed. The children would be quite stupefied, and he would laugh, teasing them. He did the trick well and fooled the eyes of even those who had seen it before and learnt how he did it (as I did). But while other adults might try the same trick, Sonnie would have a finishing touch like no one else. He would perform the trick with his right hand. But when the children gathered to demand to know how he did it, after much protest, he would show his other hand and that deformed finger, and there would be shouts and squeals from the boys and girls, and he would always laugh.

That finger trick would be used again in my novel, *City of Small Blessings*. The main character, who also endured the war and had been marked by the experience, performs the same trick. The circumstances of that fictive injury were different but the significance is shared. The victim did not only survive, he would find ways to makeover the trauma of the time into something else. The events of the war changed him and indeed all his family – not least with the killing of his father. His finger was the most visible yet smallest mark. Might all the rest that was suffered be turned into something better?

When the war came to an end, the widow Madam Goon left Penang, deciding to move to the town of Taiping. Word was sent to Sonnie at the farm. He was to take his younger brother and travel there to be reunited with his mother and their siblings. When the Japanese had invaded, Sonnie had been a nine-year-old child. Now in 1945, he was an adolescent and the eldest male in the family.

Taiping did not seem an obvious choice. In Penang or else in Nibong Tebal, they would have the rest of the Goon and Tay families, respectively, and might expect some familial support and succour. Yet, these same relatives had been unable or unwilling to really help during the war years and, while the war was over, there were further times of need and testing. The widow had seven children ranging in age from 14 to just 5 years old. A common practice in those times in such a situation would be to foster one or more of the children out to other relatives, even those more distant. There would perhaps be a married couple who were childless, or had no son to take over their business, or would want to groom a daughter to take care of them when they were older. Facing this situation, the widow judged that if she was to keep the family together, she would have to do it all on her own and in her own way.

They knew no one in Taiping. But, conversely, there were advantages to this. She would keep the children and the children would have only her. Theirs would be a nuclear family, not the extended one with many uncles and cousins that was usual at that time, but much more tightly knit. The sufferings they had endured during WWII and the stories of their father's unjust killing would provide many of the ropes and knots for their family ties. More importantly, without relatives watching on and inevitably gossiping, there was freedom to do whatever needed to be done. There were needs that would take them beyond what was conventional.

The widow's ambition was to keep her family together and do well. She understood that this would have to depend on her finding a job that could support them all. It was rare in that era for women to have any kind of job, and for widows especially. She was not an uneducated woman by the standards of her day as she had attended an English-speaking convent school in Penang until Junior Cambridge. She was used to speaking up, and used to being listened to. She believed she was more than capable of taking on a job. Moreover, she had been widowed because her husband had been loyal and decided to help the

British. She would play to these strengths and sympathies and do all she could and had to, with determination and without shame. Hard work would be needed but in itself would not be enough; she had already tried and failed at the farm. On top of effort, wiles would be needed too. The job would need, moreover, to be one that could support all the family and fund the household without a man. The widow would seek a man's job. That was the first taboo that would need to be broken.

Another was broken immediately upon arrival in Taiping. The widow reached out for help from the British military administration that had returned, and from the church. Told of their plight, the British officers and their good Christian wives provided help and she was more than glad to accept. The Tays were taken in by Mission House at the Taiping Gospel Hall. This was a church founded by missionaries in the 1880s and attended by white colonial officers and their wives, as well as the more established and well-to-do local families. They were given shelter on the church premises and lived off gifts and donations, often army rations. The general care and costs for the children were sponsored by different officers; Sonnie Tay was sponsored by one of the more senior officers.

If her relatives had known, they would have been shocked and intervened – not so much because they could have done more but simply because asking for charity carried a sense of family shame. They would not have the resources to fully assist but they would have given enough so as to keep up appearances; this had already been the experience when the widow had turned to them for help. The war relieved her of any sentimental hope that her family could and would help her sufficiently. Now relocated to Taiping, the widow had no such compunction against taking alms; she could not afford it.

Even as she took their Christian charity, she found employment. She was young and poor but proved to be anything but meek. Madam Goon was strong-willed and formidable, and those traits would be strengthened by what lay ahead. First, she was taken on as a nurse at a nearby military hospital, a job arranged by the wives from the church. But this suited neither

her character nor her ambition. She stayed only briefly before finding a more permanent and substantial position in the Welfare Department of the British Military Administration. There, she initially helped locate and channel assistance to the many needy cases that had emerged from the hard years of war, which seemed appropriate given her own experiences. Soon she was shifted to another aspect of the work that appealed to her and in which she was to excel. Her new responsibility was to track down merchants who were sharply raising prices for goods and items, especially for food and the basic household essentials. Goods were still scarce in the post-war years, and demand was increasing as the world again started to demand the tin and rubber that had made Malaya one of the most profitable of colonies. With this short supply and increasing demand, the traders were profiteering and there were also black market operations that pilfered from the supplies brought in by the British administrators.

As a local and a woman, she could find out more about these suppliers than could the white male administrators. The customers for these goods, the ones who did the buying in shops and markets were, after all, local women like her and open to talking and sharing where this item or the other was bought and at what price. There were said to have even been times when the widow would go down to the shops suspected of having black market provisions, posing as a customer, before filing her report to the administration that would lead to action. The problem was not only in the town but in other parts of the state, and a serviceable Austin and a Malay driver were put at her disposal to go around to different locations. It was a huge step up from depending on charity or work as a nurse which, unqualified by training and temperament, she had found menial. The pay was not so much but, in all, she was finding a success that, sadly, eluded many other locals in those post-war years. She had found the job that she needed. Even more important to the family, with her job she was allocated quarters. They were able to move out from the Mission House.

The house they were allocated, my Uncle Jack vividly

recollected, was at 838 Hugh Low Road, Assam Kumbang. This stood a little further out from town, near the aerodrome. It was nothing grand, just a standard British build with cement pillars, set in a neighbourhood of more or less identical buildings, all occupied by other local officers. Yet, this house was better than anything else they had known up to then. They were together and there was a roof over their heads, a refuge from their many years of insecurity and wanderings.

However, they were still poor and, with the mother at work, domestic arrangements were always makeshift. The quarters were not properly furnished and they made do with whatever they could find. There had to be a proper bed for Madam Goon but the children slept on mattresses on the floor or low book cases covered by linoleum or whatever was at hand. Meals were scraped together from what they could afford or could scrounge and cook up. There seems to have been no help in the household at first and, only later, a relative came for a spell to assist. The eldest of the children, the girl Lin, was 14 when they first arrived at the house, and she learnt to help the younger ones. The children were sent to school. Sonnie and his brothers were enrolled in King Edward VII, the grand old government school of the town.

Studies were emphasised. It would no doubt be the path for advancement. Education in the English language was especially a core belief; the widow prided herself on her facility in speaking and writing. She therefore often used English with the children, reserving Chinese dialects for the markets and dealing with local staff and networks, and her own dialect (a sub-group of Cantonese) for use with the occasional relative who would drop by. Each of her children was brought up to speak English primarily and properly, with the corollary that their dialects were only serviceable, and they had no Mandarin. Later, as circumstances allowed, the Tays would also pick up English customs, like having tea – not the Chinese way but according to what the English considered proper, often thin brews and sugared.

From the start, Sonnie did well at school. He achieved

double promotions to end up the youngest boy in the standard and still finished at the top of that class. He was outperforming and the widow could not have been prouder. For his siblings, there was admiration and also some envy at the attention that their mother gave to achieving results and spoiling those who achieved it. The eldest child, Lin, did well too but would feel that she was always held back because her grades were behind Sonnie's, and he was a son. The younger brothers felt the comparison not only at home. They had been enrolled in the same school and there were inevitable remarks by teachers and others in that small-town society.

It made things even worse for the boys that Sonnie was not only a top student but a first-rate sportsman – indeed that might have counted for more than scholastic achievement among their peers. He played for school in all the sports that mattered in that milieu, especially cricket. The young schoolboy was so good that even some of the colonial officers in the town noted it. Sonnie was not overly modest about such recognition. After all he had been through, it was something he revelled in and worked hard for, growing his intellect and also his body. He enjoyed his years at King Edward VII so much that he would adopt the school motto as his own; the Latin phrase, *Magni Nominis Umbra.*

This saying can be understood in different ways. As this long-established school intended it, the phrase might be rendered in English as being: "in the shadow of His greatness". That would evoke how limited all human beings are against the magnificence of the King, or else of God, and the reverence and humility that the school and its young students should feel.

Young Sonnie was active in church and from the Bible saw that God is referred to as a Father, our parent, and we are his children. For him, however, the role of parents was attenuated. The shock and horror of his father's death left a profound mark, as did the change in circumstances, deprivations and separation from the rest of the family that came after. As much as the elder Tay's death did cast a great shadow over him, his father's actual life cast a different shadow. He had been only a minor officer in the civil service. Even in his own family, he had been considered a distant second to his elder brother. He had died in service, not as a gallant hero, but simply a dutiful clerk.

His widow would make two different lessons from this. First, she was to win a certain amount of credit and sympathy from that in the small, colonial town – not unmerited but also quite consciously used. Second, she would always hold out to Sonnie and the other children that they could and had to do more with their lives and rise above being a minor clerk. After all, the widow, in her way, had risen by then to be more than that. For Sonnie and all his siblings, unless they excelled, they too would be judged as disappointments.

There were other lessons the widow would draw from the war. She was determined that the family, having survived separation during those years, would never again be apart. She tied them to her tightly and commanded that each be bound to the other in the fiercest of loyalties. When she was away from the home on work, the children had to fend for themselves, and Lin, as the eldest, was almost a surrogate mother. When the boys were at school, if any one of them was picked on and bullied, the others would come in to protect him. When she asked for something, it was their command.

These were essential in those early years in Taiping but would have their negative aspects, especially in later life. Even as adults, the children would dedicate every resource needed to make sure their mother was well and properly looked after, in the ways she expected, and almost to every whim. When she travelled and stayed with one or the other of them, she would expect to be the centre of attention, prioritised not only by her child but the in-laws and grandchildren. She was the ultimate matriarch. The best room in the house would be given to her, with every effort to ensure her comfort. The food at the table had to be adjusted to meet her preferences. She would often be seated next to the head of the table in Sonnie's house, where a wife would normally expect to be seated. The better her children did, the more she expected of them. Later on, when Sonnie had a car and driver, she would commandeer its use, giving herself priority over the daily routines of fetching and sending his wife to work and the children to school. When the youngest child, David, was later to do very well as a lawyer, he would be expected to bankroll all her expenses for life and her travels in some luxury. They did not do all these things so much from love but duty, bordering on fear. Those who married into the family felt it with something of a shock – especially daughters-in-law. Some would joke that they were not in-laws, but outlaws. Some of the children felt that their choices of wives were not accepted, not only initially but for the duration of their marriages. None of the children blamed their mother, but their combined record was short of enduring, happy marriages.

The widow came to stay with Sonnie after he was successful and the family had moved into a large black-and-white bungalow provided by the government at a very modest rent. In this house, I experienced my grandmother up close and how she continued to demand so much filiality from my father and dominate the household. I felt something was very wrong even then as a child. Later in life, the emotions I experienced were sufficient to provide fuel and fodder for short fiction like "Grandmother: A Horror Story" – the title might suggest the sum of my views.

My father had died by the time I wrote it, and so had my grandmother. My uncles and aunts did not remark specifically on the story although I am told that they did read it, and there was some anguish that I had not protected the family – an instinctive response inculcated by the widow from those Taiping days to stick together, right or wrong. Only decades later did one of my uncles acknowledge that he had recognised the truth about his mother that was embedded in the fiction. "Not to mention," he added, "that you knew her much later, when she was almost mellow." He laughed, and then went on to say how he had gained from her disciplines and had been saved from going wrong. That is a point that must be acknowledged.

Even if they were later to result in tensions and difficulties, the values and demands of the widow have to be understood in the context of those Taiping years. They brought to her young children a stability and discipline that they would always acknowledge for all their lives – and as they would be expected to. Sonnie, as a boy, was showing tremendous potential and with his energy, the lack of a father, and a mother too busy to supervise him very closely, he could easily have gone in a different direction. Many in that generation would not go onto university, lacking either the means and having to work and earn for the family, or simply not seeing such a qualification to be essential when most people were content to be Certificate holders. But his mother groomed Sonnie for more than that, and to deliver nothing less. In saying that, Sonnie knew then from his school motto – in the shadow of His greatness – that it could have been not "His" but hers; his predominant mother and her great expectations.

It was not just that the boy would come to recognise and try to live up to that demand. The man that Sonnie was growing up to become would internalise those same high expectations and do all he could to touch those heights – if not higher. And he would do that for himself, just as he had consciously adopted the saying: *Magni Nominis Umbra*.

Small-town Colonial Life

Meaning "everlasting peace" in Chinese, Taiping had grown in tandem with British industry and, like so many other settlements across Malaya and the Empire, supplied those industrial needs. The town had boomed from tin mining. Chinese workers arrived by the thousands to do the hard work in the mines. To administer and trade, the British built up suitable infrastructure and institutions. By 1877, there was a fine town with a mile-long street filled with bazaars and shops, gambling houses, workshops and meeting halls. There were also large detached barracks for the Sikh police, a hospital, powder magazine, parade ground, government storehouse, jail as well as some spacious bungalows for English officials;

all was neat and orderly. In 1885, the first railway line in Malaya was proudly opened to connect Taiping to the coast and Port Weld. Taiping became the administrative capital for the state and the grandest building in town was, of course, the British Residency perched on a steep, isolated hill for all to see. Colonial government departments grew, with key positions like Inspector of Mines, Harbour Master and Treasurer all held by Europeans while the Malays and Chinese took up junior posts.

But the tin mining slowed during the Great Depression, and Taiping slipped into gradual decline. By 1937, the state capital was shifted to Ipoh, which had larger mines. With the end of WWII, the British returned but prosperity and stability were to prove elusive. The challenges were not only about the tin mines or even the overall economic problems and shortages in the post-War period, the town and state were now minor parts of a larger landscape and a very different context. Taiping remained small, tidy and slightly sleepy at first glance, but it was now close to the epicentre of the Emergency, with the British trying to put down a Communist-led guerrilla war.

In the years immediately after the war, scarcities were on-going. But with school and church on top of the job with the British, with an income and housing, things were settling down for the Tays. The furniture in their home was slowly up-graded and the arrangements for the meals and the care of the children became more of a routine. The Tays adjusted to the new town, the house and their neighbourhood, a mixed area with Ceylonese, Eurasians and many others who filled in the middle and lower ranks of the colonial empire.

These early years in Taiping were to shape Sonnie and all the Tays in their outlook and sense of who they were. The English language and Christianity were entrenched, compared to other Chinese who spoke dialect and observed the rituals of a Taoist form of Buddhism. The Tays would engage with the English and many other non-Chinese. The boys grew especially familiar with the Ceylonese in the neighbourhood. The girls, in the years ahead, were all to pair up with non-Chinese and would marry into Eurasian, Scottish and Australian bloodlines. For Sonnie, even decades later, some of his closest friends were Indian and Ceylonese, and he would always be able to engage the British and other whites.

When the civilian administration returned to Taiping, many from the military were demobilised and some of the locals who had been appointed by the military in the exigencies of the post-war situation were released. But not Madam Goon. She scoured for job openings, even applying to be a probation officer for the juvenile court. Her application specifically mentioned her widowhood and the killing of her husband for aiding the British, and was endorsed by no less than the Deputy Commissioner for Perak. In the end, she was shifted from the Welfare Department but her appointment was regularised and she was appointed to be Superintendent at the Old Folks' Home – a job of considerable rank and responsibility. She kept her "man's job", and she was formidable in carrying it out, beyond the conventions of her time, gender and race.

On top of this, she was going to ensure that the children were brought up properly and would prosper. She was demanding of their school results and strict on their discipline. Much of the weight of these expectations was placed on the eldest children: Lin, the eldest and a girl, and Sonnie, as the eldest son. The widow positioned herself and the family in the right circles in the small town. There were occasions and parties where the widow would invite those she knew from work and from church, often the white officers and their wives. These included the officers who had charitably sponsored the children when the family first arrived and each child was tasked to report to his or her sponsor on their advancement at school. Their circles of acquaintances in Taiping grew to include some of the better- established families. Some of the white colonial and military officers, some who were at post without their wives, also came to visit and more than once. There were merriments with music. Sonnie, in his young teens, would play bartender to make and serve drinks.

A certain Captain Sherman was especially noted. He would

come regularly to the house and came to learn about the killing of the elder Tay. The widow was encouraged to write to the colonial administration to substantiate what her late husband had done. Sherman was sure that this would be duly acknowledged, especially as she now worked for the British administration, and this would help her and the children in the future. Letters were written and sent. A reply came in the name of the highest authorities to commend the late husband's sacrifice. Indeed, there seem to have been two. One certificate arrived to commend the late Tay Eng Hooi for help given to British forces to evade capture, and was signed by Louis Mountbatten, Supreme Allied Commander for Southeast Asia. The other was signed by Clement Atlee, the Prime Minister of post-war Great Britain. A King's commendation was even presented to the widow by the High Commissioner, Sir Henry Gurney, at a special ceremony at the Residency in Kuala Lumpur. It is not clear how much these acknowledgements helped with the emotions of losing a parent but the commendations were helpful in shoring up acceptance in the circles of Taiping town, and for the widow's continued service for the colonial authorities. There were, however, limits.

In Taiping, there is a war cemetery which is today regarded as one of the sights that any visitor must take in. At the time that the Tays were there, it was yet to be built. The newly returning British looked to mark their war dead, and the small town was selected for one of the largest memorials. Taiping and its environs had been a site of the fighting. The single battalion normally based there, augmented by two more units from India, used the town for rest and refitting. As the Japanese advanced, Taiping was on the line of retreat that the British organised, with a casualty receiving station set up together with the Indian 20th Combined General Hospital. Many died in that area. After the war, the memorial was built, interring the remains of more than 850 casualties, including more than 500 unidentified. These included not only the whites who had perished but those from the Indian and other units from various parts of the Empire. Much care and considerable planning had been undertaken, and the white granite headstones on the green lawn created a sense of dignity, order and peace – a sharp contrast to the conditions of the war that had claimed their lives.

In all this, there was no marker for the elder Tay and indeed nothing that even generally acknowledged the local, non-uniformed civil servants who had lost their lives. They would have the paper commendation, and make do with that, much as they would have to make do with their place in the society of that tidy town.

There were other limits and smaller-scale dramas that were felt acutely by young Sonnie, episodes that he would tell later as an adult about his teenage years in Taiping. They were not major calamities but neither should they be considered simple tales of growing up. Even when his career showed success and later in his life, Sonnie would retell them. These stories connected to the changing society of that period and meant something to him, about his place there. But rather than to make a specific point didactically, when he held forth on some subject the tellings of these stories from Taiping and the past would often meander in. Often there was no clear structure and were without even the simplest details of when and who, let alone how or why. Sometimes they would be told by Sonnie himself or, more often, by his siblings. The Tay siblings were all garrulous storytellers; comparatively, Sonnie was the one who spoke less, even if it was expected that, when he did speak, his words would carry more weight. If he and one or more of the siblings were together in the same room when the story came up, there might be mild disagreements about some of the details. Or else, there would be a lot of nodding as the siblings had an implicit context to the stories that escaped others present. Stories have in the course of the years been told repeatedly, but as with oral tales, are difficult, perhaps impossible, to check. Even so, they contain truths.

The first story related to church in Taiping. The Tays had been the beneficiaries of largesse through the church and, as their fortunes improved, became part of the congregation.

Attending the Gospel House church with his family, Sonnie was an active member of the Youth Movement, indeed one of the prominent ones. There, the young man met a young lady and an early interest sparked between them which might have been something innocent and normal enough. He was good looking and, while he could sometimes seem intense, he could be charming and had a sense of humour. But even as this began to develop, any further possibility was quickly smothered. Established and well-to-do families attended the church, and the young lady was from one of them. One of her close relatives was in fact a senior leader in the congregation that the young Sonnie had looked up to. Yet, when the prospective interest became known, it was this same congregation leader who summarily rejected Sonnie, explaining that he was the son of a poor widow and not a good match.

Those facts could not be denied. The family, like many others in the church, only reflected the mores that prevailed in that small-town society and the socioeconomic and colonial order of things. But to Sonnie, the rejection stung as hypocrisy. What about the values of the faith and the church to which he and the girl and their families belonged? There are accounts that the young man showed his loss of respect for the family and for the church. Trying much later to recollect what happened, some relatives suggest that the angry young man was expelled for some public disagreement with an elder. It was suggested by some that the disagreement was with one of the British officers who had sponsored the Tay children when they first arrived. Or, at other times, it was said that he loudly complained about the girl's relative who was by then a lay leader. Whatever precisely happened, there was a scandal spoken about in whispers in that small-town community. It was a fact that Sonnie then left the church. While he did not denounce faith, he never returned to regular churchgoing.

A second story concerned the extended family and an uncle on the Goon side, his mother's brother. The Goons had not been able to take in the entire Tay family during the war and, from that period onwards, were never close. Still, they had extended some assistance as they felt they could. The children were without a father and there was some sense that they needed a male figure, especially for the sons. One of the uncles took a liking to Sonnie and would occasionally invite the boy over for a visit. The uncle had a library – neither a common nor inexpensive thing to have in those days – and he had heard that Sonnie loved reading. He invited the youngster to visit and allowed him access to the books. Sonnie did have an enquiring mind that extended well beyond the texts he read at school and he and his uncle would sit and take tea, and talk about the books that they had read, discussing what they thought interesting and what was bunkum.

Before long, they met regularly. The youngster would cycle home with as many books as he could carry and read them all before the next meeting. He showed more interest in the books and talk than his uncle's own children had and the uncle promised that when it was time, the library and all the books would be left to him. Over the years, the old man promised it often enough, and not just to Sonnie; he had said that to his wife and sons at meals they had together. But later, when the uncle eventually passed on, there was no legacy of books. The old man's statements were informal and were never written into the will, and the children, even if they did not love the books, would not part with them. Even within a family, and with a relative that he had been close to, a line was drawn on the relationship, and Sonnie was left outside.

The third story Sonnie would recount concerned his own family. As his mother continued in her job and established herself, she had more time to attend to the children and make sure that they would do well. She held the children even more tightly. The widow was a disciplinarian and could be severe when her children seemed irresponsible and fell short of her high expectations. Each one was subject to this and those with high spirits were reined in – especially the boys. They were all reminded of the deprivations the family had come through and on whom the burdens of the family had all fallen. But as the family prospered, it was not so much a question of burdens but of the benefits.

The parties that the widow would hold continued and grew. They had started as a way of thanking those who helped the family to meet basic needs of shelter, food and income. As things settled and those basics were met, there were other needs and advantages which the widow sought, and those people who could next be of help. The circle widened, the parties grew larger, more social. There was a considerable amount of drinking as might be expected from a party of British colonists in this era, and perhaps there were instances when the strict propriety expected of that time might not have been fully observed. The teenage Sonnie would not only serve drinks at the bar to the guests but, manning the bar, he was also permitted and encouraged to drink with them. A young man is impressionable.

So were his sisters. At these parties, they would come to join in and mingle and meet a number of the male guests. Some started to court his sisters with the allowance and even encouragement of the widow. The eldest, Seow Lin, was soon settled with a big-sized Eurasian, Emile Nicolas. A colonial with a swagger named Brown from outside of Sydney came for Shelley, although she was quite a lot younger than he. The youngest girl, Peggy, was courted by the young pastor, Peter Ferry, to whom the widow expressed initial doubts because of the spartan life that the church offered. These matters were taken in hand and the girls were married off.

There were no corresponding efforts for the boys. A man was expected to find his own way and his own choice in marriage and in life. Sonnie would have to fend for himself and he already realised some of the obstacles. The interest in the girl at church showed how he stood in the calculations of society in Taiping – well below the whites and also behind the more established and well-to-do locals. The limits to what his uncle would leave him demonstrated that he could not count on gifts, legacies and charity; whatever he wanted would have to be earned. There could have been some element of envy against those who had more money and a father and family standing. But Sonnie did not voice it and, if he did feel that, it only drove him harder and to accept his place as being an outsider, comfortable at being something of a maverick.

There was respite and some comforts in those post-WWII years at Taiping. He and his family had been on a hard and long journey, at the end of which they secured a home and were safe and together. Yet, what had happened in the war could not be taken as a mere interruption, nor Taiping its conclusion. The concerns and resentments from this time related to colonial authority, exclusion and opportunity – of justice and equality. These were key elements in the young man's emerging sense of identity.

In the decades ahead, there was another place that Sonnie would come to call home. In that place, there would be social and political movements that would speak to circumstances that he felt about the white, colonial society. There would be ideas of society and belonging that appealed to people like him who felt an empathy and connection to others regardless of their race or religion, and a kind of attachment to the land even if they were not sons of the soil. The sense of Malaya as a country, with Singapore as part of it, would later challenge colonialism and be articulated in the calls for a Malaysian Malaysia. After the Separation, this remained, rooted in the pledge to make a Singapore that would be united, regardless of race, language or religion, so as to build a democratic society based on justice and equality. Such sentiments would crystallise for Tay and others of his generation, and would come to affect not just the young man and his family but the society and Empire.

Larger Fears and Hopes

When Sonnie was 15, the British declared a State of Emergency in Malaya. This began on 16 June 1948, after three British planters were killed in the Sungei Siput district in Perak, near Taiping. Within days, the declaration was extended throughout the entire peninsula of Malaya. The killings were carried out by Communists and was but a first incident in the battle to free Malaya from colonial rule. The Communists who emerged to fight the Japanese during the war had now regrouped to form the Malayan National Liberation Army (MNLA). The military aspect of the Emergency was a guerrilla war, fought mainly in the thick jungles of Malaya. The MNLA, operating from jungle bases, raided British police and military installations and targeted tin mines and rubber plantations to sabotage the already frail economy. Communist attacks rose sharply in late 1949 and reached a high point with the assassination of the British High Commissioner, Sir Henry Gurney, in 1951. The British responded with search-and-destroy jungle operations, deploying rapid response units against guerrilla attacks and the formation of local auxiliary forces.

The Emergency was a war in all but name. British efforts to handle the situation were later to merit some comparison to the Americans in the Vietnam War. One reason some say the term was preferred is that naming the situation a war would have excused British insurers from making payments to mines and plantations. It also differed in that the opponents arose from within the country and not from some foreign power. Whatever the term used, the Emergency was a military matter, and much more.

The Communists really gained ground in Malaya during WWII and took on energy from the British themselves when the famous British Force 136 had encouraged and enabled them to fight against the Japanese. The British valued help from all sides at that moment. But from that point on, the causes expounded by the Communists had a reach that went far beyond the Japanese and the jungle.

The appeal of Communism commingled with anti-colonialism and with racial factors, to bring together an early expression of nationalistic sentiments. The majority of the MNLA and the Communist Party of Malaya were ethnic Chinese and their calls for greater equality and for independence won sympathy. Many Chinese in Malaya were mired in poverty, and had been subject to racial persecution by the colonial administration before the war and then by the Japanese during it. Many sympathisers from among the ethnic

Chinese would lend support with money, food and shelter while some also ventured to become MNLA fighters. This meant that the British response had to address not only those in the jungle but fundamentally the many sympathisers and supporters to be found among the masses, or *min yuen*.

The main pillar of these efforts was centred on internment camps, a plan originally ascribed to Brigadier General Harold Briggs. Some 400 of these "new villages" were built to segregate the civilian population who could be sympathisers and support the Communists. The scale of the plan's ambition was considerable: over 400,000 civilians were interred there. Those identified were mostly Chinese, but there were some Indian and even Orang Asli – the original settlers of the lands. Predominately those interred were poor or felt discriminated against; the Chinese were most often "squatters" without proper documentation and any rights to housing or land.

The policy was implemented by means that would today be condemned. For while the Briggs Plan looked benign enough on paper and in various pro-British news clips, the implementation was anything but gentle. It was common that the British would detain and question Chinese with force and methods that were tantamount to torture. Accounts tell of the British forces enforcing food rationing on the civilians in the settlements, killing livestock and using chemical herbicides to destroy rural farmland. The population in the "new villages" had not been charged with any crimes but, in all but name, they were imprisoned.

The worst came in incidents when unarmed villagers were executed without trial – the most infamous case being the 1948 massacre at the village of Batang Kali, an incident sometimes called the British version of the American atrocities at My Lai in Vietnam. Despite the severe methods used, the British administration struggled to stop the sympathisers; indeed, resentment grew. From 1952, Sir Gerald Templar from the Intelligence Corps was appointed High Commissioner, and he brought a critical change in approach. He was to combine the Briggs Plan with a mode of implementation that could try to win "hearts and minds".

Much of this "war" happened in the years when Sonnie was a teenager in Taiping and these events were played out in areas nearby and familiar. The cosseted colonial town of Taiping was not untouched. More than a few young men turned to Communism and the poor Chinese men were especially drawn in. The process of recruitment was neither formal nor directly into the MNLA and the jungle. Most often, it began in casual conversations in coffee shops or at other activities that attracted the young and then graduated to cultural or sporting activities. Then there would be some dialogues and sharing about the ideals of freedom and equality, and condemnation of the deprivations that the Chinese poor suffered and the racism of the colonial system. What followed were invitations for sessions to study doctrine to instill them with the right ideology of Communism. Only some would be selectively asked to take up the armed struggle. But in this way, the Communists would woo many and win sympathy. Even short of being an active combatant in the jungle, there was a search to recruit those who would look at the issues of the day in the light of what Communism held out, so as to further the political and agitprop work. The Communists were linked not only to the *min yuen* but to an even wider movement that reached out to unions and workers, cultural groups and a political party: a united front.

Here were issues of inequality and exclusion that resonated with Sonnie, as he recounted many decades later. He was approached when he was student. It is not clear exactly when and how the approach was made. But there was a high school at Pantai Remis, a commercial town along the coast about an hour away from Taiping, with many links among the Chinese-speaking community and to China. There was some sense in trying to recruit Sonnie: he was Chinese and poor. One of his relatives had been involved around that area, in helping train the guerillas in handling small arms as they prepared to take on the Japanese. Like so many, his family had lost much in WWII and the sense of injustice over his father's killing was strong and deep. While the Tay family were not squatters, by the end of that war they had been impoverished to the point of desperation and seeking charity. He too felt unjustly treated, angry at all that happened. He had not found a strong father figure to guide his energies. At that juncture, it would not have been impossible to consider that the teenage Sonnie might be persuaded. Not perhaps into the jungle, but there were many different ways for an angry young man with nothing to lose to become involved in the movement against the Japanese and then to resist the returning colonial authorities to fight for the ideals of equality and the hope of prosperity.

Sonnie would never join the Communists but neither was he inured to what was happening. Beyond the jungle warfare and "new villages", the Emergency echoed into the towns like Taiping and colonial quarters that the Tays and others like them occupied. If the violence and shooting did not touch them directly, the rumours brought spreading fear. While Communism as whole did not appeal, there were convictions that would resonate and be adopted by the emerging post-WW2 generation. Chief amongst these was the search for prosperity for the many, and a question about the continued rule of the British.

The British relented to some degree. In the early 1950s, the colonial administration introduced local elections and the creation of village councils. Many of the Chinese migrant workers were granted citizenship. Talk of independence grew and this political expectation attracted hope and undercut the allure of the continuing armed insurgency and violence.

Communism was not accepted as the answer but the questions raised had resonance for Sonnie and many others of his generation. For him, the interest in trying to understand what happened in those years continued well into his adulthood. He would buy and closely read books to study in depth and with detachment what he had lived through and felt in the air and on his skin. It would be a clear foundation to his work for the government.

Unlike the minor Chinese traders in the street or the

market, or the squatters who did the menial work and lived in shanty towns out near the jungle, Sonnie had other ways to seek equality, a place in the sun. His hope for a better future lay not in revolution and Communism but through his studies, by working hard for respect and reward. Independence, he was sure, would change things. In Taiping, Sonnie continued to do well at school; being top of the class was the only acceptable result. Yet, this was not enough. His mother's plan was not just for him to be top in the school in Taiping. She wanted no less than a scholarship, and for that he would have to do even better to compete across the state. He would have to be much more than a mere clerk, as his father had been, and then the family would have someone to secure their future. Sonnie worked on his studies willingly, out of his own curiosity but also as his way of pleasing his mother. But he wanted more. Like any teenager, he also wanted to enjoy himself.

While he loved books and reading, he was also energetic, almost hyperactive. He would get up to all kinds of things with his brothers and others he knew from school or the neighbourhood. He was tall for his age and with sports and swimming, he was broad-shouldered and dark from the sun. Besides cricket, he took up badminton, hockey and just about every sport. He also loved the outdoors. He took up jungle trekking around Taiping for the cool air and views from nearby Maxwell Hill (now Bukit Larut).

Although the fighting from the Emergency continued in the deepest, thickest parts, there were other sections that were nearer by and safer. Sonnie and his brothers tried to understand how to survive and find their way around in the jungle, and regarded *The Jungle is Neutral* as a kind of manifesto, reading and re-reading the account of how the British officer Spencer Chapman learnt jungle skills after escaping from the Japanese in Burma. The fighting of the Emergency was never absent. One uncle would tell the story of how he, Sonnie and a few others were trekking and stumbled across the aftermath of a skirmish. Mutilation and decapitation were not uncommon. It should have been considered a war crime except that the

Emergency was not classified by the British as war. Stumbling across the corpses in the jungle reminded the young men that their lives could not be kept wholly innocent of all that was going on. Yet, the jungles would continue to draw Sonnie to them, long after he left Taiping. It was meditative for him to be in nature, and do simple things like making a fire and to cook and eat basic things.

Sonnie learnt to love swimming. While the sea was not too far away, the areas near Taiping were carved with rivers that offered many spots for swimming. His favourite was the Burmese Pool and that stretch of the river where the rocky bottom had been carved into a natural slide. It was a gathering spot for many of Taiping's teenagers. Here a boy could position himself at the right point and the swift, strong current of the river could carry him quickly forward and, as it narrowed, up the slide and he would be airborne, before landing in the deep pool below. Sonnie could spend whole afternoons there, swimming in the running cold water and emerging to dry under the sun.

Quite different from the nature trekking and swimming, Sonnie was increasingly interested in motorbikes. Fascinated, in fact. There was a function in this: they offered the means to range out further from the town and their house to forests and beaches that were further away than a bicycle could easily reach. But more, he was thrilled by their speed and freedom. They were cheap enough too, with bikes like the Triumph, BSA Matchless, and Norton left over from the British military when messengers had used them. He got a BSA and fixed it up to run fast and stop straight. He eyed other models that were more powerful, faster, and that could go further.

These pursuits – the rugged outdoors, the sea and lakes, the speed of the bikes and, later, cars – were so different from his book studies and intellectual interests. But they were more than frivolities to give him some balance. They spoke to the energy that was burning inside him, constrained in that small town and the circumstances he then faced, but straining and leaping to get out and beyond. Sonnie was kinetic, often restless and sometimes reckless. This was not just as a teenager; like the pursuits, these characteristics would continue into his adulthood. They made him at times less than predictable. These characteristics made him such a vital and charismatic figure.

Many years later, when I was about 13, he would take us back to Taiping. By this time, in the 1970s, the town seemed so small and run-down. While my father was nostalgic, he confessed he could not imagine living there, as did one of his brothers and more than a few of his classmates. How might his life been if he hadn't left? Besides seeing the town and Maxwell Hill and meeting up with his brothers, he specifically brought us to the river and the Burmese Pool. He pointed and I swam through the cold water to get to the spot where the water tumbled and frothed with such energy, and with all the stories he had told and I had heard, I plunged in. I rode that same slide, the same path, my father had. It was all that he had said it was.

In the 1990s, I would write about that place and experience in a story called, "My Cousin Tim", which became popular and was extracted in various anthologies and even taught in some schools. This was about more than a river. I could feel that even when I was in the water as a teenager with my father. I would develop that sense when I was in my early 30s, writing that story. The river that my father had so enjoyed in his childhood years was more than a place to cool off and have fun. It was about how from that quiet place, those energies could gather and sweep a young man along and up into the air briefly, and then land in a new place, with a mix of anxiety and excitement so that the goosebumps on the skin from the cold water were almost badges of courage.

Sonnie completed his full Senior Cambridge Certificate in Taiping and was sent to Ipoh, the larger nearby town, for his Form VI at St Michael's, a mission school. His results were the best in the school, no less than his mother expected. More, he was top student across the entire state of Perak. With that result, the widow contacted those she had known in the Welfare Department and others and got a State Scholarship for him. It was her wish that he be enrolled in the prestigious medical faculty at the University of Malaya. To prepare for that, at St Michael's in Ipoh, he was also to learn Latin. Sonnie wanted to study the Arts rather than Medicine but the widow prevailed in that decision, sweetening her demands with a graduation gift of a better motorbike. His mother got her way, as she most often did. But so did he.

He would leave; first for Ipoh, and then heading south to Singapore for university. Taiping was a place he enjoyed and had thought of as home. He was close to his family and would miss them, and he had friends he remembered there. He knew he owed much to his mother – that had been drummed into him. But it was not only the widow that had ambitions for her son. Even if he was unclear what exactly he wanted, he was certain that the future must be more than what Taiping had to offer. He had his own hopes and was ready to go chase them. As surely as the course of the river that ran through his favourite Burmese Pool surged and then leapt into the air, Sonnie left that small colonial town.

*

Our cousin was coming down from Malaysia. My sister messaged and suggested we all meet for dinner. Shelley is the only child of Uncle Mannie, my father's brother. My uncle had married late and continued to live and work in Taiping for many years. Consequently, my cousin was some 15 years younger than me and grew up in that small town.

I hardly knew her. She was a toddler when my father died, and did not know him. But she has grown up in the same town he had, decades earlier. She has also been the one to keep in touch with almost all of the family.

Taiping was nice, almost idyllic, Shelley recalls. She remembers with easy familiarity the streets of the town, the church, Maxwell Hill, the swimming club and the river that I barely knew and had to research. She recalls a family, the Angs, who were stalwarts of the church and very close to the Tays when they first moved to Taiping after the war. She has kept in touch with them, and also relatives from the Tay side of the family and on grandmother's side, the Goons, some of whom were still in Penang, Nibong Tebal and Taiping, while others had moved to KL or even to Singapore – and all of whom I hardly knew existed.

Shelley is affable, pleasant and easy to talk to. There was a difficult time when her parents separated when she was still a child. But she kept close to her father and to church, reconciled with her mother, and grew out of it. They left Taiping and moved to KL to be closer to the other uncles and for her school. Today, in her 40s and married with a small child, she is the main caregiver to her father – who has lost his sight quite completely. She worked in the church for years as the small Taiping congregation grew into the thousands. Now she works for a multinational bank, which was why she was visiting Singapore.

My three remaining uncles kept in close touch, seeing each other often, even every day. Short weeks before this dinner, our youngest uncle, David, had passed on. Her father is grieving the recent passing and also missing her. Almost on cue when she talks about this, her father calls. Shelley talks to her father for a while and then passes her phone to Joanne and then to me to say hullo. My uncle says he is happy we are all meeting. We take a wefie and later send it to him and also to Uncle Jack.

This is perhaps only the third or fourth time Shelley and I have ever sat down for a meal together. My sister was the one who had rekindled the cousins' connection some years back when, ever dutiful, she had gone up to KL to attend Shelley's wedding. Shelley wonders why we had been out of touch for so many years, not only with her but the family.

It would be easy to say that distance and schedules did not allow. But perhaps blood relations who ask such questions want more than easy answers. I look up from our food and cannot decide how frank to be without ruining the meal and our few hours together. We agree that talking about the generations must be subject to the acceptance that perspectives can differ.

My sister and I share what our grandmother was like in the years of our childhood, how she tried to run everything her way, tried to impose her will on me in particular and the ways she would inveigh on our father, her son. When my father died in 1980, I determined that any reason to see his mother was gone. Since she was the centre of the family, I did not see any of the uncles or aunts. My sister and mother would, now and again.

Shelley says the grandmother she knew was sometimes haughty but always benign, especially after her stroke; how the same woman could be so different in later years, a decade on. My cousin's perspectives on our aunts is quite glowing and I am glad for her. After all, she was named for two of those aunts – with Lyn as part of her Chinese name and sharing the name Shelley with another aunt. As we talk and eat together, I look across at her and decide she does bear some resemblance to my aunts.

It is for the better that there is now some connection with my cousins and their parents. Over the past decade, I have seen my Uncle Jack and his sons off and on, and occasionally met when I have been up to KL for work. My Uncle Jack was the one I talked most to over these last years and the one I contacted most often, especially when I was researching this book. He was the most outgoing, garrulous one among the brothers. He read through the chapter relating to the Taiping years and never asked me to change anything.

In writing, I have borrowed not only from him but more generally from my memory of family stories. When I was a child, there were often times that my father, uncles and aunts would sit around and recount their childhood years, things they shared. Even then, there was always something "long-ago-and-faraway" about their tales, and somewhat mythic in the tropes they themselves emphasised about what they endured in the war and the life they rebuilt in Taiping.

In writing about those years in Taiping, I had recollected what I could of the tales they told. I had borrowed, I realise, from Uncle Jack's memories and his perspectives in more recent conversations, both before and after I began this book. After our dinner and discussion, I wondered if I should send my cousin Shelley what I have written about our family. Even family myths, retold much later and from different mouths, can have different meanings; and while some might unite the family, others could divide.

After dinner, Joanne and I drive Shelley back to her hotel. When might we meet again? Oh, my sister or I will probably be up in KL sometime next year. Or she will come down. Be in touch, my cousin says. Then we are at the hotel and she is gone.

Chapter 3

YOUNG MAN GOING FAST

SINGAPORE IN THE 1950S was in a rush. The war years had hit hard. The Japanese Occupation had been short but intense and severe. The city and its port depended on the trade of goods and the movement of vessels and people, and these had been largely cut off. Post-war recovery would not come automatically, but there was a determination and urgency to bring back growth and speedily regain Singapore's place as the Empire's most important centre in the region.

Arriving in 1951, Sonnie Tay Seow Huah was a young man going fast too. He was away from his mother and siblings. Earlier, in preparing for his entry into medical school and to learn Latin, he had been in Ipoh for a year, not far away and yet still far away enough, and he had enjoyed the experience. Going to university would be for a longer spell and at a further distance. Leaving the small town and his tight family gave him a new sense of freedom. Singapore was vastly different in scale and outlook from the towns up north. These differences and distance reinforced the sense of freedom and change. So did university.

University Days
The University of Malaya was in Singapore. Without family and close friends in the city, he roomed at the Dunearn Road Hostels as did so many others who had come down from the peninsula. The hostels were newly opened and there was a teeming activity that bordered on chaos. There were also some

others who had lived and grown up in Singapore, including scions of well-to-do families. Ragging initiation rites were practised and, with British influence, were a mix of prank and cruelty, conducted on the pretext of breaking down barriers and jump-starting camaraderie. Sonnie went through what he had to and emerged as part of a lively set at the hostel, affectionately called by its acronym, DRH.

Some students were absorbed in studies, especially those who had been held back during the war years and those who had gone to work before returning for their degrees. But for many others, studies seemed secondary. After the tensions of the war and Occupation, it was not only Sonnie but the whole generation who felt a new freedom. Social life – making friends and trying to get to know the girls and especially those housed nearby but separately – was the focus for many. With the cinema and tea dances and swimming parties at the beach, there was a whirl of social activities in Singapore, all so much more when compared to the confined and quiet circles in Taiping. Sonnie was exhilarated. As surely as how he jumped into the Burmese Pool in Taiping, the young man now plunged into this new life. He lived a very full life in these student years.

He was among the keen sportsmen at DRH and the university, excelling especially in badminton. At that time, Malaya dominated the world in the sport. The top player in Singapore was Wong Peng Soon, who held the national titles on multiple occasions before and during the war. In 1950, soon after international competitions restarted, Wong went on to win the most prestigious of them all, the All-England Championship. He was the first Asian to be All-England champion and, when he went on to win the title again in 1951, 1952 and 1955, he was dubbed, "the Great Wong". Malaya – of which Singapore was then part – also won the Thomas Cup twice in that era, with Singapore playing host to this international championship three times. With Wong and Malaya's victories, badminton became all the rage. There were hotly contested matches between clubs like the Mayflower Club where Wong had been groomed and still played. There were gatherings, with the larger and richer families building courts on the grounds of their homes to host badminton parties where men and women would gather to play. Sonnie played and was at many of the competitions and, for a spell, trained at the Mayflower Club. He was good and played singles for the university. He also socialised around the sport, attending many badminton parties.

But the friends with whom Sonnie spent the most time when he lived at DRH were far from these social circles: they were motorbike riders. His interest in Taiping had grown into a preoccupation, and those closest – his *kaki* – shared this passion. Victor Gopal, a big Indian chap from Malaya, was one of them. Kasinathan was another. They would race their motorbikes along Bukit Timah Road and Dunearn Road – the main, broad and straight roads that went past the university on either side of the canal. Sonnie traded up his bikes and would eventually be astride the Black Shadow, a British motorcycle with a top speed of 125 mph. The 1953 movie, *The Wild One*, made Marlon Brando a star and cultural icon for a lifestyle around motorbikes and the young men who rode them. Motorbikes signalled the freedom of youth, and going fast in life, and taking risks. They were the trend and resonated with the fast pace of change and exciting talk in the post-war period. Sonnie would race out from the gate of the hostel and hit 100 mph before the first light at Whitley Road.

There was excitement in politics. Independence was in the air. Among the young men of DRH, more than a few were embroiled in discussions, talks and pamphleteering. The talk was not only about Singapore but, since many were from Malaya, on the prospect of independence for the peninsula as a whole. Yet, some of the British still believed that colonial rule was indisputably good for Malaya and tried to resume things as before or strengthen their position – as they did in moving for the Malayan Union to have full and direct control over all the states. Among locals of different races, however, there was no ready acceptance to go back to the pre-war days and accept colonial authority without question or accountability.

The British belatedly came to recognise the demands for decolonisation and still, as preconditions, laid out the terms and even drafted a constitution to imprint British Westminster practices and models as basic and good for all. This was their practice not just in the Far East but also in Africa, the Caribbean and across the Empire on which the sun had never set.

While the call for independence had broad appeal, opinions differed. Some accepted the British blueprint, at least as a basis for negotiation. Others embraced more radical and idealistic hopes and pushed for greater equality and equity between the rich and poor, or to find new dispensations between the races. Up north, where Sonnie had come from, there was the guerrilla war of the Emergency, led mainly by the poorer sections of Chinese. Up north too, in rejecting the Malayan Union, a movement grew to assert the rights of the Malay people, spawning the United Malays National Organisation (UMNO).

In Singapore, an Emergency was also imposed though the contest was not fought in the jungles but in street protests and conflicts and as matters of politics. Another difference from the North was that, with the Chinese making up the majority in Singapore, calls for Malay rights might have been strident but of confined appeal. It was instead the Communist appeal for greater equality that resonated more widely. This was especially among the lower-paid Chinese labourers, and also some of those from South Asia. Given this, the political differences could spark underlying racial tensions and trigger violence.

Conflicts in Singapore around this period were amongst the worst ever known: the Hock Lee Bus Riot in May 1955, and riots by pro-Communist Chinese students in October 1956. There was a mood of turbulence across the island and, on campus, the sense of activism ran high. The university students and DRH residents were part of the impulse of the times and more than a few were involved in the Socialist Club and the magazine, *Fajar*. Some were later accused of sedition against the colonial authorities. DRH alumni were prominent among those who entered politics or else the unions on the Socialist side. Some of these later joined political parties and some, like James Puthucheary, were detained by the British in the 1963 Operation Coldstore. Another activist among the DRH students was Jamit Singh, who would become a significant actor in the trade unions for port workers.

With the intense debates and a growing sympathy for the need for action, no student was unaware and yet not all students at university involved themselves directly in these protests and strikes. Sonnie discerned that some of the more vocal students were attracting attention from the colonial police's Special Branch. Some of them seemed to revel in such notice and believed that the British liberal tradition would allow room for dissent. But, from his experience of the Emergency in the North, Sonnie had seen a different and less tolerant side of the British in their prosecution of the Emergency. He participated occasionally but left the bigger, bolder talk to others. This was Singaporean politics and he was aware he did not know the place and people well. He still regarded Malaya as home.

As he settled into university, there was also the small matter of the course of his studies. At his mother's command, he had enrolled in the Medical Faculty on a scholarship. But in a matter of weeks, when dissection sessions began, he begged off. Being a doctor was a high aspiration, combining a clear good for the community and a respectable income, but Sonnie was determined to switch out from the medical school into the arts and social sciences. He preferred to read economics and the queasy sensation he reported cutting into what had been a living thing was something that excused that choice. The university had to be persuaded to allow this change. The more difficult part was with his formidable mother.

There was considerable going back and forth. The widow had set being a doctor as the goal. She had given the year in Ipoh for studies and also that first motorbike. He was the eldest boy and the only one of the family at that stage to make it to university. He would have to do well in order to ensure the whole family's future. These considerations inveighed against the change. But from a distance, there was only so much that the widow could command of her boy. At university, in Singapore, her son was finally away and could make his own decisions.

Being free did not only mean he could begin to make his own choices; he could make his own mistakes. With no father or other father figure, his mother had been the domineering one, constraining but also guiding him, for better or worse. Now on his own in Singapore, there was little to no guidance, and independence could be used in many ways. There were instances of wildness. He, Victor Gopal and others were notorious for late-night gatherings and racing along the roads on their motorbikes, loud and at literally break-neck speeds. There were more than a few drinking sessions and even an attempt to brew up alcohol in a laboratory. There were a number of cases that could have landed them in trouble with the university administration or in hospital. Yet, the mischief passed without serious mishap.

As for studies, they were something that he did easily enough when he had to buckle down. To one of his contemporaries, he was "a bit of a legend, a first-rate sportsman with a first-class mind". He lived life large and without fear of any consequences.

Cecelia from Katong

From the start, Sonnie played badminton for the university team, in singles and in the first mixed doubles. It was across the badminton net that he first saw Miss Cheong Keong Hin, whom he was to court and then marry. The young lady was not his badminton partner. She played on the other side, for the Teachers' Training College, and they clashed in the mixed doubles. Sonnie was intrigued by her from that first encounter and arranged for someone who knew her to do a more formal introduction. In a number of ways, the two were indeed on opposite sides.

She was a small, fair girl whereas Sonnie was one of the taller men of his cohort, and dark-skinned from birth as well as the years of outdoor activities under the hot sun. He was studying at university and, even when he was less than serious about studies, there was little doubt about his intellectual capacity. She was sharp in her own way and was the first in her family to get into the teachers' college. But there was a gap between that and the university. She did not have his broad-ranging curiosity and hunger for ideas.

Their family backgrounds too contrasted sharply. The Tays were a poor family from a small town up north and he had only been able to come to Singapore because of his scholarship. Her family, the Cheongs, was well-known in the Katong area, among the oldest Chinese families who had settled and done well in Singapore and the other British settlements along the Straits.

The Straits Chinese or Peranakan were bred from among the earliest arrivals from China, ahead of the later and much larger waves of immigrants. Many of them became rich under the British colonial rule and adopted Western education, customs and pastimes. Westernisation was evident from their style of dressing, as they donned ties and shirts, and they aspired to a different culture, closer to the elite Europeans and British and hence separated themselves from other locals and the more recent Chinese arrivals. The Peranakans had also hybridised their culture with elements from the Malays with spices and ways of cooking, as well as adaptations to Malay dressing, like the *kebaya* for women. A Peranakan patois developed, with many words from Malay mixed with Chinese dialect to form something unique. Many of the Peranakans also combined this with a nostalgia for China, which some continued to regard as a motherland, even when many of them were more accustomed to speaking English or their Malay-based patois, rather than Chinese.

The Cheongs were notable enough that their family lineage was later laid out in a book published about migrant Chinese: *One Hundred Years' History of the Chinese in Singapore* by Song Ong Siang. Keong Hin's great-grandfather, Cheong Koo Key, arrived in Malacca from Hainan back in 1799 and in 1833, her grandfather Ann Bee was born in that ancient port city, by then controlled by the British. He knew no English but he did well.

First working in the European firms of Messrs Dare & Co, and then in W Mansfield & Co, he started his own business to handle ships, working with different partners to form a succession of profitable firms. Cheong made considerable amounts of money and supported charities, leaving two sons. In this third generation of the Cheong family in Malaya and Singapore, the elder son was Cheong Koon Seng and, Keong Hin's father, Cheong Koon Hong, was the younger.

The two brothers worked together on a number of well-known developments of the era, like the Theatre Royal along North Bridge Road. The family had a number of houses as well as farms in the north of the island. In addition, they ran the Star Opera Co, well-known for its Malay-language entertainments ranging from adaptations of *Hamlet* to *Tales from the Arabian Nights* and Chinese legends. Much of this, especially the theatre, was managed more by the elder brother. Cheong Koon Seng was adjudged an intelligent and diligent man and would later start a successful business that bore his name, valuing land and doing property deals. He would also continue the family tradition of philanthropy and served on a number of charities, including as Chairman of the Old Boys' Association of the Anglo-Chinese School (ACS), a venerable mission school that was a touchstone of many in the Peranakan community. He was generous to the school, which reciprocated by naming one of its sports houses after him so that among generations from ACS there are "CKS " boys.

Koon Hong, as the younger brother, was less active but was still respected, prominent and wealthy. Their house in the east coast of Singapore was a grand and sprawling place where the whole considerable family – even larger than the Tay brood in Taiping – stayed. The Cheongs had the wherewithal for such a family. There had been two wives in the house. The first wife could not bear children, so it was agreed that Keong Hin's father could take a second. Chosen, she arrived from Sarawak to do her duty – bearing a total of nine children. Keong Hin was the fourth child. The eldest was a son, followed by a succession of five girls, and then another three boys. The first wife decided to adopt, picking a boy and a girl from distant relatives to be her own children.

Keong Hin's mother, the second wife, died young and suddenly, just after they had finished lunch, from a perforated ulcer left unattended for too long. The young children were raised by the first wife, but there was no close bond between the children and stepmother. The children were instead fed and taken care of by assorted family retainers and chauffeured to school by a driver. The house was always full of relatives – close or distant – and with streams of visitors. There were regular mahjong parties with many tables going on into the late night, and many outings to the beach nearby. When badminton became the sport of the town, not one but two courts were built.

Keong Hin grew up in material comfort in the community of Katong but without close parental guidance and care. Her well-known father was a proud but distant figure. Nor did she really know maternal warmth, having lost the one who birthed her and not being close to the one whom she grew up calling mother. She, instead, was drawn to the family of her uncle, Cheong Koon Seng, and was to spend a fair amount of time with them. The two families were different and that had much to do with the matriarchs. Her aunt had been to school and was much more attentive to the children and their education. She took this direction.

From her school days at the Methodist Girls' School, Keong Hin resolved that she too would aim for higher education and did her best to develop herself. She did not get into university, which drew from the entire peninsula and admitted only a very small number. Even so, when she succeeded in gaining admission to Teachers' Training College, she was the first among her siblings to attain a tertiary education. In the family, each sister would have a pet name given by the next generation of children, and she would be Aunt Teacher.

When Keong Hin was a child, the Cheongs had substantial wealth. Much of that family money would soon be dissipated. It was her eldest brother: not only did he prove to be poor at business, he also suffered many of the usual weaknesses that inflicted rich men's sons, and more so. He died young and left many debts that had to be settled. None of the other sons showed the enterprise and determination to rebuild the family fortunes. It was the proverbial curse of three generations for the Cheongs.

Land and properties had to be sold to pay off debts. The businesses were milked for short-term payments and running down. The large family house was still there for relatives and many friends to gather, but it was less well-kept and the household was less able to provide for the many mouths in the sprawling compound. Cuts were made. These deprivations were relative to all that the family once had, and not a deep and sudden impoverishment. By the time she entered the teachers' college, most of her family wealth was going or already gone. This left her with a limited horizon of life and without clear direction. The young Keong Hin – Cecelia as she was called by her sisters and friends – knew that something new was needed, something different, even if what exactly that should be, and how to get there, was uncertain.

This was when she met Sonnie. There was an early and strong attraction between them and they began to date – the usual activities like going to the beach, cinema shows, often in Katong, and also badminton parties at the Cheong house. She liked the tea dances, but he was a poor dancer and hated to do anything he was bad at. She would always play mahjong with her sisters, cousins and neighbours as much as to sit and chat and pass the time. He did not play – loathing games of chance – but would hang around the edges and drink beers with her brothers, male cousins and friends from Katong.

Sonnie was different and so was their courtship. The Cheongs were part of a receding era, extended and messy with first and second wives and second families that were widely accepted and even commonplace among the richer Chinese. This was to change in that generation, with the Women's Charter in 1961 that made only monogamous marriages legal; a progressive step. Yet, customs lagged, not only in marriage but in the courting. Arranged marriages were the practice for her parents, and the norm for Cecelia's siblings had been to marry within the social circles they knew and were comfortable with. Her eldest sister had been matched off to a young man who lived down the street in Katong, Wee Chye Khoon. Soon after, her younger sister was to marry their brother-in-law's younger brother. Her siblings did not seem to mind, did not want to strive so hard, and seemed content with life as it was in their Katong enclave.

Cecelia was not without suitors from among the eligible young men of the Katong families; she was a very attractive and lively young woman, with fine features and a slim waist. But with the British leaving and independence coming, the bubble of circumstance that created Katong was changing. It was not only that the Cheong fortune was reduced. A new world was rapidly appearing on the horizon that all would have to understand and adapt to. Cecelia tried to prepare to embrace that. It was already a major thing to attend teachers' college and thus go beyond the usual Katong circles. It was another step when, among all those she met in her college years, she felt there was something about Sonnie.

He was from beyond the limited circles she had known and a romance with him introduced her to new things. She would always recall that first time he beckoned her to get on board his motorbike and go off somewhere. To get around Katong, where everything was nearby, she would just go on foot or, if need be, hail a trishaw. If there was reason to go further, back in her early schooldays, the children were chauffeured to school by the family car. Later, when she was older and going to college, and their family circumstances reduced, there was the bus or else the pirate taxis that plied the routes. But when Sonnie waved, despite unfamiliarity, she got on the back of that large and loud motorbike. If she wanted something different, then she would have to try something different. Before long, she would ride pillion with him even when Sonnie was riding at high speed along the roads. She was just the right weight and knew how to lean into the bend, so he could ride as quickly and boldly as when he was alone. This was the compliment he would give her, and she was proud to recall it even years later.

The Cheongs did not take to Sonnie initially. Her siblings thought he was stuck-up. He thought they were a bit spoilt and silly. Perhaps a bit of both were true. Sonnie was used to standing outside of the larger social circles. He had close friends but was never to be a club man with a wide social network. He laughed and smiled more than most. At times, he could be aloof and stand off to one side at a larger gathering. The Cheongs and the social clique of other Peranakan families in Katong were a community that was privileged and could be quite closed and gossipy, and set in their ways. But the Cheong clan did not shut him out, and no father or uncle said that he was not fit as a poor outsider, a widow's son from a small Malayan town, to one day become part of the family. They were more open than the circles Sonnie had known in Taiping.

Anyway, if someone had tried to exclude Sonnie, Cecelia would not have listened. She was, in her own way, strong-willed. There were adjustments to be made with Sonnie, and she was prepared to make them. His circle of friends was something that she had to get used to. They were university students and among of the brightest minds from across the peninsula, and some of them were not shy to tout that, engaging in long, loud and often intellectual treatises when they met, getting even longer and louder after drink (although less coherent). There were also many Indians among his closest friends. That was new to her too, she would frankly admit. To be with Sonnie meant that she would have to learn to get beyond the cliques and habits of the life she had known in Peranakan Katong and move into new circles, a new society. She felt some sense of anxiety, but she wanted that change, and Sonnie would be beside her through it. Quite swept up by him and rushing so fast on that bike, she too raced ahead.

There was nothing in her life that really prepared Cecelia for all this. She and Sonnie were part of a pioneer generation not only in matters relating to the nation but even in the most personal aspects of life, in love and marriage. Their expectations of what marriage would mean, monogamous and for a lifetime, and of courtship – giving the choice to the person, rather than to parents – and to make that choice from a much wider circle: all these things were new. Unlike their siblings, where some acquaintance or parent had introduced the prospective partner and arranged a marriage, the two had chosen each other. What they chose too was neither the life in the circle of fading privilege in Katong, nor Taiping and its small-town limitations.

They may not have realised all this explicitly. It may have seemed as natural as the initial attraction and first dates. But they would live in a new way, in a new world that was emerging. That was their tacit compact: Sonnie and Cecelia were in love and it seemed that they would be together, no matter what. It all seemed like those novellas that she liked, so impossibly romantic, and perhaps it was.

Suddenly, with little notice and no reason that seemed clear or good enough, Sonnie was going. He was leaving the university and would head north, returning to Malaya.

Hard Paths, Uphill

Sonnie decided to break off from university towards the end of his third year for a considerable period. He would return later to complete his Honours year. But at the time he left, it was unclear why he did, what his future plans were, and what he exactly did in that time he was away. The explanation he would give was related to his studies.

In his first and second years, Sonnie did well in economics – his option among the social sciences – and was among the top few of the class. He had an interest in the subject and developed views. He thought that if the country – and it was Malaya that was his country then – was to prosper, it would have to do more than just produce raw resources, and Singapore would have to be more than merely a transit port. The future path would have to include processing and industrialisation. That was his conviction about the economic future.

This was not, of course, an idea that originated from the

young undergraduate. This was already an emerging idea for the economic pillar that would support the political goals for decolonisation and independence. If Malaya and other colonies were to become independent, then developing their own industries would be critical to make that independence truly sustainable. For Sonnie, the insight was more than book knowledge. It was what he had seen growing up in Taiping: a town that grew and then diminished with tin mining, that was connected by rail to a port just to facilitate the faster transit to a faraway destination which used those raw materials, and a society where so many did the hard, back-breaking work in the mines for very little income, in contrast to the colonial masters and a small elite.

Mass industrialisation was key, the young man advocated, and it would later become a central plank for the new government in Singapore after independence from Britain. But when Sonnie was at university, this was seen as an idea that was dangerous to the British interest and orthodoxy. While of good academic standing, the university was intended by the British to educate the locals and, in part, there was an implicit agenda to school them in ways that supported the Empire, rather than to undermine its prerogatives. Some of the university professors were progressive and some, rather suspiciously, even supported and encouraged the students to speak up and take sides with the Socialists. But not the economics professor that supervised Sonnie. He could have taken the young man's ideas as being different and contestable though worth consideration. Instead, he inveighed against them.

Singapore was an important port. Indeed, the port was Singapore: that was what it was, and is, and would be. In class after class, when the issue was raised, this was the vehement response from the Professor. In class after class, Sonnie marshalled arguments in reply. He was not someone who would sit quietly when he disagreed, and he had no one to counsel discretion. The Professor was unaccustomed to repeated exchanges from a local student who would not be overawed, and wrote him off as being obstinate and wrong-minded, perhaps dangerous. In the end, the Professor's final riposte was not only another exchange in class but one that affected the life of the young university student, and not for the better.

Sonnie would not be offered a place to do his Honours in Economics. He had not calculated on this. Giving up medical studies was one thing but leaving university with only a general degree and without Honours was unthinkable. It was not a disgrace. But it would place him in the middle of the pack and set him on a different, more difficult trajectory. If he were stuck on this path, he would struggle to get the right appointment and face a more constrained future ahead.

This is the explanation that Sonnie would share with some friends for his decision to break off from university. When Sonnie and his DRH friends rode their motorbikes down the Dunearn and Bukit Timah roads in those university years, they loved the sense of freedom and sensation of risk in swooping between the slow-moving cars and trucks. They felt carefree and perhaps were seen to be careless but they had measured out their risks. The road was broad and the traffic was light, especially in the night when they rode hardest and fastest. But now, he would leave the university and it was sooner than expected, and on a path he was unsure about, and on which he had no one to guide him. The only certainty was that the way ahead was narrowing and there would be bumps. Still, Sonnie was unafraid. He would find a route. He would have to.

The peninsula was home for him. When Sonnie had come down to Singapore, it was for the express and singular pursuit of his studies since the campus of the University of Malaya was there. If denied the opportunity to do an Honours year, there was no clear reason for him to stay on. It did not mean he might not return. In his mind, as for so many others then, Singapore and Malaya were intertwined, one entity; different, but integral to each other. He had enjoyed his years on the island and would miss the activity and buzz of the city, and the sense of freedom. He would miss his DRH friends but university was ending for them too, and many would head back up to Malaya anyway, and they could always keep in touch. He had enjoyed his time with Cecelia although they had really not thought far ahead of the here and now of their time together and no commitments had been made. Some words were said but without any explanation or conclusion. What could be pieced together of this turbulent time in Sonnie's life was never fully discussed.

His family were up north, and he had lived all his life there, with them or near them. Although he had enjoyed the freedom of being away from them, the ties would always be important to him. Singapore was not home. There was also the question of finding a job. With the economy still sluggish and holding only a general degree without honours, the options were limited. The job prospects were even worse in Taiping. All he had experienced and then come to hope for meant that he had outgrown that place, especially with the family and social constraints. Going back would, in a sense, be a failure, and if there were no immediate prospects in Singapore, the offer of a job in Port Dickson seemed right.

Port Dickson is a small town along the west coast of the Malayan peninsula. The British had taken it over from the Sultan of Selangor by negotiation in 1880 with the aim of developing a port. But they already had their ports in the settlements in Penang, Malacca and Singapore, and these plans never developed into anything of scale. There was a long, pleasant beach. There were still some direct British administration and military forces. In the town, there were also some Chinese who had come into the area in the early 19th century because of the tin deposits. These made PD (as Port Dickson was known) more than the usual Malayan small town, and a place that might suit him.

It is not clear what job he did in PD. One of his brothers said it was a temporary teaching position in a school. A contemporary said it was to serve as a resettlement officer, working with the British at the tail end of the Emergency in the huge effort to house many of the rural Chinese and cut off support for the Communists. In his later official CVs, it is left unstated, as if there had been no break during his university years and he went directly into the civil service.

If it had been a teaching post, the job itself was nothing exciting and would always have been intended as a stopgap until he had decided on his next steps. He was not really focused on teaching. If he had been, then he would have gone to Teachers' Training College. If it was to work on resettlement, it would be somewhat familiar to him as resettlement programmes had been run around Taiping when he lived there. The post would also have brought him into contact with the British military and intelligence servicemen who were overseeing the resettlement, now in its last years. In either case, Sonnie would not have minded. He would have some money and some time for himself. He could be amused, enjoying the beach and riding his bike on the roads along the estates, darting in and out of the heavy trunk-road traffic of trucks hefting the rubber, lumber and other resources down to Singapore to be shipped out. He could also figure out what he could try next.

He did not like the idea of business, had no background in it. Business was a world which the Chinese controlled – the real ones who spoke Chinese more than English and knew the insides and outs of trade. Business also seemed a world in which family connections, patrons and networks mattered most – and he, the widow's son from Taiping, had none of that. Joining the civil service would have been one path. But the colonials were still in charge and, unless you were white or at least Eurasian, your prospect was, at most, some glorified clerk; the expectations that his mother had so often voiced – that he must amount to more than his father, "a mere clerk" – echoed. This would be all he could expect, especially without an Honours degree.

Something with the military seemed possible. Sonnie did like the outdoors and knew the jungle well enough. He was bigger and taller than most of his cohort and, with his sports, fit. He was used to mingling with military officers from his time in Taiping. The Emergency was something he had grown up around. He admired the British forces who could navigate and fight in the jungle – to engage the enemy on their own terms. The armed forces then attracted few locals with university qualifications and, with his degree and his intellect (which he never doubted, Honours or not), this would be an opportunity to outshine other regulars. In the movement towards independence, there would be a need for an army to be headed up by locals, and he calculated that there would be many opportunities for him to move up.

There was a sizeable contingent of British military stationed in PD. Somehow (especially if he had really been working in the resettlement programmes), they had met and struck up a conversation over beers. Sonnie stood out from other locals in PD – with his height and motorbike, he had a swagger about him. Unlike many locals, he was comfortable in dealing with whites (he had to thank Taiping and even those house parties for that). What he wanted was not only to be admitted into the military but to be placed on the path to be an officer. Even more, his ambition was to be sent to Sandhurst in England, the premier military training school in all of the Empire.

The college was the most famous training ground for the British military. For British recruits, although some were accepted purely on merit, the officer class still remained skewed towards the scions of the upper class, mainly those who had proved too wayward for school or did not take to business. In the 1950s, when Sonnie looked at his options, Sandhurst was only slowly beginning to open its doors to non-white officers from the rest of the Empire. Among the first admitted were the Gurkhas, fearsome mercenaries who had followed the British expansion across much of Asia and proven themselves in WWII. For the rest, there were just a handful of openings, and local officers from the armies of the Empire were often selected on a mix of criteria that, beyond personal merit, looked at their connections to the elite of that country, with even some of the royal families enrolling their sons. It would not be easy to get a place. But if he could be admitted, Sonnie believed that graduating as an officer from Sandhurst would position him to be a leader of the armed forces in Malaya when the British were ready to let the peninsula go independent. He shared the idea with the British officers he had come to know and no one said that this was inconceivable.

He looked to them to help him get admitted and provide references. He would join the officers on treks into the jungle and up nearby hills together. The military men were good at it and liked it. Sonnie was not as good as them, nor as accustomed as the native kampong Malays. But he was exceptional for a Chinese local and a boy who had grown up in towns and gone to university, and he was willing to endure, try and learn. He had done well and enjoyed their treks. Perhaps on one of those jungle treks, the idea came to him about how to press ahead with his aim to join the military and train at Sandhurst: he would push forward on an unusual route. He would climb a mountain.

Gunung Tahan is the highest mountain on the Malayan peninsula. While the mountain is not that high, just 7,175 feet (2,187 metres), it is a tough beast of a climb. There are long days of trekking through thick jungle in humid and scorching conditions, cutting through thick foliage, crossing fast-flowing rivers and scrambling up trails in deep mud. These days seem longer and harder because of the swarms of mosquitoes that continually bite and nag at the climbers, and leeches that come out of the mud to attach themselves to the legs and feet, and some that even leap to the upper limbs, to suck blood. More dangerous are the snakes, many of which have a powerful venom that can quickly overcome a man. All this must be endured, just to get to the base of the mountain where the climb begins. Then the trail transverses mountain streams that wind through the rainforest and over narrow, pebble-strewn ridges. Near the summit, conditions turn chilly, in the low single digits, and winds can blow strong. The climb is not technically difficult, requiring more endurance than skill. In fact, the name Gunung Tahan translates from Malay to English to mean "Endurance Mountain".

Today, there is easier access for trekkers, and it is possible to even ride by four-wheel-drive to the start of the trail by the rangers stationed in the park. With preparation and some training, there are groups of everyday hikers who trek to the top. But in those days soon after the war, there were none of these amenities and support and, outside of the Orang Asli indigenous people who lived in the area, not many people knew the trail well.

The route that was chosen was the longer and harder one, some 55 kilometres (or 34 miles in the British measurements of that era). The trail was not clearly marked and overgrown. While Sonnie and his companions knew the jungle well, none of their party had been up before and there were uncertainties in finding the best way forward. While they had gotten on, there was also always a sense of competition among the men; the military men among themselves and between them and him, the local. There was a question of who should lead, and who would take which task. The military men had more experience, but he was not about to give up so easily; he believed that he was every bit as tough and capable. They all set a fast pace and no complaints were voiced.

His attitudes towards the British was changing. When he was a child in Taiping, they had been benefactors to his family, returning to oust the harsh Japanese and rooting out the Communist insurgents. In his university days in Singapore, the view changed with the question of independence and whether the locals would be up to it. He felt the drive not to simply admire and ape the British. He still had to learn from them – and not reject their schooling and ways outrightly as did the Communists – but he was determined to beat them at their own game. He would apply this attitude to many more things in his life, to learn what the best thought best and how to master that, and then go further. During that climb, this attitude drove him on – not only to match and best the military men in the jungle but to go beyond and get into Sandhurst. Sonnie had something to prove.

It was hard going. But they progressed and were near the top. After setting up camp for the evening, Sonnie sat on a rock along a running stream and removed his boots. It had been a difficult climb up, and he now knew it would be even harder back down. Coming up to this point, his feet had been stubbing against the front of the boots and his toes were bloodied, the nails impacted and cutting into the flesh. He had no other course but to show the others and, after consulting them, the consensus was that two or even three of the nails were so badly gone, it would be better to remove them immediately than to let them cut further in. It was not an easy decision to make. But Sonnie was prepared to take the hard decision, and then to live with the pain. When he first felt the pain grow, he did not complain or want to slow or turn back. The pain would be endured, he determined, so long as he could make it up to the top.

He did. Once there, he took out his camera, and carefully took a series of pictures of the view from the top. The dense forest cover below looked so green and peaceful that no one could imagine the trail and all the difficulties on the way up. The clouds were low around the peak, poetic. He had a great camera, the state-of-the-art and expensive Leica, and he would take his time to capture all this. Years later, he knew even then, this would a moment to remember.

But what then, after the summit? Heading back down, his soft, now nail-less toes were swathed as best as could be with the bandages and gauze that were at hand. Each step was painful, agonising. Yet, he would not show the pain, certainly not to the white officers. When they offered to carry some items so he could walk with less of a burden, Sonnie declined. Perhaps the hardest part was not so much the physical pain, but when the elation was fading. Such was his drive, his appetite to take on all life could offer and to succeed, no matter the cost. The nails of his toes would grow back.

The officers were pretty damn well impressed by how he had done in the climb, not even accounting for the pain. True to their implicit agreement, they encouraged and supported his application to join up. He would be accepted; joining as a local officer was not the issue. He would return to Singapore and they promised to put him in touch with some of the British officers there. They could use someone like him. But there would be no scholarship to go to Sandhurst. Another door had been shut.

Perhaps it had never really been open – that it was the dreamer in Sonnie that aimed so high. If no one really saw him as being impractical, this was only because he had so often succeeded in making outsized aspirations materialise. Success mixed in with his drive, fortitude and courage disguised a certain measure of audacious risk-taking that could, especially in his younger years, be foolhardy. He never regretted climbing Gunung Tahan. It would be a trip that he would remember all his life and he would keep a picture taken from that climb in his office, in a small album of photos. The picture showed the peak, stark and sharp except for a small cloud, and had been taken from near the top. It was an austere black-and-white image, with the canopy of the deep rainforest in the foreground. Sonnie did not dwell on his dream – that the trek would lead on from the summit to Sandhurst. Instead, he would return to Singapore and perhaps another door would open.

Returning, Rushing

Singapore was speeding, rushing headlong towards independence. Returning to university in 1955, Sonnie was admitted into the Honours programme but for history, not economics. Although he needed to get that piece of paper, he again spent more time with his DRH friends. He was also intent, after that time apart, on picking things up with Cecelia and did all he could to mend things with her. For his Honours paper, he picked the topic of the history of the Singapore Police Force. It was easy enough and he did not give the thesis much attention. Yet the academics were again not without controversy.

There were problems in how the British had grown and administered the police service. One was recruiting officers who were often Malay when gangs, the main source of police concern, were from the Chinese community. The other was the petty corruption, beneath the care and attention of the colonial higher-ups, that was prevalent at the lower level. Add them together and there was a naughty third level to the problem:

a colonial police force that was racially different and foreign to the people and potential lawbreakers against whom they enforced the law in ways that were sometimes unjust and, too often, venal. Sonnie was always unafraid to offer criticism but it was not fully appreciated by his English academic supervisor, especially since his supervisee was often absent. Sonnie would still graduate with the Honours that he wanted and needed and returned for, but it was to be a Third Class. That galled him. He deserved better, he always asserted, even if he had not worked that hard for it. Yet, there was nothing to be done. In the event, it was sufficient to get him an interview and then a job in the civil service. He was even admitted to be part of the local arm of the elite administrative service.

It was not, in those days, a highly paid job, and would remain so for all the years he was in service. But there would be a steady income. With graduation and a job, he decamped from DRH, although many of the friends he had made there would remain in contact for many years after. Things with Cecelia were moving forward. After leaving DRH, he moved into the Cheong family house, assigned a place among the men of the household, with Cecelia's brothers.

In 1957, Sonnie Tay Seow Huah married Cecelia Cheong Keong Hin. A little more than a year after, their first child was born, Joanne Tay Siok Wan. Just in three years since his return, Sonnie had gone from a student with an uncertain future to being a civil servant, a husband and father.

Their wedding was no grand affair or big dinner; only a simple civil ceremony. The Tays were never rich and knew no one in Singapore, and Sonnie did not think they needed a showy party. For her, there were some family expectations. By this time, however, the Cheong family money was a faded memory. Some of the family came, and there was a small dinner afterwards. No one from the Tay family came down from Taiping. The couple had already travelled up north and been hosted to a dinner at the clan association in the town. The widow welcomed her first daughter-in-law with a wedding gift of jewellery. But unlike the matinees that Cecelia adored and Sonnie would go along for, "happily ever after" remained a question.

Sunday, 1 June 1958, had begun much like others. Cecelia wanted to go back to Katong to her parents' house to play mahjong. So much had changed for the young wife and mother, and the old games and the familiar faces were no longer stale but comforting. She would play for hours, for small stakes but enjoying the thrills of the game nevertheless, as well as the chance to just catch up and gossip. Sonnie, restless as ever, never had any inclination to just sit by and watch. He decided to head out to Changi beach for a swim as he often would. Two of the men who were otherwise standing by idle around the house were with him. Lawrence, his brother-in-law, was one of them. The plan was that they would zip out there to the beach, take a swim, and get back quickly. Sonnie drove, and he drove fast. They swam, and even had a quick ski when they came across some friends with a boat. Then they washed off the salt best they could, towelled dry and headed back, fast along the winding coast road.

Along one stretch, at the long bend by the beach, he pulled out to overtake a car that was going too slowly. But there was a van that was making a slow U-turn right across the road. There was no time to either pull back into the lane or bring the car from speed to a safe stop. Sonnie's car hit the side of the van. It was a crushing halt, and he and his passengers were banged up, with cuts and bruises. The van suffered far worse. Hit hard in the middle, it tipped over, slowly and heavily, turning turtle and landing on the beach with a thud and a cracking sound. The passengers were injured and badly. Cars stopped and some drivers helped Sonnie and everyone else out of the car while others went down to the beach to see what could be done for those in the van. An ambulance was called. At the hospital, one of the van's passengers died – a 17-year-old girl.

The plan for a quick getaway to the beach had unfolded in tragedy. The accident was so bad that it was reported in the newspapers, and there were consequences. There would have to be a coroner's enquiry and, depending on the outcome of that process, there could well be charges brought in a court of law for reckless driving and causing death by negligence. If that were the outcome, even if there was no jail time, Sonnie's civil service career might be brought to an abrupt end as it was just beginning.

There would have to be some way to resolve matters and prevent those frightening possibilities. To defend Sonnie, they determined he must have a good lawyer. But it would take time and money – funds that the couple did not readily have. They decided not to tell his family, or otherwise the widow would issue stern instructions or even come down to Singapore and supervise, and that could only make a bad situation worse. There was no one who would really help, and Cecelia took it upon herself to do what was needed: to pay the lawyer, she would pawn the jewellery given to her at her marriage by the widow, as well as a bracelet that had been given to her by her father to mark her graduation.

The lawyer they hired found grounds to argue that Sonnie had done nothing wrong. Yes, he had been driving fast, but there was no double line that prohibited overtaking. There was no clear evidence that the car had been so far in excess of the speed limit that the driver was "reckless". Rather, it was the van that had caused the danger. It was the van that was making an illegal and clumsy U-turn. Moreover, the van had failed a road-worthiness inspection. The vehicle's poor condition was a significant factor that made the injuries to the passengers more severe than might have been. The grounds were technical and did not fully remove the scent that something awful and wrong had happened. At the end of the hearing, the coroner did not conclude that Sonnie had caused the death. Neither was he acquitted. An open verdict was returned; inconclusive but enough. The police decided there was no basis to prosecute, and the accident was shelved.

For many years, whenever Sonnie's mother would visit, she would ask why Cecelia never wore the gems that were given to her. The repeated white lie would be that they were put away for safe-keeping in a deposit box in the bank. They were never redeemed from the pawn store and, even when finances allowed, never replaced. Her dowry had gone to keep Sonnie safe. Their life as a young couple and family had been desperately close to being upended abruptly and entirely. Yes, Sonnie had survived, and their lives could resume.

There were things to be regretted, but that could not be undone. Sonnie would never talk about it. He was somewhat chastised and returned to his civil service job with a renewed effort, believing that whatever he was meant to do, he would do and do with full determination. He got a new car and would continue to drive fast. Life carried on. All that happened would just seem an interruption. The couple would continue. There were wounds – months of worries leading up to the enquiry and especially for the days during the inquest and the insecurity of their financial circumstances – and these festered. A strain in the relationship between the young couple started in those days and never went away.

Whatever they had and whatever remained now was revealed to be fragile. Cecelia had to face up to that, and the risks that Sonnie continued to run without much thought to the consequences for himself or to her and their young family. She would grow less than sure how much to rely on him. There was love and attraction still, and she would always want to stay with Sonnie. She could only hope that he would settle down, and that they would be happy together.

Settling Down

Their first home together was the small, rather dark house they rented along Kampong Java Road in an area notorious for flooding. This was all the newlyweds could afford. He had a civil servant's decent income. Hers was a teacher's salary, even lower. Together, they should have been all right. Sonnie, however, had poor habits with money. As soon as his salary was paid, he would find a way to spend it. Gambling was not his weakness (he never thought himself lucky). Nor was he driven to drunken bouts, although there were always occasions to celebrate with friends. What he succumbed to was the habit of wanting the best and newest in just about everything.

After he was married, he got rid of his big bike and got a car. None could be as fast and thrilling as his Black Phantom but he insisted that they had to have some verve and fun. The first was a Sunbeam Talbot, with an open top. Later, there was a powerful and larger Rover. This was followed by a Mini Cooper S which was all the rage then, and nippy too. He started to get into music, and soon learnt about the best stereo systems on which to play the hits of that era. He bought up a library of LPs with some contemporary music like Nat King Cole but also classical symphonies. He started buying books too, to build up not just knowledge but his own library. Many selected were printed in England: big, thick, leather-bound and expensive. He was also generous with his friends when they went out for food and something to drink. Appetites, ambitions and generosity strained his pocket. These habits were, however, not the biggest reason why the young couple was hard-pressed for cash. It was his family.

The widow had always expected Sonnie to do well and pushed him to excel not only for himself but as a strategy to pull the whole family up. She had invested in his education and although the boy had stupidly thrown aside medicine, he had landed a decent job – the investment must now deliver a dividend. Sonnie regularly sent a sum to Taiping for his mother and the family as a whole. But the heaviest cost was the money specially needed for his brother, David.

His youngest sibling was bright enough, their mother declared, and had been sent off to London to do a law degree. This was an expensive undertaking, given the value of the pound sterling at the time, so payments dug deep into each month's income. Then the family obligation got even more expensive. David fell in love with a young Italian girl named Franca and decided that he would give up law and instead go to help at her family store back in Udine.

Sonnie felt an empathy and a degree of guilt about David. There had been a bad motorbike crash that resulted in David suffering injuries that led to his right arm being amputated.

Sonnie was not there, but there was some sense that David and the third Tay brother, Jack, had been emulating him by undertaking such a fast and risky bike ride along the winding trunk roads.

On top of this, Sonnie could only sympathise, imagining what it was like to deal with their mother. When he had switched from medicine to the arts, and then not been admitted to the Honours year, there were pressures. David pulling out of law school to pursue love could only have been worse. There were so many frantic calls, inducements, pleas and threats. Then the ultimate sanction was imposed. The widow dispatched herself to London. She would make her boy buckle down and finish his law degree. No "or else" was needed. Love-struck or not, David would have to comply and did.

After graduation, he still married Franca but, rather than Italy, they moved to Malaysia where David would begin a lucrative career as a lawyer in Malacca. The couple would have a child, Ivan, although they were to separate some years after, with Franca returning to Italy with the boy. Yet, whatever the outcomes for love, the widow's intervention paid off for the family, and would keep paying off in future years. David would rise to a senior partner in a sizeable practice in KL. But, in this period before the payback, it was Sonnie who had to help foot all the bills to "invest" in his brother and the family's future. To pay for all that – including his mother's emergency journey to London – he had to borrow to get by.

Cecelia liked none of this. It was not that they had to give money to his family; she understood family obligations. In later years, she would often dip into her own savings from her teacher's income to lend money to one or another of Sonnie's family for some reason or other – loans that were never repaid, and of which he did not know. The wife and young mother worried more about Sonnie, watching her husband splurge the moment his salary came rather than putting some money away, spending grandly on whatever he thought was the best which he had eyed, when he knew that there was this family obligation. Her own family's fortune had been run down by

Above A Big Family: Sonnie (front row, second from left) is second in a family of seven children and the eldest son of Tay Hooi Eng, who was taken away by the Japanese in WWII, and Mdm Goon Goot Meng (holding their youngest child).

Right Tay Boys in Taiping: At the end of WWII, the family moved to Taiping, where the children grew up in an old but sturdy government house. Sonnie – the eldest of four sons – with Mannie, Jack and David (right to left).

Above Young Man: From his late teens into his university days, Tay (third from left) was into riding motorbikes, with speed and that sense of freedom. He rode often with his friends at Dunearn Road Hostels and with a broader network.

Left Graduating, Staying: Sonnie went to Singapore from Malaya for university and those years were formative. On graduation with honours, he was admitted to the elite administrative service of the civil service.

Right A Couple Married: Tay married Cecelia Cheong Keong Hin in 1957. It was a simple and small civil ceremony.

Top left A Couple Walking: When they married in Singapore, Tay took Cecelia to visit his mother in Taiping and this gave her a sense of where he grew up.

Below left Connected: Malaysia was often where the family would holiday, with my father driving up with plans to visit his brothers. When in Malacca to see his brother David, my father made sure he took us to the ruins of the old church by the port. He wanted us to remain connected socially, even after Separation.

Bottom Family Time: On holiday at the British-era hill station on Fraser's Hill. While so much was to be done at work, he always tried to find time for family and leisure.

Above The Beach and Sun: He always loved swimming and sea sports and, for a while, was an avid waterskier, even buying a sharp, small boat he named *The Siokwan* after his firstborn child.

Right My Father and Me: I could barely walk when he first took me into the sea. He taught me to swim here at this public beach at Changi Point and later at the pool of the somewhat secretive Pyramid Club.

Above Speed and Style: There was a succession of open-top sports cars and even the family car had to have some brio. One favourite was this sports sedan – the MK2 in a Daimler variant – which was once the world's fastest four-seater.

Right Smoking: Often cigarettes – Camels unfiltered – but when time allowed, at his desk or at leisure, he would pack and slowly smoke his pipe.

Above Useful Habits: He could hold his alcohol and this was useful for the social milieu of those years and his job. Cocktails, wine or else beer, the last of which had to be frothy and ice-cold.

Right Hunger: Tucking happily into satay in the 1950s. After the hunger and deprivations of the war years, Tay always sought good food whether in fancy international restaurants or at roadside stalls. He ate voraciously, and lived similarly.

Top left Leisure and Nature: He would often trek and camp in the jungles and hills of Malaysia, often in the Endau-Rompin area.

Bottom left Camping: The jungles were both challenging and refreshing to him. Lawrence Wee (left), his brother-in-law, was a regular companion. Lawrence could turn out a good *tumis*, adding chilli and spice to their camp provisions over the fire.

Right Swimming in the River: He had a shack built by a farmer along the river near Kota Tinggi. This he used as a base for some years.

Below left & right Connected to the Land: From a teenager to adulthood, he travelled through the jungle, always keen to see how the villagers lived. *The Jungle is Neutral,* a survival guide, was a reference book.

Above Sportsman: Badminton was the most popular game of those years and Tay Seow Huah (back row centre) was a keen, competitive player for the university team and when he first joined the civil service.

Below Family, Children: With my sister, Joanne Tay Siok Wan. Busy with work and voracious in his pastime activities, our father still made time for us children.

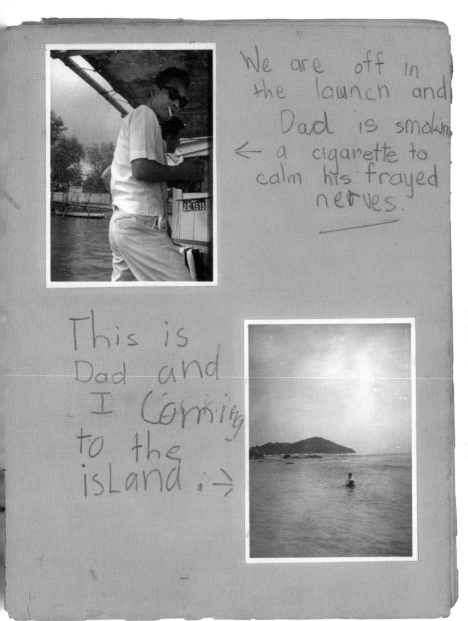

We are off in the launch and Dad is smoking ← a cigarette to calm his frayed nerves.

This is Dad and I coming to the island :→

Above Scrapbook Memories: This was of a trip my father and I took to the islands off Mersing. He was cool and looked the part, and my scrawled childhood caption is ironic.

Above Strategic Travel: Seeing my
father off as he left for another
overseas trip in the 1970s from the
Paya Lebar Airport VIP complex.
I was about 11. The two Mercedes
in the background were from
the first batch to be assembled in
Singapore, and the light green one
near the gate – my father's – had
the driver waiting at the wheel
to take my mother, sister and me
home.

profligacy. She had a terror of debt, a sense of shame whenever she owed anyone anything. Now, even when she was married and had a job, they sometimes could not pay the electricity bills so the power was cut. They borrowed from some of her relatives, which she hated. They even had to buy from the neighbourhood provision store on credit and, more than once, borrow cash outright from the owner, Khoon Guan. Sonnie did not seem to care, not the way he spent. Even after his brother's success in law practice, he never recouped a single cent. Not that she expected to; it was simply enough that the monthly sums he sent to David could end.

In April 1958, when their first child was born, there was perhaps a moment when there was a hope that their family would settle down and life would be surer, more stable. They both adored Joanne. But neither was really equipped for parenting. Sonnie had no father himself. In some ways, never a mother – the widow had kept the family together and been the breadwinner but by domination and demands, rather than providing succour and support. Cecelia was just 25 then, young and still adjusting to her work and her husband. Her biological mother had died when she was a child and her growing-up years were spent as a middle girl, passed around the maids in the sprawling household and long line of children. So it was normal for the couple to put out Joanne to the care of Cecelia's eldest sister, an arrangement that lasted for years.

The Tays then decided to economise further by sharing a house. Cecelia's youngest sister, nicknamed Gracie, had also become a teacher and married Lawrence Wee, another teacher. The Wees too had begun a family and were scraping by. The two families rented a house in Katong, along Langsat Road and close to family and old friends. A distant relative from Malacca was recommended to come down to Singapore to take care of the household chores and the children, since both the wives worked. The families were to grow close. Lawrence Wee was a canny and sociable man, full of stories and able to talk to just about anyone. He had been deprived of a university education only because his family lacked sufficient funds after his father died, and he had to leave school and find work for a spell. But after putting aside some money, he had managed to return to his studies and become a teacher. A bond of friendship began in these years.

On weekends, Cecelia and Sonnie tried to find time together. He was now into boating and waterskiing, where that sense of speed and exhilaration reminded him of the motorbikes he had loved. Cecelia used to go with him before she was pregnant, and she still went once in a while, mainly to sit on the beach with the little girl. They would ride in the boat. But she never swam well and skiing was something she thought too dangerous. Later on, the moment their finances could be stretched enough, Sonnie would buy a boat that he named *The Siokwan* after their baby girl. When the PAP government, newly in power, imposed a pay cut on civil servants, any further children were put off for two, and then three years. But then she was pregnant again and insisted on keeping the child; the second and last child in the family. In January 1961, I was born.

Sonnie, the young father, was pleased enough to watch the children grow and try to find time for them. But when they were infants, they were left to the care of others; not even to Cecelia but to aunts and amahs. He was inept with infants and there is a family legend of how he tied the diaper on his baby daughter so poorly that, when he held her, it all came apart and she ended up soiling him. As his children grew to talk and walk, Sonnie found more to do with them. He would take them to the beach with him and make sure they could swim and be active outdoors, especially the boy. He would watch with some pride when young Joanne was not only enrolled in the convent in town but would become one of the model students with the best grades, as he had been. She was dutifully also enrolled for ballet. But things really did not settle for Sonnie.

His work was pressing and remained the priority with little consideration of what is today called a work-life balance. His mother and siblings would also command much attention and have many expectations, especially when his mother would come down to visit from KL. More than occasionally, there would be large parties at his sister's house and there would be endless calls about what she was doing and wanted his help or guidance with. His wife and the children learnt to be more accommodating to the very many demands of his family.

They also would have to get used to the fact that Sonnie would give priority to whatever interest he was obsessed with at that time. These were often things – like camping in the jungle – that Cecelia and Joanne did not take to, and his son was too young for. Similarly, when he wanted to play sports – tennis and once in a while still some badminton – he was driven to compete, rather than to nurture and encourage the children. His approach was to throw them into things and let them sink or swim – quite literally in terms of swimming when it was time for them to graduate from the children's pool. That was how he himself had learnt.

When Sonnie came home from work and put things aside to finally find some moments with his wife and children, he was often tired or, later on, consumed by the headaches that he suffered with regularity and growing intensity. Sonnie, the father, said that as they grew up, he would find more time for the children. He did try and in part, did find more time outside of work. But not in 1965 or even for much of the next decade. In this, there were similarities to other men and fathers of his generation, but more so.

Cecelia and Sonnie had been much in love, in a gorgeous and romantic courtship with friends and laughter, fast and dangerous motorcycle rides, and ups-and-downs, quarrels and separations before they were reunited and then married. In this, they had chosen each other in a way that their parents had never done and which even some of their own siblings may not have experienced. That choice was made with the expectations that marriage would last for a lifetime. They genuinely had such hopes and expectations. Yet, they were less than well equipped for the day-to-day caring, cooperation and compromise that marriage requires. Neither of them had seen what a long and happy marriage with both its convictions and compromises would be like, no parent who could have been an example or counsel.

They knew this and joked about it: Sonnie was learning to be a man by watching Marlon Brando, that charismatic brooding figure astride his motorbike, while Cecelia's pretty head had been filled by romantic pulp stories from Mills & Boon. They said it and laughed. They had already gone through much, and remained together. But the reality beneath was that it was all new to them, and they were less than well prepared for more turbulent times that were to come, both personally and professionally.

*

Those early years for the country and for him rushed by. Still, my father made time – when he could, as best he could.

When Joanne started in primary one, our father took her to school that first day (our mother who was a teacher was so busy with her duties at her own school). One day, my sister bit into a hard candy and broke one of her baby molars, requiring an urgent extraction. Again, it was our father who responded to the urgent request. It was 1965, an extremely busy time for him given all that was going on in that year of Singapore's sudden independence. He must have squeezed it in, between one meeting and another. Yet, my sister recalls he did not seem rushed or even to mind the disruption to his day of work. He stayed at Poon & Phay, the dentists just across the road from her school, with her throughout, holding her small hand.

For me, I remember him always encouraging me to be active and play sports. He tried sometimes to teach me about badminton which he still played well. But I didn't really take to it. He did teach me to swim when I was only about five years old. He would get into the water to show me the strokes and, for the freestyle, even to cradle me while I tried out kicking and synchronising the arm strokes and the turn of the head. At the Pyramid Club – a place for a selection of the ministers, government officials and business leaders to meet – he would toss a coin into the deep end and make a contest to see who could swim down first to retrieve it. On the weekends, he could get away to Changi Point – a place now erased in the extension of the airport – where he showed me how to swim in the open sea when the waves were strong, and also how to pull yourself up, out of the water and into a boat.

We knew he was busy with work and his work – even if no one knew the details – was to do with security and very important. My mother told us this, not so much as an excuse but in her way to urge us to know that, even if he had less time with us, he loved us. And when he was with us, he was full of energy, making up so many things to do.

I have fond and sun-faded memories from the many times we were at Changi Point. Towards the end of a long day at the beach, the evening wind is blowing, almost cold, and I am lazing in a deck chair next to my sister and to my mother, with a towel draped over my head and body to keep warm. I am perhaps seven or eight, feeling quite happily tired after a day of sun and much activity, so drowsy and comfortable, nestled close to my mother. My father then comes along, to get me to go out on a boat for a last ride. My mother tells him that we are tired and napping, which my sister is and I pretend to be.

My father says okay and turns around to head out to the boat, and go out alone. But then I sit up and, shedding the towel, leap out of the deck chair. Wait, I yell, wait Dad. He turns and sees me running towards him. My father smiles and beckons me to come to him. He holds my small hand and we wave at my mother and Joanne, before we continue forward.

Chapter 4

THE RISING PATH

TAY SEOW HUAH was settling into his civil service job. This was what his parents had done; a common choice especially among English-speaking families of that era to benefit from their facility with the language of the colonial authorities. It was a respectable job, although pay did not match the private sector. During the colonial era, the pinnacle was perhaps to be the chief local administrator or secretary, a necessary adjunct. This could grant a local officer some degree of authority and privilege but always within the pecking order of Empire. The upper echelons and plum positions were reserved for white officers. That had been the kind of civil service that his parents had served.

Circumstances and expectations were changing when Tay Seow Huah joined the service in October 1956. Independence was in the air, heady times with many different views, hopes and fears in society and politics. He chose not to be involved directly in the political struggle during university days, as did others he knew. But there was a flux that he anticipated and welcomed.

Civil Servant and Citizen
The "Malayanisation" of the service was a long-standing promise but little had been done to allow local-born, non-white civil servants to scale up the ladder. Even in the last years with independence on the horizon, British civil servants were still given more generous terms in pay and promotion than

their Malayan counterparts – even among the administrative service officers, the elite of the civil service into which Tay had been recruited. On top of the questions of pay and prospects, what frustrated many was the prevailing attitude of superiority. The civil service of the British had become a creature of class and privilege; for postings in Malaya, many of its officers were recruited not so much on academic background as for their social background – preferring "gentlemen" of the correct class. The British self-serving estimates were that no Malayan could be truly ready for the upper tier of the civil service for ten years or more; no Malayan was good enough.

The young civil servant was not blind to this and did not accept the bias. Tay could socialise and get to know the white, expatriate civil servants as individuals. He also developed contacts in the embassy and among the military officers and would meet them every now and again. But as a group, he found them often dismissive and prickly about their privileges. With independence coming, Malayanisation would have to move faster. The days when officers sent from London ran things and reported back to the colonial office would have to end. The Malayan civil servants would administer under locally elected government leaders. Of course, civil servants would continue to be independent, in the British tradition, and serve whichever political party won power. But they were also citizens and their political masters would be Malayan too, subject to the approval of voters or else to lose power.

As Singapore moved towards independence, civil servants took a close-up look at the evolving events: what policies were pursued and the motivations and mettle of the politicians. Few had much love for the Labour Front. Chief Ministers David Marshall and then Lim Yew Hock had been elected to lead under the transitional arrangements of the time that gave Singapore internal self-rule. But their administrations were not only limited in their authority under self-rule, but also in their capabilities and quality.

Like many, Tay admired Marshall's principles and courage. But he reckoned that Marshall's stance was impractical and doomed to fail, even prior to the riots that broke out before the Chief Minister went to London for constitutional discussions with the British. Tay was to record in his oral history interviews much later, how Marshall resigned after his return and decided not only to step down as Chief Minister but to leave the government altogether. Tay felt that the Labour Front government had deteriorated rapidly. The businesses and many in the establishment from the British days were thrown off in their hopes for continuity; that, even with decolonisation, things would remain more or less the same. The Labour Front was want of wider support and Lim Yew Hock, who took over as Chief Minister, lacked Marshall's charisma. The Labour Front was further weakened when Chief Minister Lim Yew Hock agreed with the British to crack down hard on leftists. Not all the cases seemed to be entirely justified. The crackdown further strained the Labour Front's legitimacy and conversely created more sympathy for the causes of the Left.

The beneficiary of this was the then opposition, People's Action Party (PAP). The PAP's leadership were progressive socialists centred around Lee Kuan Yew, but the party had a broader appeal to the ground and with the Left. Going into the 1959 General Elections, the Labour Front was painted as a semi-colonial, corrupt and ineffectual government. There were also accusations that they had received foreign funding. In contrast, the PAP promised to be effective and clean, and to serve the people.

As a civil servant, Tay was duty-bound to be neutral but he was not indifferent. There was a need for real leadership and the Marshall and Lim Yew Hock administrations had failed to provide that. A more capable government would make a real difference and the 1959 election was the turning point. In that election, Tay served as a returning officer for the voting in the Thomson Constituency, one of the 51 constituencies. This was a predominately Chinese ward and the PAP candidate was S T Bani, an ethnic Indian. Despite being a racial minority, the PAP man had more rapport with the Chinese voters in the constituency than his Labour Front rival, a Chinese. This confirmed Tay's strong sense that the PAP would win.

The size of that margin – the PAP swept 43 seats – took many people by surprise and the result was greeted with a mix of hope and suspicion. To those accustomed to the British and the Labour Front, the PAP were outsiders and their Socialist leanings and ties to the Left were of concern. Some of the moderates in the PAP had been civil servants themselves, like Dr Goh Keng Swee and K M Byrne. But there was discomfort that the bulk of the PAP comprised many Chinese-educated working class, some of whom were already suspected to have been Communist sympathisers. There was also Ong Eng Guan who stoked populism, intent to fecklessly bringing in a politics from the street into the corridors of government. Those doubts among the civil servants were reinforced by two of the early measures the PAP government introduced.

The PAP government proceeded to re-educate the top civil servants and reorient them to understand the new social order they wished to implement. The first and deeply felt measure was to substantially cut civil service pay, impacting almost half of all civil servants. The rationale went beyond a question of trimming the budget. The then new PM Lee Kuan Yew explained in Parliament on 21 July 1959: "We wanted to show everyone in Singapore, especially the Chinese-educated majority that for the public good, the English-educated were prepared to make sacrifices…".

A second measure was to make senior civil servants go through retraining at the newly established Political Study Centre. In July 1959, Lee Kuan Yew spoke to the civil servants and warned them and "their rather inept leaders at the moment". The young and pugilistic new PM advised that, "if nothing more catastrophic happens to them than the loss of allowances and the fact that they have to face fiercer competition from the non-English-educated, then they should get down on their bended knees and thank their gods that their souls have been spared."

As the PAP moved from being the opposition into government, there was another and even more important development for the civil servants like Tay. The tensions within the PAP were growing and a split more apparent between Lee and the moderates on one hand, and the left-leaning members, including the substantial figure of Lim Chin Siong. These intra-PAP tensions were confirmed when Lee Kuan Yew addressed civil servants at a closed-door meeting. The PM admitted to the internal differences and asked those present to understand the situation. He reminded the civil servants that they no longer served in a colonial service but one that was accountable to the people, in the country itself. It was incumbent therefore that each civil servant had to consider forces that were seeking to destabilise the government.

How would the civil servants respond? More than a few of those recruited during the colonial period responded by resigning. For others, they paused and understood how the hopes and admonitions set the context for them as both civil servants and also as citizens, to decide how to act. It was a time of change for Singapore, and Tay knew from the start he would have to keep his eyes open and adapt.

Workers Unite

Tay's first posting in November 1956 was to serve as Assistant Commissioner for Labour, tasked to help mediate and arbitrate in disputes between workers and employers. From what might have seemed like disputes between two private parties, he discovered elements that had wider significance and critical implications for the emerging nation. Workers and jobs were always among the most sensitive issues. Gangs and syndicates operated as labour contractors. There were also many different and independent unions competing with each other, and they could cause any number of problems not only to their employers but in the streets. Under the British, Tay knew, there was a unit called the Chinese Protectorate that watched over Chinese migrant workers. The mandate was not, however, to ameliorate their harsh conditions and offer help. Instead, they were tasked to head off potential troubles, often through the village headmen and societies that wielded influence in the Chinese community. In many ways, the Ministry of Labour continued this function as Singapore moved towards independence. It was much-needed.

Workers were expecting a better future, a new dispensation when they became citizens, rather than being colonial subjects. A considerable part of the Chinese population were, moreover, leaning towards Socialism and there were sympathies for Communism and sentiments towards mainland China under Mao Zedong. Part of Tay's job was to keep an eye on things that went beyond the day-to-day cases brought to him. Working at the Labour Ministry, he began to uncover activities undertaken by some of the unions to radicalise workers and stoke grievances. He also gained insights about the web of relationships that linked seemingly apolitical bodies, like the Singapore Chinese Middle School Students' Union, into a united front which could support the unions affiliated with Communists. He was not surprised that the security agencies and the Special Branch under the British should have an interest in the work of the Ministry of Labour, given their close connections to workers and unions.

After a time handling worker disputes at the Labour Court, Tay was identified and sent across to help address issues faced by the sailors, dealing with some of their unions. Taking up the role as the Seaman's Industrial Relations Officer from August 1957, he could see first-hand the picture of workers and unions that he had intuited at the Labour Courts. Here, rather than working on individual cases, Tay focused more on the unions – which were fractured and often fractious; different bodies that resisted amalgamation. Behind the workers and some of the unions on the Left, there were ongoing machinations, hidden actors with motives beyond the betterment of conditions and wages.

While he could see the problems, he was also attuned to the politics and did not hold out much hope that the Labour Front – the government at this time – could or would take firm action. Problems were already popping up, and more contentions could be expected. He reckoned the coming struggle would be critical. Yet, there was little more that could be done at this time and he grew frustrated that the Labour Front government lacked the will and also the capabilities to head off these problems. For the time being, all that was possible was to map the issues and get to know the key players among the workers and how they might link to each other and also to leftist politicians and other actors who might lurk in the background, pulling the strings, and then monitor how the situation was developing.

It was during this stint at the port that he came to know another civil servant posted to help the port workers: a certain S R Nathan. He had been in the post before Tay and was older by a few years. Tasked to attend to industrial relations among the seamen as Assistant Seaman's Welfare Officer, Nathan had served immediately before as a hospital social worker, and he approached this assignment similarly, giving considerable attention and care to the seamen and their complaints.

Tay soon learnt not only to do his job but also to enjoy the port area, with its constant hum of activity, so thick with life. Before long, he learnt where to get some of the best curry puffs – the bigger, square-cut ones – and even where the South Asian workers would buy home-brewed toddy – the favoured alcohol tapped from coconut flower buds – after pay day. There were afternoons when Nathan and he would find time to sit for *kopi* at a *sarabat* stall in the port area and discuss the problems at work, and also the broader happenings across the island. While different in background and character, Tay and Nathan got on and would work well together, and they would do so again in the future.

In 1960, after the PAP government had been elected into office, Tay left the post at the Harbour Board. On leaving, he obtained agreement for the bureaucracy to meld his job with the duties that were already being out carried by Nathan, and the two men were to stay in contact, beginning a professional and personal relationship that would continue for many years. Decades later, when he was already President, Nathan was to write about this period at the port. He saw this time, at the start of his long career as helping him answer a question of purpose, "Why am I here?" and made this the title of his short memoir. Nathan dedicated the book as follows: "To the memory of Tay Seow Huah, a buddy who stood by me and shared the unpredictable stresses and strains I faced at work during those times."

Tay's next post was at the Ministry of Finance and its Division for Commerce and Industry. Here he continued, in part, to keep an eye on labour and unions. In January 1960, he was selected to represent the government at a key meeting of the United Nations Economic Commission for Asia and the Far East (ECAFE). *The Straits Times* on 17 January 1960 reported that the only other Singaporean delegate was James Puthucheary, the well-known and Left-leaning trade unionist and politician who was, at the time, manager at the Singapore Industrial Promotion Board and a PAP member. Not long afterwards, in 1961, Puthucheary would split from the moderates in the PAP to join the Barisan Sosialis.

In his role at the Ministry of Finance, Tay rose quite quickly to be Principal Assistant Secretary. It was here that he worked with George Bogaars, who was already Deputy Secretary. Tay gained the confidence of the more senior civil servant and, when Bogaars left the Ministry to take up the directorship of the Special Branch in 1961, the two remained in regular contact, especially when Tay was dealing with the politically sensitive issues with the port and its unions.

In this period, Tay also came to know the PAP leadership as they first took over the government. The key figure in the Ministry, Dr Goh Keng Swee, was in charge of all the economic agencies. He had been a civil servant too, directing the Social Welfare Department right up to 1958 when he stood for elections. Following a series of reports by experts, Dr Goh, as Minister, strongly backed the idea that Singapore had to grow an industrial base. This and other strategies were captured in the State Development Plan, 1961-64, the first and only plan of its kind for Singapore. Tay contributed to the work on the plan. In the process, his estimate of the new political leadership grew: Dr Goh was someone who had the intellect and the practical policy-making nous to get things to work. He was also someone willing and able to bring in advisors, experts and civil servants and give them the scope and support to succeed.

At this time, Tay was also to get an initial sense of Lee Kuan Yew, the firebrand lawyer who was now the charismatic Prime Minister, determined to push for independence and merger with Malaysia. Lee was only 37, younger than Dr Goh and other cabinet ministers, and just about any other prime minister, but with his character, intellect and ability to argue and inspire, there was little doubt that he was their leader. With him at the helm, the PAP was the party to deliver on the promise of independence. The larger question was which PAP it would be.

A schism was brewing within the PAP between those led by PM Lee and the Left – which was the larger part of the party – and there would be enormous implications for the national politics. There were closed-door meetings to discuss the future held among civil servants, including those who had been hired by the British colonial administration. Tay got a sense of the tensions and fissures within the PAP government. But he was careful in making his own views known, saying little even among those he knew better. When the sides formed, and the politics really required, the civil servants, like him, would have to be ready and might have to be less than neutral. This was not a colonial administration but one that had to respond to what was best for the country. It was not all settled, but Tay instinctively felt that neither the English colonial administration nor the Communists would be his preferred answer. Would he and the other civil servants stick to the ideal of neutrality as regards their political masters?

Tay shared his sense of things with Nathan, who was later to record the gist of their discussion and his response in his memoir:

"Tay Seow Huah and I began to appreciate a unity of purpose to stand up with the 'left' now evident among a small core of government ministers – people such as Goh

Keng Swee, S Rajaratnam, Toh Chin Chye and Yong Nyuk Lin, as well as the prime minister … some of us in the civil service found common ground with the anti-left-wing, non-communist group. I began to see purpose in actively working for the implementation of policies which were represented as being for the common good of Singapore. We did this more and more wholeheartedly with less hiding behind the cloak of civil service neutrality."

Tay was promoted during his stint at the Ministry of Finance. Rather than dealing with planning, policy papers and budgets, he was sent back to the port. The focus differed, however, as did the timing. The PAP was now running the government, not the Labour Front, and there would be the political backing to do what was needed. He now took on a larger role to represent the government in managing the workers at the Harbour Board as it transformed into the Port of Singapore Authority (PSA). This was a formative period, both for Tay and for the port, and the role of Staff Manager would not be a straightforward assignment.

The Port and Politics

Today, Singapore's port is known as one of the busiest and most efficient in the world, with the discipline, know-how and infrastructure to be a global player, anchoring the country as a hub and expanding outwards from Singapore. This was not the case in the 1950s and 1960s. Yes, the port was a key node in the Empire's global business and the entrepôt trade was critical to Singapore's economy. But there were challenges and these had been worsening in the run-up to independence. Perhaps none was more problematic than relations with the port workers. While running the port, British officials had exercised very little direct control over the workers. There were, instead, labour contractors who controlled their wages and living conditions. From the end of the war and into the decades leading up to calls for independence, strikes by workers – especially the port workers – were a recurring phenomenon. When the PAP was the opposition, Lee Kuan Yew, as a young lawyer, was legal adviser to one of the main unions. The port was ripe for unrest and would be a crucible for the changes that were unfolding.

While it was in opposition, the PAP might have had the luxury to simply side with the workers against the colonial authorities and the Labour Front government. But the situation was more complicated after the party's election victory in 1959. Many of the issues raised at the port related to emerging differences within the party itself. Some were over matters of national policy like internal security and the future relations with Malaya and others more directly related to the pay and conditions for work. The port was the key economic asset for Singapore at the time and provided jobs for many workers. These workers were a potent political force through the unions or if they took to the streets.

In 1961, the pro-Communist members of the PAP split to form the Barisan Sosialis, and the unions too split. The unrest that was stirring across the island was coming into the ports, and the pro-Left workers' unions had pushed for strikes and industrial action. At the same time, this was a period of adjustment, planning and development for the port to serve the country's industrialisation and development programme. While the PAP government had to deliver on promised improvements, they were also anxious to keep the port running and viable. The confrontation with Indonesia, which took place in the 1963-66 period, was already creating instability and dampening regional shipping and trade.

The leftist and suspected pro-Communists were pushing for even more pay and rights for the workers and they threatened to push the workers to bring the port to a halt. If that resulted, what happened at the ports could spread to the wider society, quickly, and not for the better. The leftists were against the proposed merger with the Federation of Malaya and would attempt to bring demonstrations and street action to rally support against it, and winning support in the unions and among the port workers would be a big boost. If that happened, the new government leaders might be undercut severely, and might lose power. To prevent that, ways were needed to deal with the port workers and unions, to keep them happy enough and working so the port would run and help boost the economic recovery. In the process, there would be the tough but sensitive work to stymie and flush out the leftist and Communist sympathisers among the port unions.

Following the 1959 elections, the port was a priority and the then new PM Lee Kuan Yew gave it considerable attention. In 1960, he attended the launch of a tugboat for the Harbour Board and said that no sector had a more immediate and direct bearing on Singapore's economy than the port. Then came more resolute actions against those identified to be leftists. In late 1962, the registrar of trade unions launched an investigation into the practices of the Harbour Board Staff Association, and two of its leaders were charged and arrested for criminal misappropriation of union funds, including Jamit Singh the Secretary-General. The Barisan staged a series of rallies but the majority of rank-and-file workers did not join in the strike as they had in past decades. Yet, not all were persuaded to accept the actions taken by government. The union was split.

Then, in February 1963, came Operation Coldstore. The Special Branch swooped down on those whom the Internal Security Council believed to be involved in Communist activities and constituted a threat to Singapore, including members of the PAP who had gone over to the Barisan and some of the more outspoken unionists.

Tay was not in the Special Branch at this time but he had kept in touch with George Bogaars, the Director in this period who carried out Operation Coldstore. Tay's work at the Labour Courts and then at the port enabled him to connect the dotted lines between workers and unions to the wider politics, and identify those who might be minded to cause problems. These factors set the context for Tay when he was sent to the port for the second time, as the government's representative to the unions and workers there.

The task to meet the fair demands of the workers while ensuring the left-wingers did not dominate was not an easy one. Both the commercial considerations and politics were more than a question of writing up the correct policies in a paper, as much civil service work required. After Coldstore and the arrests of the officials from the Harbour Board Staff Association, things were far from settled. Sentiments were roused against political interference. Explanations were demanded and questions were raised about what would come next. Working for the port and the government, Tay would expend much energy and time to respond and engage with the unions, much of it intense and behind closed doors, in endless and often difficult dialogues that bordered on ideological diatribes. At first, and for some time, trust was low and it was essential to build that up as a foundation for dialogue. But right from the start, it was clear that not all of those working in the unions could be persuaded to trust the government – nor to be themselves trusted.

Tay had to get to know the union representatives and workers well, gleaning information from direct interactions with them as well as from others who worked there. He would come to know which of those active in the unions was focused on what was right for the workers, and which might have other motivations and connections to leftist groups and political figures; between those who could be reasoned with and might be amenable to persuasion to reach a compromise, and those who were likely to prove more difficult. Information had to be gathered on key personalities and dossiers built up on each to gain some idea of how to deal with them.

PM Lee intervened to meet with representatives of the workers to try to head off industrial action. His personal intervention reflected not only the importance of the port to the nation as a whole but also the potential implications for the PM as MP for the Tanjong Pagar ward, the area around the port. As reported in *The Straits Times* of 14 June 1963, PM Lee met with the representatives face-to-face. Tay was the key person alongside him, representing the port and government.

It was not an easy time, and there was a lot to be done. There were grievances about work and pay that affected the workers, but while legitimate, could be used intentionally to stir disquiet, and not always for bona fide motives. The Staff

Association President, one Sinnatampy Markandu, went so far as to say that the government had served him with notice, and that they might strip him of his citizenship on the basis that he was a threat to the national security. A call for the port workers to strike was made. Three hundred to 400 men attended.

The Prime Minister responded by calling this a "political strike", rather than recognising it as a genuine workplace grievance. He further warned that these people had been identified and, if a strike materialised, they would "face the consequences". Hard actions – applied against an identified leadership – were necessary. The government moved to cancel the registration of the entire association – a controversial action reported on the front page. The leftist Singapore Association of Trade Unions (SATU) immediately decried the cancellation. Debate ensued in Parliament. The Minister for Home Affairs, Ong Pang Boon, warned that the matter would be brought to the Internal Security Council, accusing SATU (including the Harbour Board Staff Association) of constituting a Communist united front organisation. This warning, reported in *The Straits Times* of 27 July 1963, came just months after Operation Coldstore and was not an empty threat. The government only relented when the association reconstituted itself with a new constitution that barred any politicians from taking office. Yet, the PM knew that the hardcore agitators could not be deterred by paper rules or even threats.

Dealing with the underlying situation for the bulk of the workforce was critical. When he met them, the PM was to promise significant pay increases for dockworkers, a sizeable hike. Only thereafter was the threat of worker unrest at the port contained. These events, reported in the media as they played out from mid-July 1963 to January 1964, posed daily challenges for Tay.

Overall, compared to the days under colonial administration, the improvements and the rising prosperity and rapid development of the PAP government era were visible. Hardships remained but these struggles were linked to the collective task of nation-building and the port workers could see the reason for restraint and sacrifice. At the harbour, Tay could see such problems required new and specific solutions, and their focus would have to shift from rounds of strike action to discipline and productivity efforts. Further reforms were made to the harbour board system to improve how it managed workers, especially the ones with more skills. The mechanisation of operations in the port was also accelerated to reduce the need for manual labour, and therefore the numbers of lower-paid and lower-skilled workers. As these promised reforms proceeded, the threat of strike action receded. The port kept operating, viable and secured, but this took real effort.

Some of it was nuts-and-bolts about the work conditions. In 1964, for instance, Tay gave an interview about the board's schemes to attract, train and reward people to work as harbour pilots. This was but one part of the challenge to train up port workers in higher skills so that the port could be more efficient. The broader outlook was even more challenging, given that many port workers were still adjusting to the use of forklifts and mechanical aids. Without these, it was backbreaking labour, day and night, stretching from 7 am to 11 pm, with two two-hour breaks, and another night shift from 11 pm to 5 am. Port workers did not have it easy. Neither did Tay find it an easy job to keep the port working and head off labour unrest. By offering training schemes and other administrative improvements, Tay took a leading role in the negotiations with the unions about pay and conditions for the workers, and helped introduce progressive schemes for worker welfare, such as shift work at the wharf. There was no easy closure, however.

While the pay increase promised by PM Lee would be upheld, there were controversies about at least two key details that would again bring the situation into the newspapers. The first was a proposal to allow the PSA to have a pool of workers who could be tapped, in addition to the unionised workers. The second was a claim by the workers for the pay increases promised by the premier to be backdated to the very start of their dispute with the port.

In April 1965, as Staff Manager at the PSA, Tay announced

that the wages that were paid to workers would increase to $38 million, more than 25 per cent more than the previous total. This was part of a "step-by-step" conversion in the salaries for the 11,000-plus port workers. This was a major increase, although the union had originally asked for even more, which Tay thought "excessive". In *The Straits Times* of 26 March 1965, he explained how PM Lee had agreed to grant ex-gratia bonuses to the workers.

In these negotiations, Tay did not work alone. He had to identify those among the workers and unionists whom he could work with. He also had to persuade the PSA that the extra wages could be accepted without damaging its competitiveness. The negotiations helped set a tone in relations that was more positive than it was before, when there would be strikes and standoffs that pitted the port workers against the government. There were, again, threats to organise strikes, and he had to appeal to workers to accept a more peaceful means of settling the differences: arbitration.

Tay was to represent the port in the consequent arbitration: the 32-year-old civil servant personally arguing the high profile, multimillion dollar dispute with wider political implications. On the other side, representing the workers, was the veteran politician and National Trade Union Congress Secretary-General, Devan Nair. Known for his invective, Nair was quick to uphold the promise made by PM Lee for a pay rise, and then to accuse the port authorities for "making a liar" of the PM in the way they had calculated the pay increases and refused to meet the workers' claims for the backdate of increases to 1961. There were accusations that the port officials were "petulant", as described in *The Straits Times* on 27 April 1965.

Such acidic remarks that could play for a controversial headline with hyperbole were characteristic of the man who would go on to be the third President of the Republic. But it was also explicable in that Nair was trying to win over support from the workers for the NTUC. For even as the battle in court with the government and PSA proceeded, there was a broader war for the NTUC to win over worker allegiance from the Left-influenced union. This was not only a matter of commerce and labour contracts but high-level political theatre.

On his side, Tay stuck to the facts. There was a mistake in the union's calculations, making it $1 million more (a considerable amount in those days and in proportion to the overall claim). There had been no feet-dragging and delay by the authority, as alleged. There were vital state interests at stake, he submitted in a document to the arbitrators which was held confidential. In the result, both sides could claim some success. The Port Authority and Tay acting for them won the case on the legal merits, but an ex-gratia payment was ordered that would give the workers some of what had been claimed. The authority also had to work out some of the details in the precise calculation of pay increases to some grades of workers.

The high-profile arbitration hearing covered in the media and officially reported as IAC Case No. 21 of 1965 attracted attention and showed many of the efforts that had been going on behind the scenes. There were many and very sensitive consultations about the wages and conditions to keep the workers content, in which Tay played a role. This was both overtly in the open and in the arbitration court and media, and even more quietly in often tense negotiation in the background. In some cases, there was no easy or permanent solution; indeed the mood was restive in many other sectors across the young country. The politicking among workers and their unions was no less, and indeed often more intense. But Tay had managed to keep the situation stable enough and the port running.

Despite the considerable pressures, this second posting to the port was a positive time for Tay professionally. The result had been delivered by a mixed approach of hard policing and politicking, as well as structured and real improvements on issues of pay and working conditions. Working in this way could be seen as a small and early example of what would later be termed tripartism.

There was an even more important outcome from this time at the port. To be effective, Tay found it essential for him to know the political masters and hear first-hand what they thought and planned. He found them open to advice and inputs, and decisive in setting directions. He could see how effective the PAP government was becoming. Yet, the civil servant did not get too close and knew there was a line to be drawn; they were bosses, not friends. He was never to join their party but there were many ways a civil servant could serve in the years coming up.

In this process, he worked closely again with S R Nathan who was engaging the unions as part of the Labour Research Unit. While appointed to different sides, the two were able to find ways to progress dialogue. Often, there might be first and private exchanges on key issues, informally meeting outside of the office. Only afterwards would they bring in others, especially the unionists. From this, they would widen the dialogue, finding consensus and support to legitimise decisions reached. The two men worked on both sides of the relationship at a critical time for the port. They both understood that there was a quiet but grim and ongoing struggle.

On a personal level, the relationship grew between Nathan and Tay. Their wives and families too, came to know each other. Their paths were in fact to intertwine for many years as each progressed in the civil service. Their work at the port had been about the concerns of the unions and even about about the pay and job conditions of individual workers. In the coming years, both would focus on the security and external engagements for the country and, whatever the rank or reporting lines, their relationship remained collegial, based on mutual respect. Their long-standing ties help explain Tay's decision later, during the *Laju* Incident, to make sure that Nathan was involved. It was instinctive to bring in a known and trusted person to help in critical situations.

The time at the port also had an upside for Tay's young family. While civil servants were not highly paid as they are today, he was promoted quite quickly and this helped smooth over money matters. At the Singapore port, he was assigned quarters – a colonial bungalow at Raeburn Park, overlooking the habour, and near the railway station. It was not the largest of such bungalows but compared to their shared house in Langsat Road, it was huge. The house was a very visible marker of his professional rise and how this could be of benefit to the family. But the house was not theirs, of course. Even if things might have seemed more settled, in fact contingency and change remained.

With his key assignment completed, Tay Seow Huah was ready to move on and take up another role. Moving around the civil service, across agencies and ministries, was the usual practice among administrative service officers. In September 1965, it was made known that he was to leave his post. In response, the union for the 11,000 waterfront workers appealed to PM Lee to rescind the appointment and keep him on. The members of the union cited Tay for being: "greatly responsible for the betterment of the port workers and also for the friendly and harmonious relations that have existed hitherto between the union and the PSA for the last two years." Their petition to the PM was reported in *The Straits Times* on 3 September 1965.

Despite this, he was to be moved and it was more than the usual rotation. During his stint at the port, he had been innocuously designated as "Staff Manager". But in reality, the situation had tested his acumen in handling matters that impacted not only the workers and economy but key questions of political stability and security. This work had brought him to the attention of the senior leadership, not just within the civil service but among the politicians and especially the Prime Minister. Tay was selected for a post that was something exceptional, and at a critical time.

The year was 1965, and there was unexpectedly and suddenly an independent Singapore, with many things to be done. Immediately after the port and on an urgent basis, Tay was appointed to head the Special Branch.

The Special Branch
The Special Branch had played critical roles during the British colonial administration to maintain security and stability. First

established by the British in 1948 as the colonial government struggled to contain the Emergency in the peninsula, it grew out from the main Police Force, as the name connotes, to take on a unique role that was hallowed and feared. The Special Branch was tasked to deal with key security risks, to undertake surveillance and act preventively, and was given considerable powers to do so. Chief of these was the power to order and enforce detention without trial before a court and act, in this regard, outside of the normal rule of law processes. There was a certain awe and even fear about the organisation.

The Special Branch had notable successes before the war and during the years before the Malayan Emergency, and not always using knuckledusters. Perhaps the most spectacular success was with Lai Teck, a shadowy character thought to have been a Chinese Vietnamese and once a spy for the French. Under the British, he was planted into the Communist Party of Malaya (CPM) before the war and then ascended to become its leader. This gave the British key leverage to know what the CPM were doing and who was key within the organisation.

During the war, he was thought to then have assisted the Japanese against the Communists, even as he served as the CPM leader. In 1942, he had been the key person to enable a mass roundup of his own colleagues. When the British returned, he continued to play this double role as their key man.

That all changed unexpectedly in 1947. Lai Teck absconded, taking with him the bulk of CPM funds and, most likely, the stash he had accumulated from working against the Communists. This not only impacted the Communist Party but also the British. They had relied on Lai Teck so much that, with him gone, they struggled to rebuild their networks to understand and respond to the post-war scenario. The CPM were able to move on and to appoint Chin Peng as their head. Their networks, although disrupted, were reinstated quickly and able to bring in more recruits. But in the British security agencies of that time, only a dozen or so officers were able to carry on even a simple conversation in Chinese. British intelligence was caught looking the wrong way and had no clear understanding of the growing discontent among the Malayan Chinese. When the Emergency began in 1948 and spiralled into a full-on insurgency in the peninsula, there was a lot for the new Special Branch to do, and quickly.

From 1950, General Harold Briggs instituted a broad master plan to combat the Emergency, integrating army and police in tandem with civilian administration, and bringing in special intelligence to identify networks that were to be rooted out. This gave a key role to the Special Branch and this was reinforced by Sir Gerald Templer, when he was appointed to serve not only as Director of Operations but also as High Commissioner, effectively twinning civil administration with the military and security efforts. For wider intelligence, the Joint Intelligence Committee (Far East) assisted and, from 1954, the Special Branch was able to draw on the insights and networks from the MI5 and MI6 in the UK. This was essential, given the CPM's networks were not merely within the country but across the region and drew support from China and even the USSR.

By 1965, the Special Branch faced problems from at least four sources. The first, and perhaps the least, of these was the Communist insurgency. This had been increasingly brought under control. The threat still remained but the State of Emergency, first declared in 1948, had officially ended in 1960. Yet, Communist groups had not been fully constrained, and indeed would flare up with incidents of insurgency and subversion even into the 1970s.

The second was the Konfrontasi, a clandestine war that Sukarno's Indonesia waged against Malaysia, including Singapore. In March 1965, short months before Tay was announced as Special Branch Director, MacDonald House along Orchard Road had been bombed, with three killed in the explosion. This was, moreover, not an isolated incident; there were at least 42 bombings in Singapore from 1963 to 1966.

A third source of concern arose from racial and religious conflict. Following Singapore's merger with Malaysia in 1963, a series of racial incidents and clashes had been triggered. On

21 July 1964, there were conflicts in Singapore that left 23 people dead and 454 others injured, both Malays and Chinese. There was further unrest and, on 2 September 1964, 13 people were killed and 109 injured, and the police intervened to arrest almost 1,500 persons. The mood was restive and volatile, and there was no clear apparatus to know when a new problem among the ethnic communities might arise.

The fourth related to the leftists and Communist supporters in Singapore who were involved in a range of activities, from political parties to unions and school groups, in a united-front effort to take power. This was, in many ways, the most subterranean and complex challenge for the Special Branch, especially as questions of independence for Malaya and Singapore arose from the mid-1950s.

The heady and unstable flux went beyond the military-type Emergency operations seen up north, and approached the arena of political contestation, with far less clarity about who presented the real danger. Yet, it was inevitable. The political choices in this period of tumult went far beyond the ballot box; politics touched on the rawest points in society relating to race, religion and fundamental ideological questions concerning governance and the economy. This resulted not only in votes going one way or another but too often in incidents of foment and conflict.

There were good reasons then for the secretive nature and exceptional powers of the Special Branch. Yet, for the same reasons, it was not without controversy. Formally, the Special Branch remained a part of the overall Police Force and was apolitical. But in the context of these times, especially in dealing with the Left, a central concern was that the preventive detention powers could be used beyond the strictly legitimate concerns of policing, as well as for political advantage by one side or the other. When it was first created, the Special Branch had operated directly under the British colonial administration. Its pioneers were, accordingly, British subjects seconded from the UK and from India. But as independence loomed for Malaya and Singapore, the Branch was guided by an Internal

Security Council that comprised not only the PAP government and the British colonial administration but also representatives from the Federal government in Kuala Lumpur.

In this period of transition, the Special Branch Director had to deal with an Internal Security Council that was split among the different stakeholders. Under Bogaars, the Special Branch had carried out Operation Coldstore in February 1963. In one swoop, over a hundred persons were detained, accused of being threats to the stability of Singapore by being associated with Communist forces or under their influence. Among those arrested and detained without trial were left-wing politicians, including prominent figures like Lim Chin Siong, Fong Swee Suan, the unionists James Puthucheary and Dominic Puthucheary, Poh Soo Kai, and Lim Hock Siew.

The operation was controversial and proved to be a key moment for the PAP which, from its inception, had been discernibly split between the English-speaking moderates led by Lee Kuan Yew, and the Left, mainly Chinese-speaking camp. The cohabitation of the two groups had been widely analogised in terms of "riding the tiger" as captured in Dennis Bloodworth's *The Tiger and the Trojan Horse*. After 1959, when the PAP formed the government of Singapore, the risk arose that the rider might get thrown off and the tiger would attack. There were concerns that the Left-wing PAP, led by the charismatic Chinese-speaking Lim Chin Siong, would unseat Lee and his faction to take over. This risk had been stemmed by Operation Coldstore. Yet, there arose questions about whether Operation Coldstore addressed strictly security concerns for the country, or had intruded into the realm of politics to assist Lee Kuan Yew and the moderates he led.

In many accounts and speeches, Lim Chin Siong defended himself fiercely, stating publicly in mid-1961 that: "I am not a Communist or a Communist frontman, or, for that matter, anybody's frontman." This was headline news then and the controversy has continued. Indeed, it has since been revived after the UK released once-secret papers about how its administrators saw the situation as studied in *"Original Sin"*?

Revising the Revisionist Critique of the 1963 Operation Coldstore in Singapore by the scholar, Kumar Ramakrishna.

Tay was not in charge of the Special Branch during Operation Coldstore. However, as he took over afterwards, he could not have been unaware of effects on the institution; not least those who continued to be detained. One factor that clarified the situation was that, during his tenure, the Special Branch would no longer be subject to the different pulls and pushes of the Internal Security Council between the British, Kuala Lumpur and the Singapore government. With separation from Malaysia and full independence, the reporting line for the Special Branch had shifted. For better or worse, the Special Branch was from now answerable only to the Prime Minister of the Singapore government, Mr Lee Kuan Yew of the PAP.

PM Lee had clear views about what the Special Branch should be, and this went beyond Operation Coldstore. As merger with Malaysia proceeded, Lee and the PAP leadership felt that the Special Branch in Singapore was becoming, in effect, a sub-unit of its counterpart in KL and subject to the Malay-dominated politics at the Federal level. Lee also expressed dissatisfaction that the Special Branch was operating more like a police outfit, responding only when a crisis had risen and then enforcing matters with policing actions. Ideally, he wanted a greater focus on providing intelligence that could help foresee and head off problems. This had been part of the Special Branch's remit but as the British had other intelligence agencies, this had been neglected within the Branch itself. Yet, this need for external intelligence was underlined by Konfrontasi, waged by Sukarno's Indonesia, and the race riots in Malaysia.

Lee was anxious as Prime Minister to obtain information directly from the Special Branch as he could see that politics and security were inextricably linked. His inclination was reinforced by a certain Claude Fenner, who served as the Malaysian Inspector General for the Police during this period. When Lee sought information from him, Fenner required that PM Lee go through "normal channels" to obtain it, by routing requests through the then Police Commissioner for Singapore, Le Cain. The PM's frustrations in this period are documented in Bertha Henson's book about George Boogars, Tay's predecessor at the Special Branch.

Now free from the British as well as Federal government control, the Special Branch and its Director would report directly to PM Lee – with of course due communication with Dr Goh as the MID Minister and Bogaars as the newly appointed Permanent Secretary. The institution would need to be directed by a person who understood the unique circumstances facing Singapore, the politics of the PAP and Communist strategies, and who could be expected to sink roots in Singapore. Tay fairly well fit the bill.

Yet, when his appointment was announced, some questions arose. It was not obvious why someone who was holding the title of Staff Manager at the port authority was qualified to direct the Special Branch. Seasoned local officers were already there, including the long-serving police officer, Percy Pennefather, who had been its acting head for the short period after Bogaars left and before Tay took up the post. There is no public record of the reasons and rationale but it would seem that the selection was based on a number of factors.

There was, no doubt, a strong recommendation from Bogaars, who was leaving the Special Branch to serve as Permanent Secretary of the Ministry of Interior and Defence which would be the parent ministry. He knew Tay from their earlier spell together at the Ministry of Finance, and they had maintained contact when Bogaars was at the Special Branch and Tay was at the port. Tay was also known to Dr Goh Keng Swee, who would take over as Minister of the new and merged ministry. Third, and perhaps key, Tay had been given responsibility for the politically sensitive tasks at the port and had worked directly with the Prime Minister.

Taking on the role at this time was a considerable challenge. Changes were facing not only the Special Branch but the entire security of Singapore. At Separation in 1965, some two-thirds of the infantry battalions were non-Singaporeans, and there was an urgent need to go about establishing the army, with a core of trained regulars as well as a large volunteer People's Defence Force. To move ahead with this, one of the first acts was to immediately establish the MID. The NS (Amendment) Act was then passed in 1967 to build a conscripted army with national service, which was seen as vital to build self-reliance in defence, especially as the British prepared to withdraw their forces by 1971.

There was a lot to be done and the importance of the task was signified by the appointment of Dr Goh Keng Swee as the MID Minister. Dr Goh had already proven himself to be highly effective, doing much to jump-start the fledgling Singaporean economy and to bring in capable personnel to move things ahead. Dr Goh was known, as Finance Minister, to be careful about expenditures. As such, placing Dr Goh in charge of MID emphasised the priority of taking action, and to minimise any hesitation or financial excuse for inaction. This was a key and eventful period and challenges were met head on by the MID. After this period, when MID had grown in size and complexity, it was split in 1970 into two separate ministries – for Defence and for Home Affairs, as is the more conventional arrangement in most governments.

Taking over the Special Branch in September 1965 and serving until 1970, Tay was in the midst of all this. During these years, he would also take on key assignments that moved fluidly between the interior and external dimensions as Director of Security and Intelligence of the MID. Rather than rotating to serve on economic and diverse other issues as other civil servant colleagues in the administrative service did, from this time onwards, he would focus exclusively on security and intelligence issues. Afterwards, when the MID was split, Tay would serve as Permanent Secretary at Home Affairs and, later, Defence.

In these ways, from independence in 1965 and onwards, Tay was the first spy chief for Singapore.

*

My father's friends were many and diverse. So were his interactions with them, especially those he knew from his earliest years and university. When they visited our house, I was called down to be introduced and say hullo.

One visit I remember was by an old DRH and motorbiking *kaki*, Mr K. In all the tales I had heard, he was a giant of a man, large and fearless, full of life, a big drinker and a hellavu biker. They had not been in touch much after graduation when he had gone back to Malaysia to work. But one day, when I was maybe seven or eight, this old friend came to the house.

He was big, as I had expected, taller than my father. But he was so portly that my younger self rudely could not imagine him speeding along on a motorbike. He was, moreover, not at all lively and ebullient but quiet, even downcast. I did not stay long in the living room with him as the adults had matters to discuss.

Afterwards, I overheard my father telling my mother that poor K had some problems in Malaysia. He had come to my father not only for friendship and sympathy but advice and, if possible, assistance. My father said he had never seen him so downcast. My mother said that she had always liked K from among his loud friends and that if he could help him, my father should. Yes, my father said, he would.

Sometime after, my father reported that his old friend had been hired for a job in Brunei. There was someone he knew who needed a good person and he had suggested his old friend. That's good, my mother said, but how would K adjust with the Sultanate's constraints on alcohol and bars? Well, my father suggested, that might be even better.

Another of his friends from university days was Chan Ki Mun. He was one or two years older than my father and had ragged him when he first joined DRH. The practice, which was illegal but common in those days, was regarded as a key to either becoming sworn enemies or else good friends. It was the latter case with Chan and my father. He had a keen mind and a certain toughness in manner, and while Chan was short and small – quite the opposite to K – he too loved motorbikes.

Chan was involved with politics during university, on the active fringe of some progressive, Left-leaning groups, and kept it up even after graduating. But he was disillusioned after Operation Coldstore, when a number of those he knew were taken into detention. He was to do his Masters abroad and then moved to the UK to join the London Council as a town planner. After marrying a younger Dutch woman, he settled there but kept in touch. Whenever he returned or my father would go over, they would meet. If my father needed anything – like some odd part for one of the old British sports cars he kept, only available in the UK – Chan would assist. When my sister went to the UK to study, Uncle Ki Mun made an avuncular effort to go out to help her.

Years later, after my father had died, he was to tell my sister of the great help that my father extended. My father, he claimed, had called just before Operation Coldstore. "Stay home," was the advice, "for the next few evenings, keep clear of your usual places and friends."

This is puzzling to me, especially when in preparing this book I looked more closely at the dates of Operation Coldstore. That operation had been carried out when the Special Branch was run by George Boggars and my father was working at the port as Staff Manager. There was no clear reason why my father would have known to say anything as Chan recalled.

Another friend from university was Edwin Thumboo, the poet. He was a regular *kaki* on camping trips and jungle treks, together with Eric Alfred, the then Director of the National Museum. When I started writing in my teens, my father would show my early efforts to Thumboo, who encouraged and mentored me through my university years and for my second collection of poems, "5".

They were so close and often talked enough about DRH and student days that I assumed that they had been at university in the same years. It was only when I began writing this book and spoke in more detail to him that Thumboo told me that, while he had been at DRH, he was a few years younger and did not overlap with my father. He did not know him when he was an undergrad and riding motorbikes (unlike K and Chan). Instead, they had first connected when Thumboo was a civil servant (in the Tax Department) and my father was already working at the port. Why, I asked?

Thumboo, normally so articulate and garrulous, simply answered that my father had wanted to discuss things with people he could trust from different backgrounds and circles. He demurred on further details. One other matter was, however, to arise.

When we talked about my father's university and early days of work, Thumboo recalled what my father was doing in Port Dickson when he had abruptly left university and Singapore. My uncles had always said that my father was doing part-time teaching for that year. But Thumboo's account was different: he had been working with the British as a resettlement officer. While it was the tail end of the Emergency, this was still necessary and sometimes sensitive work, and would have entailed links to the military and security agencies.

Remembering is a complex process. There are things we say we know but what is the basis for our belief? There are things that others say they know, and this is even more complicated. In writing what I remember and hearing what others remember, there are not only questions but points of conflict between one version of what happened and another.

These differences might be innocent, especially as memories are more distant and minds age. Sometimes, the differences might show not only different perspectives and also how they were surmised differently. This is especially so with these old friends when they tell not just about my father's life but their own, and the intersections between them. They could tell me things that I had no real chance to know and either confirm or negate, as I was so young at the time as to have no real memory of what happened.

Chapter 5

SPY CHIEF

TAY SEOW HUAH'S appointment to the Special Branch in 1965 was publicly announced. From the beginning, he set about not only to direct the ongoing work but to reorganise the agency. He was to refit what the British left behind for new purposes.

Yet, he needed to know and understand more first. He went to London for a two-month senior officer's course after assuming the directorship of this storied British institution. Upon his return, he pushed for and secured agreement to reorganise the Special Branch. The idea was first discussed quite informally at the Senior Police Officers' Mess between Tay, Bogaars as Permanent Secretary of the MID, and two long-serving Special Branch officers said to be Yoong Siew Wah and Loh Hong Hee.

The history of the institutional change is often truncated to say that the Special Branch became the Internal Security Department (ISD) and focused only on internal security. It would perhaps be more complete to recognise that in the process, the Security and Intelligence Division (SID) was created. Tay would be the key actor to conceptualise and propose the reorganisation of the Special Branch. Under his charge, approval was given to specialise duties between internal and external issues. In February 1966, it was announced that, following the dissolution of the Special Branch, Tay would serve as the first Director for Security and Intelligence. This would be within the Ministry of Interior and Defence (MID), overseeing both the external intelligence and internal security functions.

External intelligence had in fact been one aspect of the Special Branch's mandate under the British. But this was less developed as the British had a number of different agencies working out of Singapore, as well as intelligence agencies in London, to look across Asia. Given this, the Special Branch inherited from the British had an existing tension, an imbalance in its functions. Internal security concerns made up the bulk of the current work and were handled well enough with existing procedures and a seasoned team, often drawn from the police. But external concerns, regionally and globally, were less in focus.

Yet, these were becoming increasingly important and impacted what happened within Singapore. More time and resources would be needed to understand and grapple with these external dimensions. From 1965, Singapore's fledgling agencies for security and intelligence would not only continue to deal with internal security, but give more attention on gathering intelligence and analysis, as PM Lee had earlier said were his hopes.

Tay's appointment to the Special Branch was known but how he and the security and intelligence agencies worked were not, and still remain withheld from the public domain. This is not only the details of specific operations and of current work, but even the work from past decades. This is, moreover, not only a matter of legal requirement but also a question of the culture. Consider the memoir of S R Nathan as President of the Republic, *Unexpected Journey: Path to the Presidency*. Nathan served as the second SID director, succeeding Tay. Yet, in his memoir of 672 pages, there are only some four pages about his time at the SID. He explained, "Some readers may wish that the foregoing brief account of my time at SID contained more details of operational matters. I make no apology for my reticence, which is driven by consideration of Singapore's national interests."

It has only been from 2021 that the SID has been more

open in recruiting staff and, therefore, having to describe what duties they are to undertake. It was so unusual that this was reported in *The Straits Times* on 19 July 2021. Even so, the descriptions of what SID does are given only in outline. Some understanding of the SID's work would help convey the urgency and often critical importance faced when Tay was Director for Security and Intelligence. Without betraying confidences or reference to secret documents, this may be sketched by looking at the key issues facing Singapore and some understanding of the roles and modus operandi among security and intelligence agencies.

How did Tay Seow Huah work as spy chief and what was done in those early years?

Security and Intelligence

For internal security, there were already officers who were accustomed and equipped to take up responsibilities and they would largely continue many of the previous functions of the Special Branch within the new ISD. It was the new SID for external intelligence gathering and analyses that required greater attention and emphasis. There were new needs. Hiring and training for the SID's external intelligence mandate, for instance, would have to look for different types of skills and people.

There was a real and urgent need for external intelligence. There were so many links that needed to be understood about the region that directly concerned the newly independent Singapore – not only in Malaysia and Indonesia but also in Vietnam and China. These external dimensions interacted with the internal security concerns in politics in very practical ways. For instance, how the leader of the Communist movement, Chin Peng, used the close cooperation of Thai, Laotian, Vietnamese and Chinese Communist parties to aid him in the hazardous journey to Beijing. In this example and very many others, looking outwards would be critical to inform decisions that were key to Singapore as a small country open to so many influences and links.

As such, the effort that Tay led to assess different capacities of the Special Branch – and then to allow specialisation – was not some bureaucratic shuffle. The change at the Special Branch was an effort to develop capacity to consider external security threats and then bring these to bear on considerations for security within Singapore. This would require both specialisation and separation, as well as synergy.

Research and analysis would have to be the core of its work. Liaison and dealing with counterparts from other countries was another necessity. Some agencies from other countries were hostile and even those who were friendly in general could – on particular occasion – have divergent interests. There was a need for operations within Singapore to keep watch over what they did here, and that this could be done. But by and large, capabilities to carry out operations in other countries were not strongly emphasised at first.

To develop those capabilities, as the first director, Tay faced the tasks of securing resources, recruiting and training, and setting up operational processes and systems. Some of these were known to him and had been part of the briefings during the course in the UK. These included ways for obtaining and then delivering sensitive information as well as how to recruit, train and supervise field operatives: spycraft and its methods such as secret drops and encryption.

The equipment for operations was also to his interest. He had always been keen on technology and equipment whether it was for the mechanisation and containerisation at the port or in his personal choices like cars, cameras and audio equipment and, later, computers. This was now applied to tools and toys, whether commercially available like the Minox camera, or things that had to be specially engineered and made, like listening devices.

All of this had to be done urgently. Yet, the situation of the government at the time was constrained and finances were tight. Furthermore, the reorganisation was taking place when there were immediate and numerous flashpoints and pressing intelligence demands. These generated pressing deadlines. It was thus a real challenge to keep up with the immediate needs while laying a path to develop the organisation. It was no small measure that the credibility of the new institution and its assessments grew strongly from its inception.

Tay was not simply an administrator. He came quickly to be known for his ability to analyse complex matters of security and intelligence swiftly. He was attested to have the rare acuity to break situations down into fundamental components so that they could be resolved, while retaining sufficient detail to be operational. A number of officers recount how he would rapidly flick through even long documents and then emerge with key points that showed he had a clear understanding of their presentation. When preparations were urgent, he also proved calm in the face of difficulties, responding quickly but in measured ways. Tay knew that what was essential for the new organisation was not only about obtaining and analysing the issues, but building up a team and its ethos. While he had been in the civil service for almost decade, this was Tay's first time to really be in charge of an institution. It was a personal challenge to the 33-year-old. Good and strong relationships were vital. Dealing with the veterans carried over from the Special Branch was another challenge. Bringing in new recruits was a further dimension.

He was not a boss who watched the clock and counted the hours staff put in, nor one given to raising his voice to issue *démarches*. He expected them to give their best and work out when effort was needed and get it done. Tay was unhurried in directing his staff, and even when issues were sensitive and urgent and Tay was tasked to report to PM Lee directly, the desk directors and junior officers could appreciate that they were given the time and room to get on with work and develop their insights. To many of these SID colleagues, Tay was not only their boss but someone whom they could trust.

He felt it important to know his own staff. That was essential to evaluate the information that they gathered and fed to him. Those he evaluated well and trusted sufficiently would be given scope. He would give them the authority and latitude to carry out the work and trust them to get it done. He would also back them up whenever problems arose, and did not seek to make them scapegoats.

He spent a lot of time and effort on colleagues at the SID; not just the more senior members but with those newly hired. He took a personal interest in their welfare and looked out for opportunities for them to develop. When there were overseas trips, he would ensure that some of the staff could go with him so they could be exposed to things, first-hand. He encouraged one to complete a Masters and helped carve out time to ensure it could be done in parallel with the work. He arranged for another to have a sabbatical in the USA, placing him at a prestigious academic institution with the connivance of a friend at Langley.

He even engaged more than a few of them personally, meeting for breakfast before work started or for a game of tennis after work, usually at the courts at the Senior Police Officer's Mess along Mount Pleasant Road. Efforts made to build up a team spirit included informal beach parties at Changi Point which Tay arranged at a large bungalow right on the beach. This belonged to the PSA and he approached his former employer to allow access. Families were included in these to build up closer ties. There were smaller events *sans* families – poker nights with small stakes with drinks and cigarettes. Tay did not gamble and was not known to join the poker games. But he was fine with the drinks and smoking and joining in casual after-office conversation convivially. He was never overly familiar, especially with the junior officers, but he was markedly relaxed, compared to the tensions in the work. An esprit de corps was developing as was needed alongside the routines and exercise drills that simulated what the team would be expected to do if an emergency occurred. People, Tay knew, were as important as policy in building up the institution.

Among those recruited to the SID at the time to undertake analysis and research, some would leave for other careers and do well. Most of them are not publicly known to be alumni of the SID. One of them was Mr N who went on to be a key executive at some of the largest government-linked companies.

Another was Ms P, who would be a journalist before joining one of the largest local banks to closely assist its top executive, and also serve as a non-resident ambassador for Singapore. A third example from the early years was the late Mr R, who would leave to qualify as a lawyer and start his law firm that was very successful into the 1990s. He was known to Tay from his stint at the Ministry of Finance and was roped in by Tay personally to head the administration and organisation, and help secure resources – perhaps the toughest and most necessary job in those years when the SID was new and the financial purse of the Singapore government less deep.

Others who joined in these first years stayed and would go on to serve for decades and grow their careers within the institution and other agencies connected to security and intelligence. Eddie Teo was one of them, then a fresh scholar who had graduated from Oxford where he had read Philosophy, Politics and Economics. Joining in 1970, Teo would rise to become Director of SID and serve more than two decades; for a spell, he was concurrently the head of the ISD, which was by then under the Ministry of Home Affairs. After that, he would serve as Permanent Secretary for Defence and, as his last post before retirement, in the Prime Minister's Office. Thereafter, he was appointed High Commissioner to Australia before returning to Singapore to become Chairman of the Public Service Commission and later, Chairman of the Council of Presidential Advisers.

As a junior officer at the SID, Teo did not engage much with Tay as he tells me when I am writing this book. The SID was growing rapidly, and there were specialised roles and a number of layers of supervision. Teo recalls being asked whether he preferred to range more broadly or be assigned to a specific country desk. When he opted for the latter, Tay responded by nodding and assigning him to focus on one of the most important and pressing neighbours.

While time was limited, Tay made the most of the interactions. Ms P, then also a junior officer, would have a similar impression. She recalls once, when Tay pressed for the basis of her analysis about the political outcome of elections in a neighbouring country, she answered "female intuition", and he just leaned back and laughed aloud with everyone – including Ms P herself – in a relaxed instance during a long and serious discussion. Later on, as she progressed and wanted to undertake a postgraduate course for further studies, Tay encouraged her.

There were, of course, those staff who had other and less positive outcomes to their careers. Some of these were new recruits who did not, for one reason or another, fit. This was not a job for everyone. There were always tensions, not only with the outside world and operatives from other governments, but also intrigue and tension within Singapore agencies and between individuals. There were many senior colleagues who had been in the Special Branch before Tay was appointed and not all of these took to the changes that were introduced.

From early on, an ethos of loyalty to the country was instilled. Trust had not only to be expected, but earned and further maintained. Even as officers were recruited and built up a sense of mission and team spirit, this was augmented routinely by surveillance of the staff, both new and old. This was necessary not only in terms of their performance and how they were dealing with the pressures of their work. It was first and foremost an effort to ensure that confidentiality was maintained; that none of those working for the Singapore government might for some reason be too friendly with foreign elements or, worse, turned. This was not paranoia. With so many foreign intelligence agencies operating in Singapore in this period, interactions were inevitable and, indeed, necessary. With that, there were temptations – like the cautionary tale of Lai Teck or others.

There were rumours of lapses that I heard as a child, without names or details, mentioned in passing; cautionary lessons. One officer opted for an early retirement and moved abroad to a Western democracy, only to turn up – as the SID was to find out – in the employ of that country's intelligence agency. Fortunately, the man had always been treated with a degree of circumspection during his tenure in the SID. Another, a senior who had been close to Tay for some time and was handling operatives in one of the most sensitive neighbours, was suspected to have been turned by money and had to be shunted to one side. A third officer, a veteran who predated my father's appointment to the Special Branch, would at one point threaten him and was even said to have waved a service pistol about in anger. These were things I remembered told around the dining table by my father to share with my mother about people she had met at the SID social events.

Yet, there were many others whom Tay knew could be counted upon to do their best for the SID and for Singapore. Many of these who served long and loyally chose not to be publicly identified; this was taken to the extent that, in subsequent years, SID officers would not be nominated for National Day awards. Pay was an issue, low by the modest pay scale among civil servants in that era, and even worse for the officers and field operatives who had no paper qualifications.

For many of those who served from those early years, it was a change not only of job but in their lives. They operated in secrecy, dealing in secrecy. Even for Tay, while his appointment as Director was publicly known, he tended not to let others know unless it was necessary. When asked what he did, Tay often described himself as a "civil servant" or, if pushed, "senior civil servant". For the analysts and even supervisors, they could say that they worked in the Ministry and be vague, given the size and range of appointments there. The situation was more complicated for the operatives in the field. They had to establish covers for their work and would continue with the secrecy even personally, so their families and spouses did not know what they really did. In some instances, they would operate under a different name and passport abroad. These operatives had to live with secrets and the stress that arose from that.

It was not enough for Tay to build up a team and put new structures and procedures in place within the security and intelligence agencies. To be successful, good links and ties were needed, both within Singapore and the government, and outside the country.

Within government, it was essential to link to the senior-most figures. Tay had the trust of the MID Minister Dr Goh but this was not to be taken for granted. The minister was always conscious about results and could be more than careful in allocating resources. Although Dr Goh had served as Finance Minister, this did not necessarily ease the steps to secure funding for the SID as a new undertaking. This was doubly so as much of the defence effort was focused on military buildup; what resources that could be commandeered were prioritised to invest in hardware and pay for the visible boots on the ground. The SID, on the other hand, would not be featured in any National Day Parade. There were real and often severe constraints in budget, despite Dr Goh's support.

Right at the top, there was PM Lee. Tay had interacted closely with him in dealing with the situation at the port and, as Director for Security and Intelligence, their interactions increased. As Director, Tay would often report to the PM directly. This contrasted to the more usual civil service practice of first being screened by the Permanent Secretary and Minister. The meetings with the PM were not only when urgent matters arose but held regularly at the Annexe to the Istana where PM Lee based himself. That access showed the priority given to security and intelligence issues, and thus the attention and time that the PM was personally willing to give to the SID and Tay. This practice would continue even afterwards, making the position of Director something akin to a national security advisor.

The privilege of that direct access, however, posed challenges. The premier had the sharpest mind for politics, fast with questions of detail, and was increasingly confident of his own assessments. By the end of the 1960s and into the 1970s, PM Lee was rapidly emerging as a leading voice for the region who could engage the major powers on key issues, especially the USA about Vietnam and the implications for the region. It was to be expected that meetings with the PM were never pro forma. Tay (and successor SID directors) would have to expect that the analysis presented would be probed and quizzed. PM Lee did not suffer fools gladly, and both he and Dr Goh were known to put civil servants in their place. Additionally, the Prime Minister had old ties with some in the British government and kept informal contact with them; this included Maurice Oldfield, an intelligence officer twice posted to Singapore who eventually rose to be chief of the MI6.

Yet, conversely, Tay would not simply await and then obey decisions. While Lee and Dr Goh did concern themselves with particulars, they also looked at broader things and would only zoom in when they thought it necessary, so Tay knew better than to bother and bore them with every small detail. He would always have his professional analyses and recommendations prepared with a preferred outcome in mind. Where their opinions differed, it was his duty as a civil servant to accept the decision – although he was glad that there would be occasions when he could persuade the leaders to revisit decisions. He did not become friends with the politicians but he came to know their habits of thinking and preferences.

Reciprocally, Tay was earning professional respect and political capital for his work as a spy chief and trouble-shooter. The clearest sign of this was the 1974 *Laju* Incident. Negotiating with the terrorists and dealing with the domestic and international media was not PM Lee or another minister or any other civil servant; the PM instead had tasked Tay to take this on and to report to him daily on developments. The trust that the leaders placed on Tay in that critical situation was drawn from an account that had been built up in those earlier years at the SID and MID.

In 1967, while continuing as Director for Security and Intelligence, Tay was promoted to Deputy Secretary in the ministry. In that same year, he received a National Day Award, the Meritorious Service Medal. His citation read that: "He brought to this completely new job a critical and enquiring mind, a robust outlook in tough situations. These together with great application enabled the internal intelligence of the Government to anticipate and meet with sensitiveness and effectiveness the many new problems independence brought to the security field."

Friends, Mexicans and Allies

Security questions are multidimensional and complex, and there is information that could be gleaned from many different interactions, including trade and education. Information sharing and some degree of coordination were needed for the SID. Yet, given the secretive nature of the work, the SID could not put up the usual memorandum from one ministry to another explaining the cooperation needed. It would have to be more confidential. The effort was therefore to have closer ties with a number of civil servants, identified to be in different ministries and at different levels, who could understand their work and be counted upon to come forward to share information when security concerns might be involved. This was common practice among security agencies like those in the UK.

Even as the SID developed these networks, no one was a closer ally to Tay and the SID than George Bogaars. This was not only because he, as Permanent Secretary at the MID, had previously headed the Special Branch.

Bogaars was an exceptional man. He had come into the service during the British administration after securing a rare first-class honours at university. He was following the footsteps of his own father, who had served four successive colonial governors as confidential secretary – a very senior role for a local within the then colonial government. His family were Eurasian, a community that enjoyed a higher standing during the colonial period than others. The Bogaars family, moreover, was connected with the Tessensohns, one of the most eminent of Eurasians, through George's mother. He was an Eurasian blue blood, and had grown up in a comfortable upper-middle-class life, albeit disrupted by WWII. During the merger years with Malaysia, Bogaars had directed the Special Branch, coming in from 1959 and overseeing the controversial Operation Coldstore. When independence came, he had expected to stay on in this post. Instead, he was elevated to be Permanent Secretary at the new MID. In later years, Bogaars returned to the economic and financial ministries, and served as Head of the Civil Service overall.

While Bogaars was senior to Tay by some six years and from a different socioeconomic background, the two men got on well from the start, working very closely together during the MID years. With Bogaars, Tay was involved in the wider work of the ministry. As the effort to build up the defence forces moved ahead, they met with officials from the key embassies. Similarly, when security officials from Asian and other countries visited, Tay would join Bogaars to receive their counterparts to exchange views and expand the country's network of contacts. The two travelled on a number of occasions abroad to meet their counterparts in defence and security. Tay was further encouraged to travel for work that combined the direct responsibilities at the SID with the broader engagement between security agencies and defence forces. A network of counterparts and broader contacts was built up including the military commanders and police. After all, in many of the countries in the region, these officers were often the power behind the thrones and seats of government.

The interactions between the two men were not only professional but grew at a personal level. Bogaar's convivial manner reinforced Tay's style when interacting with others. The two played tennis with others like Percy Pennefather, who was Assistant Police Commissioner and who reported to Tay as a deputy responsible for internal security in SID's early years. Tay had a great deal of respect for Bogaars, as well as a real liking for him – he was a highly intelligent and engaging man who knew how to get along with a wide range of people. Some upper-crust personal habits rubbed off on Tay, including the enjoyment of open-top sports cars. They were not family friends but in time the wives and children got to know each other, with meals and gatherings at one house or the other. The two wives – Mrs Dorothy Bogaars and my mother – got on and would keep in touch for all their lives.

In 1969, both Bogaars and Tay were serving at MID when riots broke out in Singapore. The violence in Singapore was a contagion from abroad – riots in Kuala Lumpur which had run out of control resulted in a State of Emergency being declared in Malaysia. In Singapore, the violence was more contained but there was, nevertheless, a tragic loss of life: four deaths and some 80 more people injured between 31 May and 6 June 1969. There had been a similar situation from racial riots in 1964 with much worse rioting. But what happened in 1969 was the first trouble of this scale and intensity in independent Singapore. The responses from the MID and relevant agencies – especially the Singapore Police Force and Internal Security Department – were put into the spotlight.

In August 1970, when the MID was split, Bogaars was transferred out. While the reasons were not made public at the time, there were some who voiced criticism of his record. There were suggestions that Bogaars did not get on with the Minister, Lim Kim San, who had come in after Dr Goh. Later, it was said that Bogaars was blamed for "a delicate racial issue" of allowing too many Malays in the Armed Forces against instructions from the Prime Minister. Whatever the reasons, Tay had learnt and gained from working with Bogaars at MID and was not among those who sniped at him. Though they no longer worked together, the two men continued to remain in contact.

Tay's approach of engaging people was not confined to those he worked with. He knew there was much to be gained by establishing a strong personal connection with his counterparts and developed strong instincts about what, who and how things worked or did not. Both personally and professionally, he was good at connecting; he had a certain immediacy and charisma. During the MID years, Tay was involved in closely engaging the Israelis who had come into Singapore as advisors on building up Singapore's defence capabilities. The contacts continued for many years afterwards.

At the start, their presence was a sensitive issue, given the predominant Muslim numbers in Malaysia and Indonesia, the active conflict in the Middle East between Israel and its Muslim neighbours, and the tensions in our own region that lingered from Separation and Konfrontasi. As a fig leaf to those sensitivities, the role of the Israelis was shrouded in

Above At the Big Desk: Posing for the official camera, at the start of his appointment as Spy Chief, in a moment amidst all that was going on when none of the four phones on the desk is ringing. The file at the side is secret as indicated by the slashes.

Left Security Pass and Secrets: Tay's security pass. From the date of issue and that Tay was given the very first one (serial number 0001), it could be that it was for the then newly founded Security and Intelligence Division.

Top left Important Relationship, Informal Interactions: In the early years, the Israeli advisors helped with both defence and security preparations, and Tay (far left) and George Bogaars (second from right) worked closely with them. On the far right is Jack Elazari, the main contact person based in Singapore.

Bottom left Colleagues: Tennis at the Senior Police Officers' Mess with George Bogaars in the middle of the front row, and Tay standing second from the right. Playing sports with others in the ministry and across government was good for comraderie. But Tay always wanted to do his best, and was proud when he won the club doubles championship.

Above A Thinker: About to speak to senior officers at the SAF Training Institute in the early years of the army. While a civilian, Tay had developed a keen understanding of strategic issues facing Singapore and how the army and police could help address them to ensure peace and stability.

A speech he gave in 1970 on "War and Peace in South East Asia" to a wider group of civil servants and teachers was circulated by the government and extensively reported in the media.

Above Intelligence Work: Information could be gleaned from news and open sources or the "gin-and-tonic" chatter of receptions. But this had to be quizzed, and askance was a useful attitude to what was said.

Below left Wife of a Spy Chief: My mother circa 1967, at Changi Point for a gathering of office colleagues.

Top right Tay and Cecelia (centre) at a dinner – a part of work – with colleagues or visitors from the region, and often with wives.

Above Toastmaster: Tay as host of a dinner with colleagues, standing to offer a toast. To his right is Percy Pennefather, who served in the Special Branch for many years, focused on internal security.

Above Factory Touring with George Bogaars: While focused on security and intelligence, Tay was interested in Singapore's industrialisation and technological development in the 1960s, especially when these might have military use.

Below The *Laju* Incident of 1974: The attack was reported in the media worldwide, including in *The New York Times* and *Japan Times*, front page.

Right National Day Award: In 1967, receiving from Puan Noor Aishah, the wife of President Yusof Ishak, the Meritorious Service Medal, one of the highest awards at that time. The citation stated that: "He brought to the completely new job a critical and enquiring mind, a robust outlook in tough situations."

Left Travels for a Purpose:
With an unidentified man, at
the Kidron Valley, circa late
1960s. Working closely with
Israeli advisers in Singapore, Tay
reciprocated by visiting them and
understanding more about their
security and intelligence services.

Below left Travelling Across
our Region: Tay would often
meet not only his counterparts
in intelligence but ministers
and dignitaries. This was in
Bangkok, but there is no verified
information about precisely whom
he met or what he did there.

Below Military Ties: Tay would
often call on military leaders who
held considerable power and
influence in broader politics.

Left Work Trips: With Bogaars (second from left), Tay would travel and visit military and intelligence counterparts. They are pictured at the old lighthouse at the entrance of Manila Bay, a national shrine that marks a battle in WWII. Years later, then Filipino security chief Fidel Ramos would present an award to Tay to thank him for the cooperation between the Philippines and Singapore.

Below Engaging the British: The withdrawal of their forces in 1971 was a defining event for security in the early years of Singapore. Tay engaged them then and after, as their intelligence remained in the region. He and Singapore had to learn their ways and rise to their level.

All Eisenhower Fellowship: In 1970, Tay was awarded the prestigious fellowship, established in the USA when Eisenhower was President, to bring rising leaders from around the world to spend an extended time in the country. He was the second Singaporean to receive the award.

Tay (top row, third from right) joined Fellows from all over the world, each with a programme individually designed for them to meet American experts and their counterparts.

That year in the USA was a time of social and political foment. Yet, on the trip, he experienced the country's diversity outside of cities, including time on an apple farm.

The EF program continues to the present and when the author received it in 2002, he was able to see reports that his father filed 30-plus years prior.

NEW NATION, Friday June 18, 1976

The dockers' best friend calls it a day

By Teresa Ooi

Mr. Tay Seow Huah, Permanent Secretary to the Ministry of Defence until he retired on medical grounds, was a highly thought-of civil servant.

Contacted at his home yesterday, Mr. Tay, 43, said he retired from Government service because of heart trouble. He declined to disclose his plans, but said: "I am on holiday and enjoying it."

Born in Penang, Mr. Tay joined the civil service as an administrative officer after graduating from the then University of Malaya in Singapore with Bachelor of Arts (Honours) degree in history.

Shortly after, he became an assistant secretary in the Commerce and Industry Division, Ministry of Finance, and was later seconded to the Port of Singapore Authority as staff manager.

In 1965, when Mr. Tay was appointed the new director of the Special Branch, the 11,000 waterfront workers appealed to Prime Minister Mr.

Flashback ... Mr. Tay (right) keeping reporters informed of Laju developments in 1974.

the friendly and harmonious relations that have existed hitherto between the union and the PSA for the last few years.

month senior police officers' course before taking over as director of the Special Branch.

Laju hijack in 19
The Laju dra
February 1974 w
second anti-hijac

Left Moving On: Tay's early
retirement in 1975 was covered
in Singapore media. This *New
Nation* headline harked back to
the accolade given when he left
the Harbour Board to direct the
Special Branch. The picture shows
him briefing the media during the
Laju Incident.

Right After Life: After his surgery
and early retirement from the civil
service, Tay was a visiting Fellow
at the History Department of the
University of Singapore. He is on
the far left, and a bit removed.
Former Minister and then
Department Head, Wong Lin
Ken, is second from the right.

Below With the Prime Minister:
In early 1978, PM Lee (centre)
went on national television to
discuss bilingualism, a sensitive
topic and one he pushed. For this
important forum, Tay (right),
although already retired, was still
trusted to moderate the discussion.

Above To be Remembered:
An official head-and-shoulders
picture from the early 1970s.
This was used in many different
circumstances, including for the
newspaper announcement of his
death in 1980, and then on his
colombarium niche.

Right Snapshot: This was taken
during the Singapore trade
mission to Bogor, 1961.

secrecy and the advisors were referred to from their first visit in 1965 as "Mexicans". Lee Kuan Yew is reported to have said they looked "swarthy enough". Among the SID officers, there are some who tell how Tay helped coin the term "Mexicans" and, rather cheekily, tested that on a senior colleague to see if it was credible.

In July 1967, the Israeli advisors were invited to the commissioning of the first batch of Singapore officers who graduated from the Singapore Armed Forces Training Institute. The "Mexicans" had helped to conceptualise and plan the training of the trainers. The secret was allowed out into the open – the Israelis attended in their defence force uniforms – and Dr Goh, as the minister officiating at the ceremony, made plain the reason for their attendance, stating that the Israelis were "advising us (Singapore) on how to build an army". The message rang all the louder because of the context of the Six Day War that had just been fought in the Middle East, with a decisive victory for Israel over much larger neighbours. The message was clear: Singapore was prepared to deal with military threats that might emerge in the region. The point was amplified in the National Day Parade in 1969, when 30 AMX-13 tanks, purchased from the Israelis, were featured in the military review. Yet, the ways and extents of cooperation continued to be masked.

Tay was one of those who got to know the Israelis better. The focus was on building up military capacity and training for uniformed officers, but the understanding of security was broad and included intelligence aspects from the start. When the Israelis agreed to assist, Major General Rehavam Zeevi was given charge and assembled a team for the purpose which included Meir Amit, the then head of the Mossad, the Israeli intelligence agency. They scoped what they felt was necessary to be done in a masterplan for the Singapore military, which came to be known as "The Brown Book", and provided further advice on the formation of the intelligence agencies in "The Blue Book". Tay was to visit Israel in the late 1960s, and made a wide range of contacts in their military and intelligence agencies.

Among the Israelis Tay worked with was Jack (Yaakov) Elazari, the most senior of those who were based in Singapore. Elazari, then a colonel, stayed to advise from 1966-69, and was later promoted to brigadier general. After leaving the Israeli army, he became a consultant to the Singaporean army. Again, Tay ensured that the ties, while professional, were close and even personal. Interactions were not only in the office but included informal dinners at the Tay home at Mount Pleasant for Elazari and his wife, Niurut, who was included in outings with Tay's wife. The children played together at the Tays' or in the apartment near Balmoral where the Elazaris were accommodated. Even after the Israelis returned home, Tay and Elazari remained in contact. Tay would visit Israel for work to understand the Mossad operations more closely, and to broaden networks with the agency. The Elazaris even welcomed Tay's daughter, warmly hosting her for weeks when she visited years later, and arranging for her to have a short stay in a kibbutz.

Another link that was important for Tay to cultivate was with the UK. Ties were never that smooth or easy. The British withdrawal of their bases was moving ahead and there were tensions. For much of the Singapore public, the main issues from the British withdrawal were economic. The British military bases were contributing over 20 per cent to Singapore's gross national product, and it was projected that about 25,000 workers in Singapore would be rendered jobless as a result of the military base closure. But knowing the impacts, the government redoubled its effort and achieved considerable success; by the final withdrawal, Singapore had achieved strong economic growth and nearly full employment.

The withdrawal also caused concerns about the military and security commitments. During Kronfrontasi with Indonesia under Sukarno, the British were engaged in jungle warfare in Borneo. At that time, the timing for British withdrawal was left unclear, with some even suggesting that it might happen as late as 1975 and that some contingents might be kept on. But when Konfrontasi ended and the situation stabilised, reassurances of

British commitment were less ready and the talk was that the withdrawal would be sooner rather than later, and complete. With the timeline still unclear, the question of British withdrawal was among one of the first issues the SID had to cover for the recently decolonised and independent republic.

This involved analysis of the British press, platforms of the two main political parties, and readings of public opinion in the UK as well as the overall economic pressures on their government. Readings of the British intentions and activities in the region were also needed. Yet, whatever the pace of withdrawal, whether sooner or later, it was clear it would happen. To cater for this, the new government strengthened Singapore's defence through military cooperation with other countries and tripled military spending.

By the time most of the British troops moved out of Singapore in October 1971, the Five Power Defence Arrangements had already been signed in April the same year to anchor defence ties linking the UK with Australia and New Zealand to Malaysia and Singapore. What could have been a huge gap in the economy and security of Singapore was filled in and patched over.

The situation facing the SID in intelligence was somewhat different and, in some ways, more challenging. In parallel with the Five Power Defence Arrangements, intelligence liaison increased with the other agencies, especially Australia. Moreover, the British continued to have interests in the region and, while military forces were departing, the old colonial masters thought it fairly obvious that it would be best for all that their influence should still be felt across the region. To that end, the British continued to maintain their intelligence networks and touchpoints, especially in Malaysia, Singapore and Brunei, where they had many contacts. There was a sense that the British believed their operations superior to Singapore's fledgling security organisations, not only in the ways they operated but in the quality of their intelligence and analyses of the region, and their capabilities to run operations of influence.

A lot of the British knowledge and capacity had been put

in place by Maurice Oldfield, who was later to become the overall head of British Intelligence, codenamed "C". Oldfield had been based in Singapore twice, first during the start of the Emergency and then again in 1956 as head of station. In this period, when David Marshall was Chief Minister, Oldfield had recognised the rise of the PAP and cultivated a relationship with the then opposition leader, Lee Kuan Yew. Although he left by late 1958, Oldfield was to claim a long-lasting relationship with Lee. Thereafter, even as the British armed forces prepared for the 1971 withdrawal, British intelligence remained active both in gathering intelligence for analysis and in seeking influence.

The Singapore government was not anti-British, as some other post-colonial governments were, and there was broad agreement on many issues. But while friendly, the then new Singapore government was not unconscious of the need to think and act independently. Some of the British priorities might have run counter to what was thought best by Singapore. Even where there was agreement, Singapore had to ascertain for itself what could or could not be achieved now that there were no longer any bases as evidence of British presence and their guarantees of stability. It was critical that Singapore develop its own intelligence capacity. This was imperative even as Tay established good working ties with his British counterparts and when he sent SID personnel over for exchange and training. The converse of those close ties was that Tay had to keep watch to make sure that the British MI6 influence on the SID and other relevant agencies in Singapore would be limited and transparent. Influence in those Cold War days involved a multiplicity of actors and interests and it was Tay's duty to ensure that the SID and all its operatives worked solely for Singapore's interests and for no one else.

Tay had a number of touchpoints within the British intelligence community in Singapore, a few even arising prior to his appointment to the Special Branch and SID. One of these was a man named Philip Osmond, and he ensured that ties were convivial and professional. By cultivating close and long-term ties with Osmond and others, Tay and the SID were able to exchange notes with the British informally and have a degree of access to the wider networks that they had. Singapore would never be admitted into the Anglo-American security arrangements dubbed "five eyes" that had started during WWII and was deepening during the Cold War years. But in this same era, Singapore's security intelligence institutions were increasingly engaged and also respected; ties built from that time would continue and grow into the present.

As the British withdrawal approached, Tay worked on developing another key relationship: with the USA. With the departure of the British troops, the USA would be the major power in the region. American policies to the area were uncertain, especially with the entanglements in Vietnam. For Singapore, the question was whether they could see any value in the small island state; it was in this period that the first real engagements between the USA and Singapore grew. PM Lee, of course, led this effort personally, undertaking personal trips to the USA from early on and even having a short sabbatical in the USA. For Tay, he was awarded the prestigious Eisenhower Fellowship in 1970, named for the American president and funded by his supporters. This enabled him to spend six months in the USA on an extensive programme to meet security agencies like the CIA and FBI, as well as experts in related fields. From this, Tay could understand the country better, first-hand, and build a strong American network that he and the government expected would serve for the next decade or longer.

Thoughts and Actions
In his best work on politics, Shakespeare writes that, "The evil that men do lives after them; the good is oft interred with their bones." Tay Seow Huah knew his Shakespeare and the play *Julius Caesar*. When I studied the play for junior college, we would discuss it and he would have perspectives that no teacher taught.

The words are spoken by Marc Antony and while the meaning is clear, it was a plot twist whether the person he referred to was the dead Caesar, or else to Brutus and others who had killed him. Broad thinking and Shakespearean ambiguity appealed to my father. Yet, the work he undertook in those early years dealt not only with security and intelligence in broad abstractions of geopolitics; it intersected with political ambitions and individual characters and lives in very concrete ways. Yes, thinking and analysis were critical. But matters were handled not simply in terms of speeches or by cabinet papers leading to policies and new laws. The work had to link to decisive action. In directing the SID's work, Tay had to ensure that its work focused on very practical things, while considering actionable alternatives and taking decisions about what to do or not do, and often urgently, and by what means, secretly or openly. He also knew that the work would require deciding on what to do (or not to do) when facts and intentions were less than clear – sometimes secret and often disguised even if in plain sight.

Making those evaluations was not applying some preset formula on a narrow set of facts. What was necessary was to exercise judgement in the context of what was relevant. Determining what was relevant, moreover, depended on being able to identify what the relevant considerations were and this might include what, at first glance, seemed faraway and unconnected. Conversely, it might exclude things that were happening concurrently and yet, upon closer reading, were mere coincidence or epiphenomenal. Judging those events, in real time and not in hindsight, would depend not only on proven and impartial facts. Decisions would be informed by the values of the decision-maker and how he saw the world. Conversely, the outcomes of those decisions would become experiences that the decision maker would learn from, to reinforce those decisions or else to be lessons learnt and highlight mistakes to avoid in the future.

For internal security, Tay had inherited operating protocols and seasoned staff who had carried out operations under the colonial and pre-independence years. The methods were not perfect and improvements could be made to attune to the new realities of an independent Singapore. The use of the Internal Security Act and its powers of preventive detention were particularly controversial. But their use, in combination with other police powers, had proven effective against the Emergency, dealing not only with insurgents and terrorists but those who supported and enabled them to pre-empt the dangers. Given this, the net might be drawn more widely, just in case. Tay might well have turned again to his *Julius Caesar* to note how Cassius argued that Caesar had to be stopped before he was crowned – to act preventively. But most of the practices, built up during British times, would set the pattern and any change would need to wait, given the exigencies of those first years.

The demands for the SID to deliver external intelligence were new and qualitatively different, and pressing. Modes of working were more fluid and so were the objectives. From considering what other intelligence agencies did, much of what was done could be set in four main areas of work: the collection of information, its analysis, informal diplomacy, and efforts to influence.

Much of gathering information about external threats and concerns came from the public domain and domestic newspapers. Additional insights and gossip could also be gleaned from diplomatic sources, in what some called the "G&T (gin and tonic) circles". Networks were also cultivated of contacts and "friends" to gather further information and insights that might be confidential and could prove critical. There were covert operations, often to gather information or else to communicate it, and it was the SID's task not only to identify and plan those but to put them into action. Within the SID, a degree of separation was maintained between the internal and external units, and between research and operations; it was a basic method to minimise the risk of information being leaked out. But Tay, as Director for Security and Intelligence, had to have the overall perspective – and in sufficient detail – to connect the different parts.

Tay was conscious of laying down a foundation; so many

things in those pioneer years were new. Standard ways of operations and procedures were not always in place, and resources were thin and stretched. Yet, the culture and commitment to doing the best had to be cultivated. There was a need to recruit operatives of the quality, character and commitment that was needed for a serious mission at a most challenging time. To set up and handle these networks, operatives had to be recruited, with supervisors who reported to Tay.

Tay had recruited the best staff that could be found. Soon enough, through both formal and informal interactions, he knew their measure – who could be relied upon and for what. He himself was not an operative. Yet, as spy chief, he was able to master detail and to assess the quality of the information and analysis at briefings. He was known to listen carefully and discuss the reports of his staff in detail. If an officer was wasting time in the briefing, he would be polite but firm in interjecting with questions and points. Building up the SID started essen-tially with the staff and the quality of their work, and as Director he had to ensure that quality, indeed insist on it. He would not lecture or berate his staff and analysts but would share some of his own views and insights. Once the assessments were done and agreed upon, Tay would have to distill these into key insights and, with acumen, convey essential points to the leaders and other agencies on a need-to-know basis.

Understanding Malaysia was bread-and-butter and was almost second nature to Tay, as it was for many of his generation. But it was not enough for the new republic. He extensively expanded the networks for collecting information, both covertly and openly. He travelled considerably in the region and met officials of those governments as well as the SID officers stationed in those countries. On some trips, he would travel with Bogaars; on others with a deputy, including Lim Chye Heng whom he trusted and who would later be appointed Internal Security Director. As SID Director, Tay would personally build up official channels and meet with counterparts in the police, defence and intelligence and also some key politicians. He would attend some official and embassy functions, where diplomats and others networked and shared gossip and occasionally useful insights. He understood that the vast majority of intelligence could be gleaned from open sources and these interactions with officials. But Tay went further.

It was essential to have a first-hand impression of the events and key figures. Venturing beyond the official channels, he would meet some of the key contacts and "friends" who had been cultivated. How was this done? It is on record that some intelligence agencies, including those from the great powers, can on occasion obtain information by blackmail and making unrecorded payments from slush funds. Tay found that it was often more effective to be subtle, that a contact might be cultivated by favours done – like a scholarship given to a member of the family or a donation to a charity that is politically important. Often, he found that information could be directly exchanged between intelligence officers where there was no direct conflict between the two countries. Meeting those in the region, he would occasionally find attitudes similar to those he had experienced as a young man – of reactions to colonial rule, injustice and the desperate hope for life to be better. Sometimes, it seemed that those who knew so many things wanted little more than to have someone who could empathise and appreciate the knowledge, and you had only to ask the right question and listen appreciatively. Of course, no matter how the information was received, it would be subject to verification from other sources.

In his movements across the region, Tay liked to move out from the offices and get around to other parts of the city, to towns and even villages. He had to understand motivations, networks and also the practical nitty-gritty of things like how sensitive items could be supplied and moved across borders. The travels were not cushy tours and there could be tense moments, fraught instances. He came quickly to understand how, "Agents do of course take great risks" – although he was only to say so much later, in the 1975 publication *This*

Singapore, which marked the 10th anniversary of the Republic.

Our family would welcome him home from these travels into the hot spots of the region and, when he told us some of the things he had seen, we could see that my father was refreshed and broadened in mind, even if often he was tired in body and there were tensions that would remain within him.

From these travels and experiences, he took the opportunity not to look only at issues in the headlines but knit together observations and pieces of intelligence from the different SID desk officers so that he could develop a wide-ranging view of the region, unconstrained by national boundaries, and form a robust and forward-looking assessment. In ideas and analysis, Tay never shied away from historical and intellectual frameworks, or being considered "brainy" or intellectual. He would think broadly and then find different angles and ways to probe deeply to get to the core of the situation, often focusing on the unstated, hidden motivations of the main actors. He knew details mattered and spent time to ensure he connected directly to the men in the field who would gather and comb through the information, and read their briefs closely. In this way, Tay tried his best to combine broader contextual ideas to the specifics of the key people and situations and worked on mastering the security briefs from the ways that operations were implemented to the analyses of situations, and to the dynamics of the broader politics. He came to admire and adopt the ideal that the man of ideas could also be the man of action.

Even decades after he left, SID contemporaries would remember Tay smoking his pipe as he pondered the complex situations presented for consideration and then, always unflustered and often with a small smile, making a decision.

What issues were in focus in those early years, from 1965 and into the early 1970s?

It was a most turbulent time in the world. In our region too, almost every country was undergoing severe stresses and struggling, perhaps failing to cope. In Cambodia, for instance, a civil war was beginning that would lead to the Khmer Rogue and "Killing Fields". In Thailand, the military regimes and elites that had run the country were facing rural unrest and growing calls for democracy from students. On the radar of problems and risks, there were many and very red dots. But for Singapore, its new intelligence agencies and Tay, the spy chief, four key concerns would have stood out: the Emergency, race and religious tensions especially in relation to Malaysia, Konfrontasi with Indonesia and its aftermath, and the Vietnam War. The context of the period was singular: the Cold War.

Neighbours, Not Friends

From the end of WWII, the Emergency had been the pre-occupation of the British in Malaya, and not without reason; it amounted to a full-on guerrilla war. By 1965, the situation was relatively contained after the efforts to wage counter-insurgency operations combined with better intelligence to cut off supplies from sympathisers to the combatants by interning many of the poor Chinese masses. This was assisted by the return of growth, with renewed demand for Malaysian primary products as industries and factories began again to hum, and a broader effort to win "hearts and minds" among the Chinese Malaysians. Even so, the Emergency would continue for years up north, with continued fighting in the jungles of the northern reaches of West Malaysia and across the border into Thailand.

Tay had read up extensively on the Emergency from both open and confidential sources, and had grown up in Taiping, in the north of Western Malaysia, where many of these events had played out. By the mid-1960s, the threat of the Communists taking over the peninsula had diminished, and the guerrilla warfare tactics used in the jungles could not be replicated in urban Singapore. But their tactics were adapted to deploy covert operations to carry out selected killings and bombings. This shift necessitated even more effort from the intelligence networks.

The challenge of dealing with the Communists was further complicated by race, culture and inequalities. There were affinities for the Communists among the many Chinese-speaking Chinese in Singapore and, for some, there was a degree of pride in events in the Mainland, where the Communists seemed to be finally cutting away the deadwood and moving ahead with reforms on issues that had held China back since the last century. (At that time, the suffering of the Great Leap Forward was not apparent.) Beyond the links in race and culture, Communism also held considerable appeal in view of the huge inequalities that underpinned the colonial system and that had been revealed by the war. This was especially in the early years when jobs in Singapore remained scarce after Separation, with between 10 to 12 per cent unemployment. These were issues that Tay had faced at the port in dealing with workers and left-wing unionists. But now, they were writ large across the country.

Moreover, independence had raised expectations. Separation from Malaysia made the Chinese-speaking Chinese in Singapore the vast majority. They might give succour and support to the Communists and the Barisan Sosialis – formed when the left-wingers left the PAP – as their political representatives. Following Operation Coldstore in 1963, Lim Chin Siong and many of the left-wingers had been detained, leaving the leadership of the party to fall on Dr Lee Siew Choh. In 1966, the doctor was to lead the party to abandon Parliament and take up an "extra-parliamentary" political struggle. When the Barisan boycotted the elections, the PAP were to have a monopoly. But as the political struggle went from Parliament into the streets, there was even more need to keep eyes on things across society. The Communist use of "united front" tactics meant that troubles might come from many different angles and sources.

In Singapore, there was an operational network, as demonstrated by the operations under the Lim Yew Hock government and then Operation Coldstore. This included some who had themselves been within the local Communist ranks before being turned and then persuaded to help keep an eye on their former colleagues.

Post 1965, the watch over security issues was not only internal but, instead, required the effort of the external intelligence capacity of the SID in relation to the Communist networks outside the borders, across the region. The role that the Communist Party of China was playing to actively support Communist movements abroad was unclear. The Communist Party of Malaya (CPM), after all, had grown from local grievances and not as a franchise from the Mainland. Yet, rhetorical support ranted across the region with the ideology of a global struggle, as well as the charisma of Mao. Even if they did not control the CPM, China was known to flex a muscle now and again to assist.

Trying to understand political developments within the Mainland and its networks across the region was therefore a key priority for the external intelligence efforts from the beginning. To that end, the SID was developing listening posts for insights into the many and often subterranean developments in the Mainland. Ties with Taiwan were useful for this. Other efforts were made to involve those who knew China close up, or even from the inside.

As a child, I remember my father mentioning one man who had been in the People's Liberation Army who had fled the Mainland and another who, although Singaporean, had fought in the Chinese civil war on the side of the Kuomintang. With so much of China closed in those years, information was gleaned from Chinese public statements, their press and radio broadcasts, as well broadcasts of Voice of Malayan Revolution. Intelligence was also supplied and traded with other friendly intelligence services who watched China closely.

Even as China-watching was necessary, the most immediate concern for Singapore's security was still Malaysia. The connections were so direct among the communities. There were also many who had moved to Singapore in the months leading up to independence and merger and had stayed on afterward, as Tay himself had. Yet, relations with Malaysia were strained post-Separation. There were ongoing political disagreements and difficult working relations on many fronts, including the military. One particular issue related to troops under Malaysian command that remained in Singapore itself and were under

KL's command; an odd arrangement that continued until 1967. More broadly, after Separation, politicians on both sides continued to voice their differences and there were more than a few instances when playing off the other side would be a ploy to stoke support amongst their domestic constituencies.

The intelligence agencies on both sides of the Causeway attempted the opposite: to develop ties for cooperation that would endure even during high-profile political tensions and disagreements among the leaders. In relation to dealing with the Communists, the SID was able to build a solid working relationship with its Malaysian counterpart. Much information and analysis was shared and there was even close coordination in a number of operations. Some of this grew from old school ties for Tay and others in the SID who had family and friends up north and included those who had studied in the University of Malaya and lived at the Dunearn Road Hostels as Tay did. The habits that grew in this critical period have since been institutionalised, withstanding subsequent periods of political difference, and continued to grow as the Communist threat receded to include other areas of common concern, like extremist and terrorist groups.

In those earlier post-1965 years, one pressing need for the SID was for additional contacts and networks to gather information and perspectives about Malaysia's domestic politics. These were critical as the situation with Malaysia was still settling. A reading of what its leaders intended could help shape how the Singapore government might respond to pronouncements on such sensitive issues as reminders about the supply of water, or the conduct of military exercises in the South, nearest the border.

There was also a need to understand the internal dynamics of Malaysian society and among the political class because of the implications for inter-racial relations. The riots of 1964 were the worst, both in Malaysia and in Singapore, and had followed rising political tensions between the PAP government in Singapore and the UMNO-led Alliance government in Malaysia as a result of their electoral competition. Despite

Separation, there were still ties of race, religion and between families that linked the two sides of the Causeway. These were underscored by the 1969 riots, seven days of communal riots between 31 May and 6 June in Singapore that were a spillover from the much larger May 13 Incident in Malaysia.

Racial issues are at the core of the politics within Malaysia itself, with political parties based on race. As such, unlike efforts to contain Communism, cooperation with Malaysia on these issues could not be expected to be easy. There was always much suspicion and sensitivity about Malaysia and Singapore spying on each other, given the deep and long ties between people on one side and the other, with so many of the civil servants, business families and even politicians having close friends, old classmates and family on the other side of the Causeway. Yet, there was a practical understanding in those years that issues between the two neighbours could be downplayed because the larger concerns were faced in common: this was not only about the Communist threat but the situation with Indonesia.

Started in January 1963, the Indonesians had undertaken a clandestine war – Konfrontasi – against Malaysia (of which Singapore was part). There were sabre-rattling statements by the charismatic President Sukarno, decrying Malaysia as a neo-colonist and illegitimate entity. There were guerrilla warfare campaigns of incursions and skirmishes, as well as bombings. The danger was most vividly marked by the bombing at MacDonald House along Orchard Road that killed three people in March 1965, just months before Tay was assigned as Director of Special Branch.

However, by October that same year, a coup in Jakarta, blamed on Communist elements, failed. This was followed by a counter-coup, a military takeover that eventually, after a period of deep uncertainty, deposed Sukarno. What unfolded in this period of flux were mass killings across the archipelago. The real actors in this remain controversial and even the extent of the resulting deaths is still debated today – at something between 250,000 and 1 million.

As General Suharto consolidated power to assume the

presidency and install the "New Order", the situation improved with Indonesia's neighbours, Malaysia and Singapore. A formal peace treaty was concluded in August 1966 to officially end Konfrontasi. Yet, the situation in Indonesia remained uncertain and violent and, for a period, it was unsure who would prevail within the country.

With this, there remained the risk that it might seem convenient for the new administration to again play to nationalistic sentiments, as the charismatic Sukarno had by fanning Konfrontasi. This danger was further increased by the Singapore government's decision concerning the Indonesians who had bombed MacDonald House.

The two marines – Osman Mohamed Ali and Harun Said – were put on trial as criminals, whereas Indonesia saw them as combatants in a war and therefore subject to protection under the laws of war. Since there had been fatalities in the bombing, after a due trial in Singapore, they were sentenced in 1965 to death. Despite pleas for clemency from Indonesia, including from President Suharto, the penalty was carried out in late 1968. To retaliate, some in the Indonesian military urged a seaborne invasion of Singapore. While this did not eventuate, the Singapore embassy had been sacked and set ablaze. Relations were far from stable.

Yet, there was an opportunity with the rise of the New Order and General Suharto becoming President. Ties could normalise. Efforts had to be taken. The critical step in the public eye was taken in 1973, when PM Lee personally went to Jakarta to meet with President Suharto. The meeting – held just between the two leaders on a "four-eyes" basis – began a historic stabilisation in relations. The Singaporean leader made the further effort to scatter flowers on the marines' graves at Kalibata Heroes Cemetery, as a symbolic act in the Javanese tradition to pacify the souls of the executed marines. It is a matter of public record that the then Ambassador to Indonesia, Lee Khoon Choy, a PAP politician, was a key player in convincing PM Lee to make this gesture. He did much to assist the repair of relations.

What is not publicly known were the other efforts made by Singaporean intelligence before that visit; these must have considerable. After the immediate aftermath of the MacDonald House bombing and before the subsequent execution of the two marines, Konfrontasi continued and indeed seemed to be gaining ground. That bomb – while the most deadly – was by no means the only Indonesian operation against Singapore, nor the last. The effort to stem Konfrontasi required not just a reactive policing action or better surveillance of the borders – always porous in those years to small craft from the Indonesian islands just south. As was the case in tackling the Communists, the SID would have had to identify and map the networks that enabled the Indonesian operations. Some would have been stopped and arrested, while with some others – the more difficult ones – the aim was to capture and try to turn them.

How the SID operated is not in the public realm. But methods used by other intelligence agencies in the West during the Cold War have now been revealed and help illustrate the spycraft of developing networks on the other side. Sometimes, this could be done by simple persuasion. Otherwise, pressure could be asserted or else payments made. If that could be achieved, an operative from the other side could become an asset.

But before the person could be returned to the field, every effort had to be made to ensure that he would not be compromised. This could even mean that, say if the operation was to bomb a target, an explosion would be set off in a controlled way and without injury. This would be followed by headlines the next day to show that the operation had been a success. Such methods had been used, for example, by British counterintelligence during WWII.

The efforts did not start or end at Singapore's borders. In this same period, from 1965 to 1966, trying to read what was happening inside Indonesia was the critical thing. The coup and the counter-coup that favoured Suharto led to a prolonged period of internal conflict, with intrigue as well as bloody campaigns against those considered Communist. Anti-

Chinese riots and killings also broke out in this period. So did a purge across Bali and much of the archipelago. It was a time vividly described in the title of a well-received novel and movie observing events there, *The Year of Living Dangerously*. It was only in 1968 that Singapore established an embassy in Jakarta, headed by Ambassador P S Raman who was in charge when the mobs set fire to the embassy.

Throughout this period, the SID would have been trying to understand what was happening inside Indonesia and within different circles of power and influence. Some accounts have tried to portray the waves of killings across Indonesia as a spontaneous outpouring against the Communist party members that the new military could not stop. Other analyses point to a collaboration between a number of key generals supporting Suharto, deploying student protests and other means to create the conditions to corner and dispose of their opponents and seize power decisively. In this, intelligence played pivotal roles – and not only in trying to discern the likely outcomes and key actors.

From the outside, many efforts were made to weaken Communism in Indonesia. British government officials play-ed a role in stoking anger against those in Indonesia who were thought to be Communist, by authoring and delivering propaganda in Bahasa into Indonesia. Influence and even agitation were tools of the trade and included bald-faced incitements to violence. One operation by the British was carried out by the innocuously-named Information Research Department which, moreover, had a small team that worked out of Singapore.

There were also elements within Indonesia itself and its military intelligence who were increasingly convinced that Konfrontasi had been a mistake and were determined to stop it and replace President Sukarno. These included figures such as Sarwo Edhie Wibowo, who led many of the attacks against PKI supporters who were deemed Communists, and Ali Moertopo who ran a clandestine organisation within Indonesian intell-igence itself, using OPSUS (Special Operations Unit) to undermine Konfrontasi. To provide resources for this effort, Moertopo is said to have smuggled rubber and other goods and accumulated secret funds of some $17 million, which were then held in banks in Malaysia and Singapore. Whether or not the intelligence agencies of Singapore learnt of this from the banks or other sources is not in the public domain; nor is how the funds in the Singapore-based accounts were accessed and replenished.

In the effort to understand and respond to events in Indonesia, Tay and the SID could not afford to see the situation academically, from afar. It was touch-and-go for a while whether Indonesia would become Communist or if Suharto would be able to stabilise the situation. It was essential that the SID could tap into people inside the country who would provide insight and potentially be of influence. There were some Indonesians within influential circles who were sufficiently realistic to see that any Indonesian ambition to increase trade, investment and growth would mean that relations with Singapore would need to be friendly enough. These Indonesian interlocutors would quietly share their views and even, within limited and private discussions, speak sometimes in favour of improving ties with Singapore.

Consider the circumstances when Konfrontasi was finally ended. This was done quickly and key actors on the Indonesian side included some from its military intelligence, such as Moertopo and Benny (Leonardus Benjamin) Moerdani. Both were known entities to their military intelligence counterparts in Malaysia and Singapore during and after this period. Moertopo would afterwards be entrusted by Suharto to under-take operations to ensure Papua would vote for integration into Indonesia as well as, later, similar efforts to deal with a restive East Timor. As for Moerdani, he would rise to become the right-hand man to President Suharto in the 1980s. His ties to Singapore (and Malaysia) would grow in parallel, and during his visits in this period, he would regularly call upon the country's top leaders and was seen as a key actor in relations between the two governments.

Cultivating ties with these and other Indonesians was critical and, given the key role of the military and military intelligence officers in that era of Indonesian history, it can surmised that the SID played a key role in this. Their exact operations remain classified. But the spycraft practised by other countries in the Cold War context may suggest some of the methods that could have been used during the Konfrontasi years.

To develop and then to support these networks who could operate within the country, the operatives would have go regularly into the country on the pretext of doing trade and business. These efforts were aimed more to understand and sometimes perhaps try to influence, and were relatively innocent compared to the sabotage and bombing operations carried out in the years before that by the Indonesians.

Nevertheless, given the tensions and the blood-letting in this period, any foreign agent in Indonesia during this era – whether from Singapore or even more from other powers – ran considerable risks if they were exposed. Any intelligence agency in those years had the duty not only to support their operatives to find a way to access different circles in Indonesia and by different means to grow their networks, but – more importantly – to make sure that, if the operatives were un-covered, they could be exfiltrated from the country quickly and safely.

Years after, by the time Prime Minister Lee visited Indonesia to normalise ties and scatter the petals at the memorial to the marines involved in the MacDonald House bombing, these efforts – not only to analyse but to influence – ensured that beyond symbolism, there was a foundation for stability and cooperation on which the leaders could stand.

Cold War, Hot Spot

The Vietnam War was another key issue for Tay and the SID. While it was not as immediate as Malaysia or Indonesia, it was in many ways more important in terms of geopolitical implications. With the USA and the Soviet Union present by proxies in South and North Vietnam, the situation was the main lens for Western powers to see the region and Singapore.

American involvement in South Vietnam was predicated on the Domino Theory. This encapsulated the belief that the loss of Vietnam to Communist control would lead to similar Communist victories in neighbouring countries in Southeast Asia – most immediately Laos, Cambodia and Thailand, and then perhaps elsewhere where there had been Communist insurgencies, like Malaysia and Singapore. This term was first used by President Eisenhower and grew in common use during successive presidents to justify the American presence. There was no reason for Tay or any Singaporean official in that period to undermine the theory publicly; it was embraced as a logic to keep the Americans engaged and active, to ensure that the dominos did not fall.

In this context, it was necessary for the SID to gain its own insights into each of the relevant countries, and also to track movements between them through the very porous borders. In the process, efforts had to be made to build networks in these countries and Tay was to personally undertake trips in this tense time, with a focus on the situation in Vietnam.

As the "frontline" state in the Vietnam War, Thailand was of particular importance. The Americans recognised this by pouring in huge amounts of economic and military aid and assistance. The Thai military was essential to the situation as they ran the country, riding an economic boom that the American support had jump-started, and were able to monopolise power in this period after General Sarit Thanarat took power.

For Singapore, there were links to the Thai military and intelligence circles because of the Emergency and when the Communist Party of Malaya decided to go into the jungles and, eventually, cross from the north of Malaya into southern Thailand. There would be a considerable effort to increase and widen those circles within Thailand. This was especially so given the direct and close attention that the USA gave the Thais in this period. There was also the question of Thailand's internal politics with much of the benefits from growth sticking to the military and commercial elites, to the exclusion of the still-underdeveloped rural areas. Political angst was growing and would lead to the student protests of 1973 which ended the military domination and ushered in efforts to move towards democracy. The ability to gain insights into developments concerning the Vietnam War and therefore Thailand was a key currency for the intelligence agencies in the Cold War – much as the US dollar was supplanting the British pound sterling.

The SID placed a number of its officers at the Embassy in Bangkok as diplomats, "declared" intelligence officers that were known to the Thais. This was and is a common practice among many countries. A number of these were able to build up strong and useful networks among the Thai military, political parties, media and even business interests who had influence on the political situation. In this early period, the SID networks were primarily aimed at liaison and research. But some of the information and intelligence networks built up in those years would be of use later, in 1979, when the North Vietnamese had won and consolidated. When they helped push Pol Pot out from Cambodia, the SID would more actively run operations at the border with Thailand, building up from the networks and contacts initiated in the earlier decade.

For much the same reasons, many other governments had intelligence operations out from Singapore in this period, active in trying to gather intelligence about the situation in Vietnam, the wider Indochina and the influence of China. British intelligence was especially active with its evolving relationship with the USA and CIA operations in Southeast Asia. It was not the only one. From the 1960s and into the 1970s, Singapore was a hub for many intelligence agencies and spies from across the world, much like a Switzerland or Vienna of Asia. There was a need therefore not only to liaise with these agencies to share and receive information but also to keep a watchful eye on their operations in Singapore.

A View of the World
The years when Tay served as Director of the Security and Intelligence Division within the Ministry of Interior and

Defence were tumultuous. This flux continued in the 1970s. Malaysia and Indonesia were to remain core concerns. So was the Vietnam War, with its implications for the USA and the balance of powers in the region. Building upon this, Tay was to develop readings of the wider region and a world view. By 1971, he had travelled to every country in Southeast Asia, building up his own first-hand views. He also gained from the broader readings he undertook as a mix of work and satisfying his own intellectual curiosity. Many of the ways he and others in the pioneer generation thought about security and international relations grew from the context of those decades and would become key pillars in Singapore's strategic outlook, continuing as baseline assumptions for even current thinking.

In 1969, Tay was asked to accompany PM Lee Kuan Yew to London for the Commonwealth Heads of Government Meeting (CHOGM). It was significant to be selected for the trip: it was seen as a sign of acceptance and standing with PM Lee. This trip gave Tay the opportunity to engage the PM in a relatively closed and small group for an extended period. The trip included, on the return leg, a stop in Egypt, a leader in the Non-Aligned Movement (NAM), where Lee and the delegation met with President Gamal Abdel Nasser and toured the pyramids. Engaging with the Commonwealth and visiting one of the early leaders of the NAM broadened Tay's world view. His role in CHOGM with PM Lee continued into its 1973 Ottawa meeting.

In August 1970, Tay was asked to be the plenary speaker at a large and prominent forum run by the Ministry of Education to help teachers and other civil servants learn more about Southeast Asia. Within the SID itself, his officers found their Director knowledgeable and thoughtful yet concise in expression. Many discussions among the staff were built on implicit knowledge, perspectives that had been developed, and zoomed into the details of a particular situation. The Director did not lecture. This request was to do almost exactly the opposite: an opportunity to outline the thinking he had developed – his view of the world as Singapore saw and engaged it. This was an occasion to share that perspective with a wider audience outside the SID that would necessitate more explicit and longer explanations.

Subsequently, an extensive report of his speech was published in the media – *The Singapore Herald* of 25 August 1970, and the full text by the Ministry of Education with the title "War and Peace in South East Asia: A Singapore Perspective". With an endorsement from the political leadership, this circulated widely among government ministers and civil servants. While it was by no means the only talk Tay was to give, the text was useful to reveal his views about key issues, indicative of what the thinking was among policy-makers in that era. His speech, looking back, was given at an important juncture of that period.

Parts of Tay's lecture bear consideration. To be clear, it did not pioneer the thinking and directions for Singapore – so much depended on the political leadership and PM Lee. But Tay's talk does suggest that a consensus was developing at the time, among the political leadership and those like Tay, on key strategic and security issues. There is even reason to reflect on this, more than 50 years on, not merely as a record of thinking at the time but in the current strategic context. The years ahead will not be the same as the 1970s. Analyses and policy prescriptions will differ from those that served a pioneering generation. Yet, looking back at an arc of 50-plus years, there may be useful wisdom. History does not repeat itself, as many say, but, as some wisely acknowledge, it can rhyme.

To Tay, the region had always been the scene of conflicts – within individual states, between them, and between regional states and outside powers. He also cautioned against conflicts between major powers outside of the region playing out, for various reasons, to use Southeast Asia as their battlefield. While the conventional view was to distinguish between internal turmoil and interstate conflicts, he recalled that this distinction was very blurred – especially in the archipelagic Southeast Asia of Indonesia, Malaysia, Singapore, and the Philippines – because the states had resulted from colonial rule; maps drawn in Europe. He assessed Southeast Asian states were "beset with formidable problems arising from political, cultural and racial pluralism and also faced the basic question of how to build the political and social institutions to integrate the heterogenous elements into a single nation".

In looking at the countries of the region, Tay employed a longer perspective of history that went back into the colonial and pre-colonial periods. Having studied history at university, Tay continued to deepen his knowledge of the history of Asia with academic books that went far deeper than the newspapers or the reports and analyses from the field. He was comfortable to discuss China's modernisation efforts, or turn further back to consider Srivijaya and Khmer kingdoms and the Indianised states of the region. In this, he looked not only for the particulars of the past but also to try to discern patterns that could help understand what was happening and might develop next. Even in that period, Tay saw the use of technology and communications that could extend the reach and authority of states over their territory or beyond.

In surveying the region, Tay differentiated three security areas: the northern, continental states, a central Straits area of West Malaysia, Singapore and Sumatra, and a southern zone comprising Java and the rest of Indonesia. The situations specific to each country were referenced with some detail. Looking at Burma, his view was that the conflict with ethnic minorities, which had already gone beyond two decades, showed no prospect of ending in the foreseeable future. The situation in the country, now named Myanmar, continues and, in fact, has been exacerbated in the wake of the coup of 2021. Tay was concerned with internal conditions of still-weak states, fearing that the art of "people's war" would become more common.

The lesson was that the central authority in each of these new regional states would have to "deliver the goods" and that they faced higher expectations than ever before. Rapid economic development was an imperative. It was naïve, Tay warned, to assume that this alone would deliver peace. Moreover, economic development itself was dependent on resolving some of the social and political problems. He did not see that there were quick or easy solutions for the region to move forward quickly. Instead, efforts to establish peace and advance economic development would be mixed with tension and conflict. In this, he was implicitly explaining the emerging approach that Singapore under the PAP was taking. He saw this not as a tradeoff to prefer economic growth over efforts to address social and political tensions, but the challenge of doing both in tandem. While this was a public lecture, it was not within Tay's nature nor his penchant as spy chief to theorise. He did not allude to the concept of comprehensive security, as scholars studying the region later would (and still do). Yet, it was implicit in the ways that he saw the links between internal factors and external threats for the different countries.

More than surveying the region country by country, Tay's speech also connected wider issues in Southeast Asia to key outside factors – China and, as the British were withdrawing, the USA. He helped map out the risks like red dots on a radar scope and sketched a world view that connected the countries of the region to the largest questions of geopolitics.

Understanding China's intentions for Southeast Asia and Singapore was especially critical. This was changing as the Communist insurgencies in the region were fading and Peking (as it was then referred to) rethought its own priorities. Notwithstanding internal convulsions intensifying, Tay's assessment was that China's intention was "to change the present status quo... which means essentially the removal of the American presence and the evolution of indigenous regimes". Not all in the region would be swayed but the concern was countries would adopt, "at the minimum a China-leaning neutrality and therefore permit a considerable Peking influence in the entire area." He saw this ambition not only as a manifestation of the Cold War between Democracy and Communism but in historical context as "traditional Chinese policy of seeking to exercise predominant influence in mainland Southeast Asia".

The key to this, with the weakening of the Communist insurgencies, was Vietnam. While aware of Hanoi's differences and caution against the Chinese, Tay reckoned that they were now the primary lever for China to remove the USA and were likely to succeed. On the other side of the Cold War line, Thailand was a key front-line country in this situation. With its decision to ally with the USA and even pursue "forward defence" with bordering states, it was serving to resist the influence of Vietnam and China. But Tay cautioned not to take this for granted. He noted antecedents when the kingdom had accommodated outside powers to preserve its own autonomy while allowing them to dominate areas to the South – thus remaining independent while the rest of the region came under French or else British colonial control, and also accommodating Japan in 1942. One of the key factors to ensure that Thailand continued to buffer the situation would be the degree to which the USA would provide military and economic aid.

While the British had yet to exit their bases in Singapore when Tay spoke, his analysis already took the sharp puncture in UK military power as a political given. The regional balance that had prevailed for 150 years (bar WWII) was unhinged. The withdrawal of British troops from Singapore marked the end of Empire and a geopolitical shift. "Today, British power… is no longer the size as it was in the Fifties during the Emergency," Tay remarked mildly.

He believed that this vacuum of power would be filled: "The involvement of outside powers cannot be ignored. The region has from the earliest times been subjected to outside influence and intervention." The USA could, obviously, be expected to play that role and was already present in the region. But there would be limits to its commitment. While the departure of US forces and the fall of Saigon was still to come only in 1975, Tay was speaking after the Tet Offensive and he was of the view that: "it appears highly improbable that the US will in the future involve itself in war on the mainland of Southeast Asia with large numbers of ground troops."

Singapore was coming to grips with the British departure and the recognition of the USA as the new dominant power in the region. This would require the Singapore government to respond adroitly, to maintain good relations with the UK while increasing efforts to engage the USA. It was clear that the USA would be different from the British, as their conduct in Vietnam was showing when compared to how the British approached the Emergency in Malaysia. So, Singapore would need much closer, personal ties with the USA to be able to understand them better.

Much has happened since Tay spoke. Remarkably, some factors have remained quite consistent and have resurfaced. The competition between the USA and China that is playing out across the region is one. Some domestic conflicts have also remained – such as the internal tensions that Tay observed in Burma, now called Myanmar.

Other things have changed and largely for the better. Perhaps chief amongst these has been the relations amongst Southeast Asian neighbours, both bilaterally and in the collective of ASEAN. In 1970, ASEAN was barely three years old, and the thaw was just starting in ties among its five original members – Thailand, Indonesia, Malaysia, Singapore and the Philippines. Nevertheless, Tay had held out the need for the countries of the region to respond to the Cold War and shifting geopolitics by acting on their own initiative "to find a new balance and develop ways to cooperate to mutual advantage". He felt a degree of optimism in the formation and activities of ASEAN as well as the improving bilateral relations between Singapore, Malaysia and Indonesia, and thought all members could find a common cause against Communism. Such efforts were indeed made and helped to create a foundation for ASEAN that has endured and been further developed in ways that no one might have predicted.

In the year after Tay spoke, the USA announced a startling geopolitical move – the opening up of ties with China. Over the following decades, the USA and its allies would prevail in the Cold War, the Soviet Union would collapse, and the dividing line across Southeast Asia would be erased so that ASEAN would expand to bring in the northern countries that had been opponents or else isolated in the Cold War era. Whereas Vietnam in 1970 was feared as a Communist and expansionist power, it is today an investment darling, with Singapore its largest investor. Moreover, while the USA was to leave the battlefields of Southeast Asia as Tay calculated was likely, it would continue to engage the region.

Today's level of investment and growth into the region was unforeseen in 1970. Countries in the region were poor and more than a few proclaimed that the region would Balkanise from both external and internal problems. Investment and trade with Japan have played a larger role than Tay or anyone who had lived through WWII might have expected. Ties between Tokyo and ASEAN grew especially after anti-Japanese demonstrations in 1974 and, following the Fukuda Doctrine announced in 1977, Tokyo has become perhaps the most consistent economic partner for the region. For ASEAN, while far from being perfect, current efforts to integrate as a community have created many economic opportunities for the "mutual advantage" Tay called for. With that growth, ASEAN today offers some political ballast and space amidst the great power rivalry that has resumed – albeit on different lines from the original Cold War.

Other changes at the global scale were things that no analyst of that era could have foreseen, especially the collapse of the Soviet Union and the rapid growth and change in China. However, by that time, some things were clear enough. For Singapore, the situation in the 1970s would continue to be challenging but there were more experiences in handling vola-tility and insecurity than there had been in the 1960s, and things were settling down, more under control.

This was a key period for Tay and 1971 was a signal year. This was the year that the British pulled out from its bases in Singapore. In April the Five Power Defence Arrangements were signed to come into effect in November, just one month after the British closed their bases. This was the existential change which had driven the Singapore government and the MID to drive forward with such urgency and Tay had played his role in these intense preparations so that an independent Singapore could stand on its own. This was also the year that Singapore hosted the first Commonwealth Heads of Government Meeting held outside of the UK. It was the first time that the new country had hosted not only the British leader but so many from across the world.

Tay had accompanied Lee Kuan Yew to the 1969 Commonwealth meeting in the UK that preceded this, and was involved in aspects of the preparations for the 1971 meeting. The 1971 CHOGM was significant not only for Singapore as hosts but for the grouping. The 1971 Singapore Declaration of Commonwealth Principles set out core political values and membership criteria such as the goals of peace, individual liberty and egalitarianism, the eradication of poverty, ignorance, disease and economic inequality, support for free trade and the United Nations, and the rejection of coercion. The Declaration of 1971 would guide the Commonwealth for decades and help lay the foundation for the Charter of the Commonwealth adopted in 2012.

Perhaps the final and somewhat idealistic article would serve as a touchstone not only for the Commonwealth but also the hosts, Singapore: "These relationships we intend to foster and extend, for we believe that our multinational association can expand human understanding and understanding among nations, assist in the elimination of discrimination based on differences of race, colour or creed, maintain and strengthen personal liberty, contribute to the enrichment of life for all, and provide a powerful influence for peace among nations."

The British base closure and the hosting of CHOGM in 1971 created a special context for Tay and the pioneer generation. They had grown up under British colonial rule, been shaken by WWII and the Japanese Occupation, and then took the turbulent path to independence. These events, in combination, brought much of the pioneering work of the past years to a culmination.

For Tay personally, there were two other notable markers. First, in 1970, it was announced that he had been selected for an Eisenhower Fellowship. This was a prestigious award that would allow him to spend months in the USA, with access arranged to get to know his counterparts professionally and to know the country on a more personal level. In that era, trips to the USA were rare, especially one like this fellowship which would be for an extended spell and with a curated itinerary. The opportunity to understand and engage the USA could not have been more timely.

Tay saw this not only as a benefit to his personal advancement but through the lens of the wider concerns facing Singapore and its region. In a speech he gave in this period, he said: "The precise magnitude of the change in US policy that will occur is still not clear and would depend to a large extent upon changes in US domestic attitudes." The trip would give him an exceptional opportunity to better understand the country and people who were now assuming the dominant role in the region around Singapore and the world.

It was PM Lee who had personally led the effort to engage the USA from 1967, and relations grew from 1969 with the presidency of Nixon and of Henry Kissinger as National Security Advisor, with whom Lee struck up a long-term relationship. No one foresaw the surprise of 1971, when Nixon announced he would visit China, and Tay was able to get a first-hand sense of the thinking and context that had led to this epochal decision and help think through what it might mean for Singapore and its neighbours. The Eisenhower Fellowship was intended to not simply be an educational sojourn, but another step in building Tay's view of the world and in what he could contribute to Singapore.

Secondly, the government announced that Tay would serve as Permanent Secretary of the Ministry of Home Affairs, a ministry created as the MID was split. He would have to relinquish his directorship of the SID. Tay had put much into the agency and come to know many of his staff, and so leaving was not without some sentiment. But he was confident that the SID was on a good footing.

There had been just five years from the date he was appointed as Director of the Special Branch through the revamp of security agencies, the creation of the SID, and his promotion to become Permanent Secretary. These intense years saw him advance in public service, develop his skills in administration, managing people, dealing with difficult situations, and running the mechanics of secret operations and detentions.

His appointment to the Ministry of Home Affairs would continue to allow him to play a key role in the security establishment. It was, moreover, a promotion: for a civil servant, appointment as permanent secretary was the topmost position that can be attained in a career. In combination, these two announcements of the Eisenhower Fellowship and the promotion confirmed the recognition of what he had done, his high standing in government circles and the potential of further contributions. Tay was 38.

*

He was busy in those years, and the discipline of his days set the tempo for our household.

I would wake early, at 6 am or so, before the sun to be in time for school. Ee Ee, the amah who looked after the house (and me especially as the youngest), would usually come up the back stairs to make sure I was awake, sometimes having to nudge me gently.

As I got ready in my bathroom, washing up and changing, I could hear my father in his. He had the habit of brushing his teeth thoroughly to try to keep off the stains from smoking. This extended to brushing his tongue quite roughly and so far back into his throat, he would gag – the sounds reverberating, loud, urgent and awful.

I would go down to have breakfast with my mother, where my father would join us. He would flick through the newspapers. I would have Milo, and my father, coffee. I had orange juice from F&N cordial or else a powder called Tangs (touted as a drink for astronauts). He drank Jaffa orange. Friends in Israel sent him cans of it. In the 1950s and into the 1960s, it was an emblem of the Israeli state. Curious and with a child's adulation of his father, I had to try it. Unsweetened, to my young taste buds, the juice was teeth-achingly sharp.

The same was true of the grapefruit they would send when it was in season. My father ate the fruits sliced into half and dusted with sugar, spoon after spoon. I tried one spoonful once and returned to my papaya (sometimes grown in our own garden). Just watching my father eat the cut, pinkish segments of the fruit and gulp down that juice would make my mouth feel an edge and my lips pucker. I could not understand how my father could, literally, stomach it. Perhaps the acid in the gut was an essential in Israeli martial training?

Yet, even at the busiest times, he was not an absent father. He paid attention to what I was doing in class and sports and who my friends were. He didn't tell me what to do, but did encourage me to mix around different groups and to play sports. When I mixed with kids from richer families – and there more than enough in Anglo-Chinese School (ACS) – he didn't encourage it or stop it. But he would remind me that we were not rich, and never would be.

I would go off to the car with my mother. She taught at a government school near the house and I attended ACS at Barker Road. The driver – Choon Chye and then later Alwi – would drop us first, before heading back to pick my father up and drive to his office in the city.

I liked being with my father. From my earliest years, I knew the times we had were not to be taken for granted. In the evenings, I would look forward to his return and sitting down for our dinner. Sometimes, often, he would shower, change and then head out for a dinner appointment.

But at other times, we would all be at home. At the dining table, we would discuss many things, not only what was happening in the lives of us children but also what he was doing, and what was happening in the country and the world. He would tell you things that made you pause and wonder how on earth he knew that. He was also a person to say the funniest things.

Sometimes, I would incur the disapproval of my grandmother about something I had done, or had not. I knew that she would complain about me to my father either before or even sometimes as we sat at the table having dinner. On such days, the anticipation of his return and our meal together was, to say the least, mixed.

Most memories of our evening meals as a family are, however, happy. It was my father, rather than my mother, who would initiate games or outings. After dinner, we would go into the living room and play. There were card games – Russian poker or bluff – or else more elaborate ones like racing cars on the Scalextric track or table tennis. Whatever the game, we played intensely, yet with much teasing and great joshing.

Then we children would go up and prepare for sleep and the next day, and he would go into his study. He would smoke his pipe and play his music, usually classical, sometimes jazz. I would come in to say goodnight to him, and he would be going over some paper at the desk or, in his reclining chair, reading a book. We would talk again for a spell.

Once, I asked him why he worked at home, at night, and if he wasn't tired and should just sleep. He told me that was the best time when all the things of the day might be quieted and revisited and he could connect one thing to another and see if things really fitted, and how. Afterwards, upstairs in my bed, I would hear the music softly playing. When I closed my eyes, I could almost see him still at his desk, working and thinking until late.

Chapter 6

"PROGRESS FOR OUR NATION"

AS SINGAPORE STABILISED and began to prosper and boom into the 1970s, so did the aspirations of individual citizens in their careers and personal lives. While he focused on work and the bigger questions that arose, Tay Seow Huah was not exempt from these hopes. How did he live? What changed and improved for him and the pioneer generation and how would they live and define the good life?

Progress for the nation, he hoped, would also mean better lives for him and others of his generation as individuals; after all the concept of a nation is based on "people" rather than only the state. He wanted a place in the sun. He was adventurous, even voracious, in seeking out what life had to offer.

Suddenly Singaporean

The early and perhaps biggest change for him had come in 1965. The young man from the peninsula of Malaya was suddenly Singaporean. He was not alone in this. With Separation, an entire generation was; the referendum of September 1962 had been on the basis of merger with Malaysia, which the PAP leaders had proposed and pushed for and the Left had opposed.

But if it was unintended, Singaporean identity was not to be left to accident and circumstance. Nor was it a question only of personal choice and preference. Much as the civil service had been re-educated and repurposed after the PAP came into power, the Singaporean nation-building effort was an explicit government policy. This was not only about security but was twinned to a social agenda; indeed, those aspects were often much more visible with campaigns and slogans.

There was the call for a "Rugged Society", combined with more practical admonitions to learn to swim (enabled by the building of public swimming pools). Perhaps the most significant campaign was the "Stop At Two" policy for population control; so successful that it would be one reason for, subsequently, the failure to have more children, with impacts on the demography of Singapore.

Tay did not ignore these efforts, nor did he respond cynically. He had made his choice. But some of the changes in being Singaporean did not always fit him entirely. He felt quite abruptly cut off from where he had been born and always regarded as home, where his youth had been spent, and where his family still resided. A part of him would always long for Malaya, although he enjoyed Singapore. For many years, when time allowed, he would drive up north with his wife and young children, road trips leading to KL, Ipoh and (although less often) Taiping to see his brothers and his mother for rounds of food and catching up. He took his children to try to make sure they were not only city folk but comfortable with the larger, more rural Malaya, able to trek in the jungles. He also used the time to catch up with classmates and other contacts and get a first-hand feel for what was happening, and to develop his own perceptions of the situation back there.

For the same reasons that he looked with fondness up north, his views were critical of the emerging political and economic system in Malaysia. There would often be mealtime debates with his brothers, especially David and Jack, that were vociferous and opiniated, even if good-natured. This was not only about whether food was better in Malaysia or Singapore, but about which country was doing better in terms of the economy and life, and the relative merits of their airlines, and the *ringgit* versus the Singapore dollar. In the early years, these were lively, even heated, debates. Yet, after a while, the terms of engagement changed. His brothers who had chosen to remain in Malaysia knew it was best to restrict banter to the quality of the food and durians, and the ease of life. On almost all other matters, it was increasingly clear where the weight of evidence lay.

Sonnie would always remain interested in Malaysia. There was a book about Malaysia's history edited by Wang Gungwu, who would become the pre-eminent academic of that generation and whom he knew from university. The handsome, leather-bound work had taken years in gestation and the contents were almost made obsolete by events of the Separation – events that had happened so suddenly and unexpectedly though the tensions were known. It was a history of what might have been. Nevertheless, it was a book that he read when it was published, and one which he kept on his shelves for many years.

He did not give himself undue credit for the wisdom of choosing the right side. Like many at that time, he had simply reacted to events where he was, rather than considering the question *de nouveau*, on a blank sheet. There was so much to do and so little time to do it. He had felt that since 1959 and, in 1965, when appointed to the Special Branch, this was redoubled. Rushed or not, he had made the choice to be Singaporean, and the consequences would be felt over and over again in those pioneer years. For Tay Seow Huah, there had to be a clear commitment to Singapore and no other country. There would be issues where the interests of his former home would clash and have to be subordinated to Singapore's. Still, he would stress the need for cooperation to continue between the security and intelligence agencies on each side of the border and aimed for this to be resilient, even when there were disagreements between the political masters; this was a tradition started then which would continue into the future.

For years after he had become a Singapore citizen, he continued to keep his blue identity card – its colour instantly contrasted to the light red of the Singaporean equivalent. When I first enrolled in school, my teacher – like any proper bureaucrat – refused to accept that a blue IC might nevertheless belong to a Singaporean. In a letter dated 27 February 1970, marked confidential and stamped as being from "Director, Security and Intelligence, Ministry of Interior and Defence", my father wrote to the school to explain: "My identity card, No. 2024154, was taken when I was still a Malaysian citizen. Subsequently, on 27th August, 1966, I became a Singapore citizen by registration, certificate No. FF.19177. I have not changed my identity card because it allows me a certain degree of access in my present duties which I would not otherwise have."

The last sentence was deliberately vague so the school did not know anything but would not ask for anything more. What was clear was what it indicated about his identity. Beyond the colour of his identity card, elements from his early days in Taiping continued. That was when he had first felt the social and political movements and grown his own sense of self-identity – distant and distinct from both China and the white colonial society. He had felt an empathy and connection to others regardless of their race or religion, and a kind of attachment to the land even if they were not sons of the soil. There were ideas of society and belonging that appealed to him and others like him, a Malayan generation. He had hoped for this to emerge with calls for a Malaysian Malaysia.

After Separation, those hopes and aspirations were enshrined in Singapore and its pledge to be united, regardless of race, language or religion, so as to build a democratic society based on justice and equality. Those words, now so often repeated and memorised by generations of school children, were for him and the pioneer generation still fresh and bold promises. As both citizen and spy chief, he could see the challenges: to secure the fledgling democracy against internal and external threats, to create conditions of equality, justice and equity to ensure people progressed, and to help the young country find its place in the world. In this, he had found not just a job but a sense of purpose and belief.

Housing and Family Life
Yet, it took him a much longer time to make a home in Singapore. The hardscrabble days and make-do accommodation eventually gave way to days of greater comfort. As he progressed

in the civil service, he was allocated government quarters.

At the port, it was the bungalow at Raeburn Park from the British days, built on thick, brick pillars with cool stone on the ground floor and solid wood for the upper storey. It was not the largest though there were enough rooms not only for his young family but also one set aside for a proper study with a handsome desk and the books he was accumulating. What he especially liked was its site. The house stood high on the hillside overlooking the busy port and the railway and while there could be noise from the trains and from the ships when they blared their horns, he could see how Singapore was connected to the world and, by the rail, up north to the Malaya he had known.

When he was appointed Director of the Special Branch, our family moved to another government house. This was larger and grander, a pukka British black-and-white bungalow that the British administrators had designed for themselves as a matter of prestige and to accommodate the privileges of a colonial lifestyle. While now old and not always pristine, the bungalows continued as a sign of status. Spacious and airy, with dining halls and living rooms designed for hosting grand parties and entertainments they were, to say the least, a considerable step up from the small houses that he and Cecelia had rented before. The new country was still struggling to put up HDB flats in sufficient number and quickly, and there were still kampongs with make-do wooden structures and standpipes by the side of broad *longkangs*.

The bungalow was set in a green area that was convenient not only to the Police Academy and one of the facilities of the Special Branch, but also to the Senior Police Officers Mess, where Sonnie would play tennis, and to the upper-crust Polo Club. It was a place set in some tropical version of the English counties and the name of the road, Mount Pleasant, seemed to sum up the situation well. This was to be home from 1966 to 1974; the longest spell he and his family would ever spend under one roof.

The road to the house sloped upwards and led through

broad gates to a covered porch. The entrance hall of cool, reddish stone was high-ceilinged and grand stairs led upwards. There were just three rooms upstairs, but so large that each could have accommodated an entire family. Downstairs was a spacious living room on the left and, on the other side, a separate and handsome dining room for formal dinners. From here, the house opened out to a covered patio where there were large, comfortable chairs of rattan and stuffed cushions so you could sit, take tea or an after-dinner drink, and look out over the garden. The grounds of the house were big enough for parties, perhaps an acre including a lawn tennis court (discernible from imprint of the lines), and this was useful and used more than a few times.

There was much effort to cultivate a range of contacts like the "Mexicans" and British in these years. There would be black-tie, official dinners and receptions at the embassies and there were other parties hosted by Bogaars at his home, another grand black-and-white. Living in this Mount Pleasant colonial bungalow not only enabled Sonnie to follow suit, but even seemed to demand that he too offer entertainments and upgrade his lifestyle to host parties and gatherings.

There were sometimes sit-down dinners among the adults only but there were more occasions when their families and children would be invited and the house would be full to the brim, with many spilling out into the garden. At other times he and his guests, including the "Mexicans", might be more convivial, in short sleeves and sitting under the trees, no longer representatives of this government or another but just men drinking and laughing.

There were also occasions when he and Cecelia would host their own families and siblings or to hold parties for the children and their friends on their birthdays or other occasions like Children's Day and Easter. Sonnie was doing well and had felt it incumbent to put up a good show of his newfound circumstances, for colleagues and family. It was in fact expected that he should live the good life and share it – and the relatives who came were properly impressed by the place.

His British habits from the Taiping years were reinforced when engaging the Americans and Europeans. On weekends, the family would have tea in the afternoons, served with a lot of sugar and sometimes the thinnest of lemon slices, and sandwiches or biscuits. Or, for a special treat, with Black Forest gateau and curry puffs from Mont Dór. Dinners would be around the grand and polished table in the formal dining room, big enough to seat twelve. Often, especially on weekends, there would be Western food: Birds Eye peas and fish fingers bought from Fitzpatricks, the latter fried up crisp in a *kuali*, or attempts at rump steak.

The housekeeper was an amah who had joined them earlier and would try to cope with the much larger house and higher expectations. She was particularly to look after me but also continued to look after the entire household for many years, bringing down two of her children from Malacca to join her and go to school in Singapore. There was a driver, and a full-time gardener who stayed in the servants' quarters at the back of the bungalow with his whole family. There were the makings of a comfortable, good life.

When no urgency detained him in the office, the driver would bring Sonnie home at dusk, when there would be the smell of burning grass and leaves from small, smoky fires lit by the gardener. There would be just enough time to go upstairs for a shower and change out of the starched, white office shirt, and into something more relaxed yet presentable for dinner. There might be a cocktail before, which his mother made a habit of, and a chance for the children to talk with him. Then, dinner would be served.

For these home dinners, also at the polished table in the large, formal dining room, the food was most often the Peranakan dishes that the amah cooked best, and that the family liked most. There would be a fried, crispy fish with an oily, roughly pounded chilli *rempah* that Sonnie especially liked. At other times, when his mother wished, there was steamed fish with ginger or other dishes from the Cantonese cuisine that were her heritage.

After dinner, he would always make time for the family and especially the children. He took the trouble to contrive games to play with them, as a way to interact and amuse one another. For a long spell, there were table tennis games – at first played on the long and broad dining table after the meal was over and the plates all cleared and, later, on a proper table that he bought and kept folded up in one corner of the long, covered porch off the living room. In these sports, Sonnie wanted his children to always try hard enough to win but to accept that they could not always control the outcomes: be a good loser, but not a great one.

After that, when the children went up and got ready for sleep, he would go into his study. There, he would clear more work, opening up the tidy hard-sided Samsonite brief case, and taking out the files with the bold stripe across the front that signified their classification was secret. On other evenings, when work relented, he would do much the same, except that the reading would be a book of history or politics. He would, in such moments of relaxation, wear a sarong and simple white collarless T-shirt or singlet; a habit of that era that he knew was already becoming an anachronism.

I lived here with him and our family from my early childhood to early teens. It was a fine house with the space to run around inside and out, and imagine so much. Living there, even when things were busy and he was tired, my father would try to find time for us as children, and my sister and I would often sit expectantly in the evenings, waiting for him to return. There are many and large, etched memories of my childhood from that time, in that house. After so many years since I have moved and the place demolished for a highway, it is the place I return to in my memories and sometimes in my dreams.

While I was a child and happy enough, I was not entirely ignorant that some aspects of home and family life were not doing so well, even amidst these comfortable settings and the moments of laughter and dinner parties. He and my mother had known tensions from their early years and, while some of that centred on the lack of money, these were not resolved when Sonnie was promoted and the house was bigger and there was more. His habits meant that the more he had, the more he would spend. But their tensions were about more than money.

Issues escalated when his mother moved in to live with them in the large black-and-white on Mount Pleasant where she was accorded the master bedroom. The children would be subject to the widow's commandments about discipline. Even the amah would receive instructions. The widow was a domineering woman, and there was no one to stand in her way in that house. Certainly not Cecelia, not with Sonnie always giving in to his mother's demands.

Yet, the fault in a marriage cannot be laid entirely on one person, especially one who is not even a party within it. If it were otherwise, Cecelia and Sonnie might have endured having the widow live with them and even laughed about her privately. But they themselves were proving less than compatible.

He was so busy at work and everything else that while she was often there with him at functions, they found little time for or focus on each other. The activity, the guests and the children took up attention. He was exploring new things and widening his circles. She was not at all closed to trying some new things, and would welcome the foreign guests into their home with interest and even warmth. But she could not keep up with his energy. While she was not without education and wit, Cecelia struggled with the wide-ranging and often intellectual discussions. He was no doubt the smarter of the two and she was not competitive about that; she only asked for some basic respect but Sonnie would never be shy about outshining his siblings or anyone else, not even his wife. He was going up and heading out into the wider society and the world beyond, and she could not keep up.

Cecelia tried to find comfort in the two children and was a loving mother. In this, she was poorly equipped by her own experiences. She worked hard as a teacher, giving a lot of attention to the students and rising to be vice-principal of the school. But by now, Sonnie's success in the civil service led some of her colleagues in the government-run school, including the principal, to unfairly suspect that any recognition she got was only because she was his wife. There was once a special evening at the Istana and when the newspaper ran a picture of her seated next to Prime Minister Lee, this honour was appreciated but did not help perceptions at her school.

There were many evenings for her alone in the large house on Mount Pleasant when he would be out and the children were asleep and the widow would be in her room, and Cecelia would just sit and brood. There were many weekends when Sonnie would make plans to do this or the other, go up to Malaysia or all the way to some part across Singapore, and while she could go, she felt neither needed nor really welcome. Increasingly, she would go back to Katong and join her sisters and the old, familiar faces around the mahjong table. This was a circle and life she had known from before, and it brought her some comfort. Now there was no great excitement when Sonnie came to pick her up. She would just close off her hand, muster the children as quickly as she could, and run off because he would often just sit in the car with the engine on and didn't like to be kept waiting.

He could be impatient in the house. This was a contrast to the way he approached work and colleagues – perhaps its corollary. Sonnie focused on work, and found a meaning and purpose that was central to him. In the circles he interacted with, there was excitement and novelty – new horizons to explore in tastes, culture and ideas. He never had a traditional home life and his mother, while keeping the brood of children together, had not been a traditional mother. He had no model of what a family life looked like. In his headlong pursuit of all life had, he understood little about contentment and quiet; only after he was satiated and wanted nothing more would he sit alone and smoke his pipe and listen to classical music.

He tried and did make time for family. He would be the one to find enjoyable excursions that could include Cecelia and the two children, still young at the time. Weekend excursions to Changi Point to swim and boat were a favourite.

There was a bungalow at the far end of the beach that they

could use. Before the Changi airport construction began, there was a long, flat stretch of soft, off-white sand and a fringe of tall, pine-like Casuarina trees. For a while, Sonnie had that speed boat used for skiing or just for him to race along the coast with the exhilaration of the wind and the blow of the engine. Skiing was in vogue in that era and any number of people would come to join him off and on, including relatives from the Cheong side. He was getting more used to them and they to him. His brother-in-law Lawrence Wee would join in that too. He was never that keen or good at the skiing but was steady at the wheel of the speedboat when it was Sonnie's turn to ski. Another was Steven, the son of Cecelia's oldest sister, then a teenager. The young man skied well and would later continue with his own boat and, in the 1980s, teach his cousin, Sonnie's son.

Cecelia was happy enough to come along and would sit in a deckchair on the beach to mind the children, sometimes in the sun with her hat and sunglasses on, or at other times in the shade of the Casuarinas, dipping into the water now and again with the children. At low tide, after boating, it would be Sonnie who was in the chair while she took the children out meandering on the sand to spy what the receding waves exposed and sometimes to help her dig and see if there were cockles to bring home to cook. There was also a small snack shop further along on the beach where they would gather in the low deckchairs. Sonnie would order them sandwiches and drinks – coffee or, for the kids, Milo or Horlicks. An entire Sunday could be spent this way before heading back home, after dusting away as much sand from their legs and feet, and sitting on towels or newspapers to prevent the damp of their swimming costumes seeping into the car seats. This was one of the main things that the family did together in those years.

In some of this, Sonnie would mix work with leisure. The drive up to Changi beach ran past the prison and perhaps more than once, after his family was settled at the bungalow on the beach, he would drop in to speak to the Prisons Director and have a look around. Similarly, when the government got coastal patrol boats (on independence, there was only one wooden ship in the navy), Sonnie would make it part of his work to go out to sea.

On weekdays when there was no time to get out to Changi Point or the beach, he would sometimes take the children for a swim at the Pyramid Club. The club was the brainchild of Dr Goh Keng Swee and was started to select and bring together an elite from among the politicians, civil servants and those in private-sector business – who formed the top of the three-sided pyramid structure in Goh's mind. Tay had been asked to join soon after his appointment to SID. He would use the club recreationally, as it was just a short drive from where he lived.

There were other excursions and activities he planned, like performances at the National Theatre if there was something suitable, like *Swan Lake* when Joanne was taking ballet lessons. There were also occasional outings to MacRitchie Reservoir on weekends to walk around and enjoy the outdoors, and especially if there was a band playing. He liked the bandstand there with the striking, Southeast Asian-inspired roof – better than the one at the Botanic Gardens from the British colonial period, even if the latter was more famous.

But more often, he would go out without the family, with friends or else alone.

He had many pursuits. Some were carried over from his days in Taiping and the undergraduate years. Others were new, things that took his fancy so that he would master as much of each and as quickly as possible. As work took up more and more time and attention, he would continue to try to enjoy his life. He attacked life on all fronts, someone who believed he could do it all. What he did, the things he accumulated and the friends he had, spoke about him and those times.

Pursuits, Buddies and Distractions

He enjoyed culture, literature and learning, and he would scour so many books and so many types of books from different traditions. There were friends with such intellectual interests too, and many exchanges of ideas over drinks. He would go to some art shows and later, when he had more time and money, would buy some pieces he admired by artists of the Nanyang School, or of the Singapore River and landmarks of that era that seemed fresh and different, like the Woh Hup complex near Kallang with its distinct "cash-register" profile. On many evenings, there were formal dinners and events associated with the diplomatic circuit in Singapore or for civil servants and the government. Or there might be private dinners at the best restaurants of the time to entertain foreign guests. At other times, he liked little more than to search out places to go *makan* with buddies.

He was always doing or learning something, most often out and about in Singapore, driving here and there, with some friend or to see someone, or up to Katong to visit his sister. Or he might be travelling, whether for work or else in a camper van up to Malaysia to go trekking

His circle of friends and acquaintances was diverse from the start and widened further with time and often associated with one pastime or another. Many had nothing much in common or did not get on with each other. Some were regular *kaki*. Others might meet up only very occasionally, but once there, were greeted as dear and long-lost friends, especially some of those who had come from Taiping or the Dunearn Road Hostels. It did not matter what they did or how well or poorly they had done. As Edwin Thumboo was to remark, "He formed a number of friendships and it is significant that almost all of them strengthened and enlarged over the years. For he was that very rare person who made many but hardly ever lost a friend."

For sports, the cricket and especially badminton that Sonnie had played so passionately continued but were displaced by a newer interest – tennis. There were courts at the Senior Police Officers Mess that were convenient, and he would play there with Bogaars and other people from the ministry and the police. He enjoyed playing with people he knew from work and with friends, but he was more than a social player. His attitude was always competitive and he was delighted to win the club competition and was insulted by the idea that any of the younger officers had ceded him some advantage because of his seniority.

He continued with the jungle trekking and camping. He never forgot his climb of Gunung Tahan and thought of making the trip to Kinabalu in Sabah, which was higher. The big dream he held was of Everest, which Hilary had made in 1953, and he kept a stack of *National Geographic* magazines that covered the expedition in the greatest detail. Sonnie never got there and always knew it was more of a daydream. He fished once in a while at Kukup. More regularly, he would be in some stretch of the still-considerable forests near Endau-Rompin that straddled the northern part of Johor state and Pahang.

There was a particularly epic trip to Tasik Chini, the large lake in northern Pahang. There were villages where the Orang Asli lived, much in the ways they had for centuries, as well as the extensive swathes of water lilies just past where the river met the lake. There were the legends of ancient Khmer ruins sunken underwater, and of the Naga, a mystical giant serpent.

The trips required a lot of preparation and equipment and he would enjoy selecting and buying the latest and best. For a time, he had a sturdy wooden shack built for him along a small river past Kulai and near Kota Tinggi. He and his friends who regularly went up camping pooled money to buy a sturdy VW Camper and the vehicle or else the shack served as a base for many walks deeper into the jungle. He was always raring to go and there were good buddies who would be ready to get up and go with him.

One of them was Eric Alfred, whom he had known from DRH back in university. Eric was a trained zoologist and curator with the Raffles Museum (which preceded the National Museum), and later appointed its director. He was especially proud of the enormous whale skeleton mounted on the ceiling above the staircase of the museum; so striking and something any child would remember. The other buddy who would regularly come up camping was Edwin Thumboo. Although Edwin was destined for the University's English

Literature Department, the expats then in charge had been stroppy about locals, and Edwin first had to slog nine long years in the civil service. From those years, and especially the camping excursions, they became very close.

What rich and unusual camping expeditions they must have been, with one companion being able to discern the calls of different animals at night, while another might recite poems by the fire. Only when one or the other of these two could not make the trip would there be other companions. Of these, his brother-in-law Lawrence Wee was companionable enough and could be depended upon to improvise and add spice and *tumis* the otherwise plain provisions, like sardines from tin cans, into a very satisfying campfire meal.

Thumboo helped feed Sonnie's long-standing interest in English literature and expanded his horizons to read Yeats with the Irish quizzing of the English, and then anti-colonial African literature (on which Thumboo obtained his PhD).

Another pursuit Sonnie kept from his Taiping years was swimming and the sea. There were longer trips to the islands off the coast of Johor for snorkelling and diving, with assorted friends and friends of friends, a mix of locals and expats. He liked few things better than to be out in the sun, on a boat or the beach. Scuba diving among the coral had a special attraction and he liked the equipment, making sure he had a good and sharp diver's knife to pry open sea urchins and even a speargun for fishing, as well as custom-made goggles to compensate for his spectacles. Rawa was one favourite when the accommodation was still new and decent, or else he would arrange to camp at Pulau Hujong. He enjoyed roughing things out, so long as there was beer and they could have a fire on the beach over which fish could be grilled.

Speed was something that he always enjoyed and pursued, acting on Aldous Huxley's dictum that "speed provides the one genuinely modern pleasure". He had given up motorbikes even if he would always reminisce about the fun times, riding with his DRH friends and, once in a while, borrow one from someone for a few days. By the late 1960s, he reckoned there was too much traffic on the road to ride really fast with any degree of safety as there would be some moron in a car or truck. He found something of a substitute: cars.

After marriage and that terrible accident, he had cars that, while practical and safe enough for a family, offered performance. His favourite was the Jaguar Daimler Mark 2. This had four doors but an engine under the long bonnet that was powerful enough to earn the right to match its claim to be a sports saloon. The car had lovely curves and a deep exhaust, as well as comfy leather seats and a smaller, all-wood steering wheel that was responsive. Sonnie was especially pleased his was badged as a Daimler, with the more subtle hood icon.

When he would drive up to Malaysia, he would get the car up past 100 mph, to the very end of what it could do. Even with Cecelia or the children along, he would speed on the winding trunk roads and overtake the large and slow trucks, with his son cheering. Later on, the government would provide a driver and a Mercedes which he used most of the time for office and official functions. But Sonnie continued to drive for enjoyment and would keep a succession of sports cars for that.

One Malay term for leisure enjoyment, *makan angin*, translates literally as meaning "eat air", and Sonnie did that with those sports cars, almost all open-tops. Sometimes, he would head out to Changi, even on a weekday evening, or drop by on his sister or a friend out on the East Coast in Katong or Siglap. There were otherwise winding roads that he really enjoyed, along the ridges in the West (where the Kent Ridge campus of the National University of Singapore is now). Cecelia would occasionally go along; there would be a scarf kept in the glove compartment that she could use to try to keep her hair tidy. Other times, it would be us children, small enough then to squeeze into the rear seats. Or there were times that Sonnie would drive out alone, just to unwind, for a while, away from everyone and everything.

Compared to the austerity of the 1950s, the sports car was impractical and impossibly glamorous. They were all the rage in the West; this was the heyday of the British sports car. One of the first was an MGA that had nice lines but not much power. It was also a pure two-seater so he ordered body alterations to make two little back seats. After he sold that, there was a succession of cars, one after another, so many that only some stand out in memory. One was an Austin Healey 3000 that, with that size of engine, had real power, and even then he had the garage put in a supercharger that, at the flick of a long metal switch, would emit a high whine above the low note of the engine and add even more kick. Another was an Italian Lancia open-top, which he might have bought from Bogaars who also liked sports cars.

Perhaps the favourite was the Mercedes 190SL, which Sonnie thought quite classic and faultless. The car was a left-hand drive, made for Europe and not the right-hand drive system of Singapore. New rules were tightening to disallow left-hand drive cars and yet Sonnie was so taken by the car that he looked for loopholes that might allow him to keep it. After some time, someone (perhaps Bogaars) called and he accepted that this could not go on, selling the car to an old friend in Malaysia, where rules remained more flexible. He was to think back on it wistfully but Sonnie knew what he had to do, properly.

This small incident spoke to something broader in his character as it related to his pursuits and other distractions. Sometimes exuberance could get the better of him for that moment, but whatever the distraction or how intensely he pursued it for a time, his judgement would normally come around about what he could and should do, and he would undertake to put matters right. It was also habit that after the initial period of intense pursuit, he might relegate that interest to another. He was not just energetic but restless.

And after those episodes of great enthusiasm, he would come home where he would often retire to the bath to soak and then sleep deeply, and then to putter around the house and his study, with his books and music before dinner with the family, spend more time in the study and more sleep before the work of the next day.

Just as often he would sleep deeply but briefly, and his eyes would open quite suddenly – full of energy again – and he would ask us children and our mother: "Who wants to go…?" and be off on another excursion.

The Good Life

As he rose up the ranks of the civil service, Sonnie would try to learn about the best things, and to savour them. He worked hard, and why should he not enjoy the rewards? After all he had gone through in the early years, he felt he deserved nothing less. There was also a sense of seeking and learning, and in engaging the world outside, especially with the British and Americans, to learn about their lifestyles and the finer things. This was particularly after things were more settled from the 1970s.

He dined out often for work and, when he did, there were meals at the hotels and the best international restaurants at that time. The 1970s would be a boom for the country in many measures, and the quality of restaurants showed it. The Shangri-La had just opened, with its foyer grand, lofty and large grounds. The Mandarin too was new, a good place for a drink in the lounge (famous for beautiful and tall waitresses in cheongsams). Its expensive Chicken Rice was also something of a treat, especially when there were foreign guests. The Marco Polo was convenient and had a good bistro. There was Hugo's at the Hyatt and Chesa at the Equatorial, where the local maître d' Johnny always took care of him and the guests, and would flambé a spectacular Crepes Suzette at tableside. He also liked Le Chalet at Ladyhill Hotel for the Swiss fondue (traditional cheese or else beef cubes) and Gordon's Grill at the Goodwood. Sonnie was pleased to be a regular at such places.

Of these, only the last remains at the time of writing but these restaurants have not really gone; their European and Western dining DNA is now so much of the norm that it is hard to imagine how these were rarified treats in their time.

When Joanne and I were older, and especially on our birthdays, he would take us to share the experience. I was just ten when I first went to a proper restaurant with him and our family, and he made sure to tutor me beforehand on the placement of knives and forks.

When he was young, my father had been a hungry boy selling *kueh* by the roadside, and now he had his wish to run off to consume those cakes and so much more. You could see the delight in his eyes. At these dinners, his manner was relaxed, his laugh deep and real.

There were favoured eating places at the other end of the spectrum. Singapore was still taking hawkers off the street in that era and trying to get the coffee shops to be more hygienic. But Sonnie had quite an opposite response: that it was the old places that retained the best food and if that meant less than ideal conditions, so be it. If Cecelia and the children did not feel so comfortable in these types of places, he would go with friends or else buy and pack it back home for a treat.

The same man who would relish fine dining also loved his southern Indian food and was entirely comfortable to eat with his fingers off a banana leaf, adept enough that not a single curry smear or grain of rice would show on his palm (in fact not beyond the second phalange of the fingers). He relished Fish Head Curry when it was fresh and succulent and there were enough eaters at the table to do a big one justice. He also loved dry curried mutton and enjoyed the famous Islamic Restaurant. A less well-known haunt was Ujagar Singh's at St Gregory's Place, just off the then-busy Hill Street. Up the winding, creaking staircase, there was hardly any room to eat and the whole place reeked from years of oil and spices, but the fried mutton chops were out of this world.

There was also a place off Rochor Road, defined at that time by the smelly canal that ran down the middle. There were hardly any tables in the coffee shop, the smell of oil was overwhelming, and the floor slippery with grease and strewn with eggshell fragments so he would always buy food to take home. Sometimes, the driver would run this errand for him. But otherwise, he would go in and queue near the giant *kuali*, giving his order in understandable Hokkien to the sweating man in a singlet who would throw noodles into a stock of prawn shells and pork bones until they were slightly soggy and glistening, add squid, some prawns and roast-pork strips, and eggs, and serve this up, topped with a palmful of crisped pork fat nuggets, with cut limes to squeeze over and a sharp hot chilli sauce on the side. Sonnie would drive down to Koek Road to buy turtle soup when his mother was in town. This was an expensive dish, prepared quite gruesomely from live turtles (which are now a protected species). But it was what she demanded.

When there were visitors from abroad, Sonnie might take them to the then-famous Satay Club, the rows of Malay stalls lined up at one end of Queen Elizabeth Walk along the shore in front of the city. But there was another special place that, while not as famous, he preferred: the Batik Inn. This was just off Orchard Road and had tables set with white tablecloths and candlelights, laid out in an open-air courtyard that was bordered by leafy trees and Traveller's Palms, the tall elegant fan of a plant associated with Raffles Hotel. It was much pricier but the chicken was whole (rather than minced) and juicy. There were prawn satay, and beer served properly cold.

He brought these habits into his travels, even when it was for work. When he was on the Eisenhower Fellowship, he and Cecelia would dine at the Four Seasons at the top of the Chrysler Building in New York that was famous among the American celebrities and elite, and fabulously expensive. They would stay and dine at the Mark Hopkins in San Francisco.

In the 1970s, Sonnie was enjoying life – like others of his generation and perhaps even more so. The mood of the times encouraged that. In the West, Britain was finally finding its post-war feet with the swinging Sixties. James Bond movies were the rage – watched by rapt audiences generally and, surely, not without some amusement and perhaps longing for those working in security and intelligence. On the European continent and in the USA, with which Tay had increasing contact, there was a sense of better, happier times amidst the tensions of the Cold War. Indeed, there was a contest of lifestyles and consumption between the USA and the Soviet Union and, by extension, whether capitalism or socialism was best.

The good life for Tay was more than just indulgence in food or cars. In building up his library and reading after work in his study, he would equally devour books and then, talking with friends, share strong views not simply on their content but style. He built up a huge collection of classical music, LPs mainly bought from Beethoven Record House, where he would rack up bills each month. Many of the books he bought were related to his work but at a deeper level. He read up a lot about Malaya and the region, with a wide range of readings including many by colonial officers and authors. There were studies of China, both contemporary and historical – all of course in English since he could not read Chinese. More than a few of his books ranged widely into Western culture and, immediately before and especially after his Eisenhower Fellowship, there were many books about the USA and its political leadership and values. He also read a considerable amount of poetry, ranging from the old Romantics like Keats and the heroic Byron to Yeats. Many of these were borrowed from Thumboo and would remain on his shelves for years. In classical music, he started with light symphonies but showed a taste for Tchaikovsky and Beethoven. Later, it was often Mahler he listened to; he liked the story of how his work had almost been forgotten before there was recognition.

He was always trying to decide for himself which he thought was the best. He could sometimes offend people with his opinions. Some of them, including other civil servants, might think he was full of himself; the line between self-confidence and outright arrogance can be thin. But there were others with whom Sonnie would quite quickly make an impression and make a connection. He had the character and the intellect and was attractive, not just physically but as a whole. There was a verve and vigour that was inherent to him.

Living With Secrets
During this era, there was a popular culture fascination with spies of the James Bond type. The Bond movies in the 1960s

represented a kind of fantasy that played off the realities of the Cold War to present a chimera of impossible glamour, and led to dozens of imitators, including some that were filmed in Singapore and even featured Singapore stars. As Singapore's spy chief, Tay knew such representations were far-fetched illusions so different from the realities. If anything, he preferred the works of Le Carré.

He knew the famous section of the film based on the *The Spy Who Came in From the Cold*, and what the burnt-out Leamas, played by Richard Burton, said about spies and what they did. He had seen parts of this reflected in his work, in those around him. "What the hell do you think spies are? Moral philosophers measuring everything they do against the word of God or Karl Marx? They're not. They're just a bunch of seedy squalid bastards like me, little men, drunkards, queers, henpecked husbands, civil servants playing 'Cowboys and Indians' to brighten their rotten little lives."

Yet, he remained convicted about what he did and that it needed to be done. He believed that it could be done with some regard to principles and values, a modicum of decency and even humanity. Like so many others, he was not immune to some of that lifestyle popularised by the Bond idea of spies and made possible by increasing affluence. He may have enjoyed cultivating that image of sophistication and derring-do. More than one person was to remark that, in the ways he lived, he looked the part of a spy chief.

But it was not all fun and games. As with many pioneers in those years, there was no strict demarcation between personal and professional aspects of life. What he got and valued most from his work was not the pay or perks but the sense of purpose.

Another aspect of his work that shaped Tay's life, with the focus on security and intelligence, was inevitably secrecy. There were not a few pressures, and these flowed into his personal life. There were many tensions in living a life of secrecy. This was clearest in the life of those working in the SID, especially the field operatives. Many failed or else could not take it and gave up the work. Some leaked or tried to palm off bad information as good. Other colleagues succumbed to weaknesses like drink, money and women. It was not without reason that a normal function within the security agencies was to keep watch over their own operatives.

Those running the operations too felt the tensions and disagreements vividly, with instances when differences boiled over, threats exchanged. These were never confirmed and Tay never said anything that he thought might cause his family, and especially his wife, to worry too much. This applied to everyday practices. Our driver Alwi was a plain-clothes police-man, instructed to always accompany my mother and sister against the risk that they might be kidnapped. For my father himself, there were instances when he was directly targeted by the remaining Communists. Yet, he said little, betrayed no concern. Not even the time when he returned home one evening with a special officer detailed to provide him protection. Tay simply asked to arrange meals for the man and a bed for the night. Only later, when his wife pressed, did he let on that the Communists in Malaysia – increasingly isolated and on the retreat – had struck at senior security officials up north, and there had been intelligence reports that there was a list of potential targets with his name on it. If my mother had not asked, he would not have said anything – even when there was the unusual circumstance of an armed security officer living in the house.

Cecelia felt a sense of insecurity, especially as her relationship with Sonnie drifted and he widened his circles and accrued so many different friends with the many different pastimes, and would so often be at the office or out for dinner until late. Such secrets that existed could affect not just his work but also their personal lives, if and when they were to emerge in plain sight, undeniable. Yet Cecelia would not confront him, not without basis and unless she was prepared to know and deal with what might be revealed. She knew the common joke that when someone asked a question that you would rather not answer, you would reply: "I could tell you… but then I would have to kill you." Cecelia knew this all too well to ask, and she fretted even if she would try not to nag – as was his ideal in a spouse. She could not but speculate, however. Many years later, giving an interview to the media about being a spy chief, he was to pay tribute to his wife as someone who "never worried", taking the view that, "This is a quality our wives have… They don't nag, they allow us to pursue our ambitions without holding us back."

One secret was perhaps about Tay's own connections with the security and intelligence agencies. Officially, these began only in 1965 when it was in the public domain that he was appointed Director of the Special Branch. Before this, on the record, he was simply part of the civil service. Yet, as recounted, his work at the port and even before at the Ministry of Labour contained considerable elements of security, beyond what might be expected of a more usual appointment. It might be more than a coincidence that he was to work with S R Nathan at the port, and Nathan was to succeed him as SID Director.

Looking further back, there was his time when he was in Port Dickson, before returning to university to complete his Honours year. As noted, it is an unrecorded period during which he might have served as a resettlement officer and interacted with the British military and intelligence at the tail end of the Emergency. When he turned to Singapore, before the Special Branch appointment, he had contacts with British officers, both from the military and the High Commission. These connections were not apparent to his wife at the time nor to me and my sister. Only as information and stories have been gathered for this book, might these tangents be drawn together, tentatively as suppositions without clear proof. On the public record, to reiterate, his first connection to the world of intelligence was in 1965, when he was appointed to the Special Branch and, even then, he was the Director, not an operative.

There was also the odd circumstance of Tay's brother-in-law Lawrence Wee. He had been a teacher after graduating from Teachers' Training College. When the two families had lived together, the two fathers had got on and, even afterward, Lawrence was a reliable companion who might join in skiing or trekking and camping. He was smart and shrewd, among the top handful of students at Raffles Institution in his year until family circumstances after his father died forced him to go out to look for a job. He had an everyman style of bonhomie so he could talk to just about anyone. Some eyebrows in the family were raised when he decided to leave his steady, iron-bowl job of teaching to go into the business of buying and selling books, with trips into Malaysia and Indonesia. It was the late 1960s and his wife, my aunt, sometimes voiced concern that travel in those countries was not always safe. But Lawrence was street-smart and did well enough – he spoke Malay and could reach out to the widest range of people in these countries. Soon enough, he had a large, new car to showcase a growing success and to ferry his sample books when he drove up north.

Worry and mystification returned some years on, when it was announced that the teacher-turned-bookseller – by now in his 40s – was suddenly to become a journalist. It beggared belief, even in the family. Not long afterwards, Lawrence Wee openly joined the Ministry of Defence as a mid-level administrator of a department, where he stayed on until his retirement. These twists and turns in his jobs were unexpected, to say the least. No explanation was proffered. There was some speculation in the family if there had been a secret all those years, kept not only by Lawrence Wee but by Tay as his brother-in-law; a secret not only from the public but open and in plain sight to all the families, yet still unseen, even by their own wives.

A Change in Life
In 1973, there came a change that affected not just my father but the personal lives and circumstances of all our family. We would move out from Mount Pleasant. The next place would not be another black-and-white or anything so grand. Government policy had shifted to emphasise home ownership and, quite belatedly, they would stop the practice of allocating senior civil servants bungalows to live in at low rents. Moreover, the particular house that we lived in, near the start of Mount Pleasant, was slated to be torn down as part of the link between

the old Whitley Road and the then new Pan Island Expressway.

As permanent secretary, my father could possibly have finagled another bungalow but the policy was shifting and he thought to take the opportunity to make a change. A considerable one. He would, finally, buy a home. He had never bought any place before. He had shuffled from one rented property to another, whether private or government-allocated, quite itinerant. But now with a growing family and an established career as a senior civil servant, it was time.

He could not afford a bungalow. The salary of a permanent secretary was still not very much, and he had never saved much, almost nothing in fact. Nor had he acted early enough, when the prices were starting to climb with the stability and growth surge of the early 1970s. He had seen it coming, and his work in security had helped create the conditions for that. But my father was too busy to think of it, and having the government bungalow was so comfortable and affordable that, when other civil servants and his junior colleagues had made their purchases, this pioneer was not one who took that step. He shrugged and looked forward.

He secured a place that would be comfortable enough and that he could afford without a huge mortgage and monthly repayments. It would be an apartment, modern and so different from the large, rambling house at Mount Pleasant with its immense grounds. The flat was at One Tree Hill and it was his joke to wonder which was that one tree. The PSA had built up a small block, very central, just off Orchard Road and Grange Road, and large enough to have three bedrooms and an airy, open-plan living-cum-dining room. Given his past association, a unit was offered. He was thankful and embraced the change.

As the first place he actually owned, he took considerable time and no small pleasure in supervising its design and renovation, and in all details. Although he valued history and had studied it, he had always wanted to be modern and forward-looking; earnest to understand the latest trends and what was best, and to turn on a page and move on. None of the old, heavy wooden furniture would be carried over. The new flat was outfitted with completely new things and in the latest ways.

There were bean bags and high-gloss fiberglass furniture by Italian designers and a lovely Noguchi coffee table. A designer was engaged and delivered fitted, floor-to-ceiling shelving that was functional to provide a lot of storage, and furniture that would maximise the space, all in a pale tan pinewood, with light-coloured leather upholstery. The only concession to the old ways was to have the contractor install wood beams into the cement ceiling when there was no need. To him, this made the otherwise bare space something that could evoke the ceilings of those old houses with the beams needed to lend support.

In all, it seemed something out of the latest designer magazines, with more than a touch of mid-century style that, at that time, spelt modernity. He was ready to jettison the old things and the flat showed it: a departure from the old ways and a willingness to own a place of his own permanently and in modern style. The rest of us would have to adjust too.

As the mid-1970s approached, a decade after independence, the tumult of early politics and the worst of insecurities seemed to be behind. There were more stability and jobs, and quite heady growth for the country and for him. Professionally, he was doing well. Personally, like many others of the pioneer generation, my father looked forward with optimism to it all. Yet, rather than being able to live the good life, the years ahead would turn out to be his most difficult and testing times.

For, outside of work, there was another and even larger secret Tay kept. The tensions from work were feeding into his personal life and health. It was not just that he was sometimes short-tempered. The long tense hours at the office and headaches were normalised. So was disrupted, fractured sleep followed by long periods of deep slumber, when circumstances might allow, like the sleep of the dead. This built up in high blood pressure from his 30s, with prolonged spikes after some of the more difficult and stressful periods and after trips overseas into the region. He did go to the doctors but the medicines of the era were only able to do so much and the advice would have been either to stop the work – and that seemed impossible during the years of exigency – or otherwise just to monitor. There was a time when he was hospitalised for a protracted spell, complaining of the worst of headaches. But he continued to work from the ward and recovered after a few days. There seemed to be no aftereffects, so the doctors put the episode down to a period of heightened stress and perhaps a virus picked up during travels.

No one in the office knew about this in detail. No one suspected how deep the problem could run. For Tay himself, perhaps he did not really know either, and did not want to admit it. He seemed so physically fit and energetic, full of life at work and in so many aspects of his personal life. There was no sign of any adverse medical condition, no instances of a flare-up. Even at the times of the greatest tension, my father had a manner to keep up a calm front and smile.

Chapter 7

SENIOR CIVIL SERVANT

TAY'S OFFICE was at Pearl's Hill, at the edge of Chinatown and the city. This was familiar. The Ministry of Interior and Defence (MID) had been based here as it grew and so was the SID. When the MID was split in 1970, the Ministry of Home Affairs (MHA) would remain at Pearl's Hill. While he was newly confirmed as Permanent Secretary, Tay knew many aspects of the work. Yet, in a number of other ways, things were new.

First started in 1959, after Singapore gained self-rule, the MHA ceased in 1963 upon merger with Malaysia, since its responsibilities was transferred to the Federal government in KL. At Separation in 1965, the decision was then made to place both interior security and defence under one single ministry, the MID. It was not until MID was split – on 11 August 1970 – that there was again a separate Ministry of Home Affairs.

In splitting the MID, there was also a change in personnel. The Prime Minister and cabinet decided not to carry over the senior leadership of the MID to either of the two ministries created; both MID Minister Lim Kim San and Permanent Secretary George Bogaars were sent to other posts. The minister would head the Public Utilities Board with a mandate to build up the reservoirs and address the critical and perennial water insecurity of the country. Bogaars was to move back to Finance, where he had been before the MID. In their place, there would new names. Tay was named Permanent Secretary at first on an acting basis; that was shortly confirmed. There would also be a new minister. The PAP veteran Ong Pang Boon served for a scant month. Then Dr Wong Lin Ken, a professor of history recently elected as MP, was named. In the split of the MID, it was also decided that the Internal Security Department was to be placed under the Ministry of Home Affairs, while the external intelligence functions would remain with the SID, which would be from then on under the Ministry of Defence.

For Tay, there were both continuities as well as changes. One of the continuities was that, notwithstanding the focus on Home Affairs, he was to remain broadly involved in security issues, even relating to external matters and defence, much as he had in his previous role as Director for Security and Intelligence in the MID.

Among the changes, two bear special mention. One was that as the ministry supervised the Police Force, Tay as Permanent Secretary had charge of a large staff. The Force, as the staff liked to refer to it, was very public and its actions related very directly to the lives of ordinary people every day. This character was a sharp contrast to the relatively small and tightly staffed SID team and its secretive work. Another change was that much of his work would shift to the broader policy-making functions of a permanent secretary, rather than a direct operational role. This was particularly as the Police Commissioner, while reporting to the ministry, had to be respected as the professional leader within the Force.

There were many things undertaken in the MHA in the years Tay served as Permanent Secretary. But, of course, this cannot be attributed solely to him. Indeed, it was usual to ascribe most initiatives to the minister then in charge, recognising his role as a political master. There were decisions that might be evaluated to have been in the direct responsibility of other officers, such as the Police Commissioner in respect of the Force and its staff, or to the Internal Security Department. In the latter case, when considering specific operations and decisions taken, there was a culture to keep decision-making processes and attribution behind closed doors. However, for any detention order under the Internal Security Act, this had to be authorised by the signature of the Permanent Secretary, on behalf of the Minister, and not the ISD Director. More broadly too, there were the responsibilities and initiatives that a permanent secretary took up, even if it may not have been clear to those outside what that role encompassed, as opposed to the minister in charge of that portfolio. Perhaps the question of what Tay did as Permanent Secretary would best be considered both in general terms and by considering the specifics of the contributions of an individual, and the thinking and personality of that person, in the context of the times and other colleagues who served.

In general terms, a permanent secretary is the highest position for a civil servant in government and is responsible to run the ministry to which he is appointed. While this much can be simply stated, there is always some degree of misunderstanding, both generally and in particular in Singapore, where the context of that role has shifted from the pioneer generation into the present. The question of what permanent secretaries did is a larger one than can be addressed by looking at the life and work of any single civil servant and is absent in writings about other pioneer civil servants. Some may understand the role as merely bureaucratic, that the politicians decided and the civil servants implemented. This may be inadvertently supported by what has been written about a later-generation civil servant, Philip Yeo. By saying (as the title of his biography does) that he was neither servile nor civil, it may be taken to imply that less exceptional civil servants perhaps were. On the other hand, there may be others who somehow suggest that while the politicians give speeches and claim the credit or else be blamed, it is the bureaucracy who actually determines what happens. The British comedy *Yes Minister*, so popular in the 1980s, supports this view and more than a few acknowledge there is some echo of truth. Some might say that the pioneer generation of senior civil servants shared many of the same values and hopes of their political masters and, as such, were given considerable latitude to get things done.

Specifically, looking at Tay's time as Permanent Secretary, much depended on the timing, issues and personalities. As a pioneer generation civil servant, he was working in a public service that was considerably smaller and had much less capacity than today. Many of the systems, institutions, and standard operating procedures were just being put into place. Consider the organisation and reorgansation of the Special Branch and ISD and the start-up of the SID that he had undertaken. Also consider the broader issues relating to the creation and then splitting up of the MID, between the ministries of Defence and Home Affairs. Both allowed and required the leaders and the senior civil servants to make decisions where there were few or no precedents, and to build up systems rather than simply follow existing procedures. These conditions must be read into the full meaning of the term chosen to now acknowledge this generation of Singaporeans: pioneers.

What about the lines connecting and also delineating the political pioneers from the civil servants? In his recollections, one pioneer permanent secretary, the late Ngiam Tong Dow, intimated at least one situation in which he and other civil servants disagreed with their minister and won the day; no less than Dr Goh Keng Swee, who preferred to bet on buses to provide public transport than commit to trains and the mass rapid transport system. Writing later about his contributions, Philip Yeo let it be known of his effort to push through – without the blessing or clear ministerial acceptance – the buildup of Jurong Island as one example of exceptional civil servant initiative. Yeo also makes broader and more controversial claims: "Today, ministers overwork – doing everything and appearing everywhere…. Now, the Admin Officers are quiet. That is a sad thing. In my time, permanent secretaries were permanent in their postings. Today, we should call them "temporary secretaries" because they get rotated every few years. There's no reservoir of experience… they are constantly rotated and they have no depth."

While many will admit and admire what Yeo did during his public service, it is perhaps unnecessary to enhance the contributions that some of the pioneer generation civil servants made by such a contrast to the present. Nor is it necessary to claim a particular instance of defying one's political masters or moving things without their agreement. For Tay, he always acknowledged the need for the oversight and judgement of the senior political leadership. Perhaps this was especially because he worked on security issues, rather than economic development as Ngiam and Yeo did. Few doubted that PM Lee personally gave close attention to the Home Affairs portfolio in those years.

This did not mean that Tay was confined to being an eternal typist (as one might translate permanent secretary). Consider that, during the *Laju* Incident in 1974, it was Tay who oversaw the ground situation and shuttled back and forth to brief the Istana. It was, moreover, also Tay who was exposed to the intense spotlight and briefed the media every day during that crisis. Before this, as Director SID, Tay anchored the tradition that he would have direct access to the PM and not simply report to another civil servant.

In many ways, this carried over to his role at the MHA. During the first four years, there were no less than four different ministers. Ong Pang Boon was first appointed but stayed barely a month before being reassigned to Labour. His successor, Dr Wong Lin Ken, was to serve only for two years. The veteran Law Minister Eddie Barker is recorded to have then stepped in as minister for all of a month in 1972. Then Chua Sian Chin was appointed, beginning a tenure of nearly a decade.

There was a question of expertise. Leaving aside Ong and Barker (who were there only for one month each), consider the backgrounds of the ministers. Dr Wong, a former history lecturer, was briefly Ambassador to the USA before entering politics as an MP. After he stepped down as minister, he returned to teaching history at the university before leaving politics entirely in 1976. Chua was, in comparison, a veteran, having been a minister since 1968 (at the time only 35 and the youngest minister), but he had no previous experience in a security portfolio. As such, in his appointment as Permanent Secretary, Tay would seem to have been the one who provided continuity and security expertise to the new ministry. Tay would also serve to contribute within the broader security agenda, to link internal security issues and key external developments – none more so than in engaging America.

Engaging America

Tay remained involved in issues relating to external security and relations. During his Eisenhower Fellowship and the six months he spent in the States, he developed extensive contacts that would be of use as Singapore positioned itself to engage the USA. In the decades to come, the US relationship with Singapore would develop into a strategic partnership, with military hard-ware from the USA, as well as having training fa-cilities in the States. Some units of the Singapore Armed Forces would begin to exercise with their American counterparts in Asia, and arrangements were made for US military logistics to be carried out from Singapore and for aircraft carriers and other critical naval assets to dock in Singapore. The arrangements were termed as "places, not bases" but, in many respects, what had developed was only slightly short of an alliance, dubbed as a "strategic partnership". Economic ties grew over subsequent decades too. The small island became the largest location in the region for American investment and the sole ASEAN country to have a free trade agreement with the USA.

This was not the situation in the 1970s. Defence capa-bilities had been mustered since 1965 but the Singapore Armed Forces were still not at that time sufficient to be able to conduct exercises together with the superpower. There was less interest from America, which already had alliances with Thailand and the Philippines in Southeast Asia, and with Japan and South Korea in the North. With bases in the last three of these countries at that time, there was no clear reason for the superpower to need the tiny republic. On Singapore's side, PM Lee had at times voiced criticisms of the USA to the point where some media felt him to be neutral or even anti-American. This was buttressed by Singapore's decision to join the Non-Aligned Movement formally, and to open ties with the Soviet Union, starting from an agreement in mid-1968 with the Soviet embassy in Singapore permitted to begin from January 1969.

But another truth was emerging for relations between the USA and Singapore. While the Singapore leadership had misgivings about American involvement in Vietnam, there was great concern about the consequences if there was a hasty US withdrawal. PM Lee would often refer to the concerns about the region falling to Communism in what the Americans called the Domino Theory. He wished to keep the USA engaged in the region; he would hold this fundamental view, even as circumstances changed, right to the end of his life. While it did not wish to be an ally, Singapore would welcome the American presence and do what it could to support that. By 1966, Singapore-US relations had improved considerably. Meeting with the newly appointed US Ambassador to Singapore, Lee sought to signal the opening of a "new era in US-Singapore relations" and to invite Americans to invest and help the economic situation in Singapore. This effort to engage the USA continued to grow, not only in what was said but in practical ways.

During his first visit to the USA in 1967, PM Lee confidentially offered the use of facilities that the British would vacate from 1971. These would include aircraft maintenance and ship repair, together with highly trained staff to man the facilities. It was declined, but this offer showed that Singapore was prepared to welcome the USA – notwithstanding some of the statements by PM Lee and the country's Non-Aligned Movement membership. This was followed up in different ways and at different levels, including efforts at the MID led by Permanent Secretary Bogaars and Tay. One such meeting with US embassy officials was in January 1968, when Bogaars explored whether the USA might be willing to step into the bases that the British were leaving behind. Bogaars and Tay sounded out the opinions of American officials based in Singapore, discussing it quite informally as the pair travelled with two of the US officials in Tay's car to visit the SAF Training Institute (SAFTI) in Jurong, as declassified American memoranda record.

Engagements with the USA grew markedly; PM Lee even personally spent a five-week sabbatical in the United States in November to December 1968. From this period, Singapore became intimately involved in almost all aspects of the American war effort in Vietnam, short of sending troops. This included exporting virtually all of the oil from refineries in Singapore – including the Pulau Bukom Shell facility that the *Laju* Incident terrorists had targeted – to keep the American and South Vietnamese armies, air forces, and navies functioning.

The months in the USA on the Eisenhower Fellowship helped Tay build a wide network among the American intelligence agencies and beyond. He visited Langley, where the Central Intelligence Agency was located, and spent time with those thinking about Vietnam. The issue was no longer simply a foreign policy quagmire but an enormous schism in domestic politics and the society. The decision of President Lyndon Johnson not to seek a second term and refuse to contest the presidential elections of 1968 showed this. The protests against the Vietnam War had grown to embrace calls for a wider and more radical change in the USA. At the same time, the Cold War contest with the Soviet Union was far from over and, as Vietnam showed, it was far from clear that the USA would emerge the victor. In 1971, President Richard Nixon was beginning to pave the way for an agreement for the USA to withdraw from Vietnam, a move carried out in 1975. When it was done, the withdrawal was not without a degree of chaos and dismay for those who believed that US engagement would be critical to Southeast Asia remaining non-Communist.

Tay had watched the USA increase its commitments from 1965, the year that he was appointed to lead the Special Branch. He had also pondered the revelation of American atrocities in Mai Lai and then the shock of the Tet Offensive when the superpower seemed anything but super and all-powerful. Under Nixon, the tactics had been to increase bombing while pulling out men from the ground, and those policies must have stirred doubt in Tay's calculation of what might work. They had indeed proved largely ineffectual and, worse, heightened protests across America. If the USA were to pull out its troops, as Tay and others believed likely, there would be considerable implications not only in Vietnam itself and Indochina as their theatre of operations, but all of the region, including Singapore. What were the other arrangements that would be needed to help Thailand and the other Southeast Asian countries continue to be secure and stable, and to have a chance to prosper?

Tay was trying to triangulate another and perhaps bigger question during his time in the USA: the emerging American thinking about China. These were beginning to shift quite fundamentally. In the aftermath of WWII and as the Cold War started, the ideological schism had put Moscow and Peking (to use its name of that time) in one camp, while the USA extended recognition and assistance to the rump end of the Kuomintang, now retreated to and ensconced in the island of Taiwan off the Mainland. However, events in 1969 had shown that China was no longer a junior partner to the Soviet Union and indeed, there was evidence of conflict between the two Communist states. Given this, there were rumblings that the USA might change its stance on China in order to further distance it from the Soviet Union, which was viewed as America's main threat and competitor.

The Singaporean perspective differed. In Southeast Asia's Cold War, China had been more directly involved and active than the Soviet Union. Many of the Communist elements and parties in Southeast Asia had direct links and interactions with China during the 1960s, even if they were indigenous movements and not offshoots of the Chinese Communist Party. While these links seemed to have receded by 1971, China's support for Communist movements in Southeast Asia and for North Vietnam had not officially ended. As such, any abrupt shift in US policy to China could impact Southeast Asia, especially if this occurred in tandem with a full American withdrawal and disengagement from the region. Tay was mindful of these possible negative linkages, and he was uncertain if the Americans were equally mindful. Great powers, he knew from his experience with the UK, had their own calculus. Facing domestic upheavals over Vietnam as well as seeking advantage against Moscow, the US administration would view the situation in its own way. As a visitor, Tay could try to inveigh against the worst by sharing perspectives of the wider impacts on Southeast Asia and America's standing. But it was equally necessary and, perhaps, more useful to listen and get a sense of the pulse in the USA on these issues.

It is not clear how much foresight he gained about the American opening of ties with China. These started in 1971 under President Nixon and moved quickly. In the first public sign of warming relations between Washington and Beijing, China's ping-pong team invited members of the American team to China in April. Soon after, in July 1971, US Secretary of State Henry Kissinger made a then secret trip to China. Shortly thereafter, the US administration shifted its position at the UN, allowing the People's Republic of China to be recognised, instead of Republic of China on Taiwan – a policy held in place since 1945 – and to take up its seat in the Security Council. It was also announced in 1971 that President Nixon would personally travel to China, which he did the following year.

To get that sense of America, Tay spent time not only in government offices of DC but roamed more broadly, to other states and cities, visiting think tanks and campuses and even farms that seemed so far removed from the world he knew. Given the fellowship was for six months and that flights were less common at the time, the Eisenhower Fellowships leased a car for Tay to drive across much of the country. This allowed him to experience the size and diversity of the different states and locales. He enjoyed some the great sights, especially when Cecelia joined him for some months. He returned not only with strong and positive memories of the country but also an extensive collection of books about the USA and American views of the world. The trip reinforced his view that what the USA did (or did not do) would matter more to the region and Singapore than any other country.

It convicted him that the USA was a complex and multi-faceted polity, capable of quite sudden changes internally and in its policies abroad. Singapore would need to work hard to try to understand America. At the same time, there would be the need to develop Singapore's own reading of China and its policies and actions across the region and in Singapore. This would be critical to engage the USA and its policy-makers. The exchange between the USA and Singapore on these issues had its beginnings in this period with the Nixon administration, well before the security relationship grew in terms of military hardware and joint training. In the years that were to follow, Singapore, and especially PM Lee, would come to develop closer ties with the USA, valued not simply for Singapore in itself but in its views of larger events concerning the region and, especially, China.

In his report from the Eisenhower Fellowship, Tay was to write: "The U.S. is withdrawing its military presence in the Asia-Pacific region and there are large uncertainties abroad about when and where this retrenchment will stop. U.S. declarations that security commitments will be honored inspire confidence only when it is clear what capacity there is to honor them. The American forces on the ground have always been regarded as an earnest of intent and it was assumed that the U.S. would act quickly to protect its own ground forces in any event of threat. It was also assumed that domestic opinion (in the U.S.) would support such a response. These two assumptions on which the confidence of allies rested are no longer tenable as the major underpinning for national security planning."

There were decision-makers in that era who built up the foundations for the new country's engagement with the USA and the rest of the world. The then Foreign Minister, S Rajaratnam, stated that "foreign policy was shaped more objectively by myself, the Prime Minister [Lee Kuan Yew], and Dr Goh [Keng Swee] where there were economic implications...." Clearly, Singapore's engagements with the world were largely dependant on a small circle. The early part of the statement – setting out the sequence and balance between these three pioneer generation ministers – might however be questioned. There is no doubt that as the Foreign Minister, Rajaratnam was a trusted stalwart and spokesman and an intellect to be reckoned with. But in its early years, the Ministry of Foreign Affairs was a smaller ministry and, beyond protocol, diplomatic statecraft and crafting statements, its capacity for providing analysis was more limited. By this time, PM Lee was growing not only as the leader within the country but in his international standing in reading the regional situation and serving as interlocutor with the Americans. As for Dr Goh, his role and that of the MID and its agencies under him should not be narrowly confined and, even after he left MID, Dr Goh's influence was not limited to economic issues. Perhaps the effort of these three political leaders in shaping Singapore's foreign policy and engagement with the world is best seen as a joint effort, led by the PM. Contributing to this was the work of senior officials, with Tay amongst them.

He continued to report to PM Lee during the years after he left the SID and was focused on the MHA portfolio. The record of these exchanges is not in the public domain but what little that is available does indicate that the wider remit continued. One recorded example, relating to the Commonwealth Heads of Government Meeting, may assist. Tay had been with PM Lee at CHOGM in past years and he continued to advise for the meeting held in Ottawa in early August 1973. At that conference, Lee had debated Australia's then new Labour Prime Minister, Gough Whitlam, on his policies and statements, and not without some heat. Tay followed up upon returning to Singapore by meeting the then Australian High Commissioner, Nicholas Parkinson. The note that Parkinson sent back to his government (since declassified) is worth some consideration, not only in terms of Singapore's relations with Australia at that juncture, but also in understanding Tay's scope of work after moving to the Ministry of Home Affairs.

In engaging the Australians, Tay was frank and extensive, even more forthright than his PM had been in the formal setting of CHOGM at Ottawa. He expressed that the government and PM Lee were both "puzzled" and "troubled" by the new directions in foreign policy that the Australian government was taking vis-à-vis their relations with the USA and the UK. Whitlam had publicly criticised President Richard Nixon and Prime Minister Edward Heath and, Tay felt, seemed to be intent on "weakening Australia's links with the United States and Britain". Tay added more criticism about the Whitlam government's "hasty cancellation of defence aid and political and moral support to the non-Communist Indochina states"; its "rapid recognition" of both the People's Republic of China and the Democratic Republic of Vietnam (North Vietnam); its "attempts to undermine the United States position in Thailand"; and its backing for "neutralist type statements in regard to the Indian Ocean" and "the Malaysian concepts of neutralisation of the South East Asian region". He was especially critical of Whitlam's plans to withdraw Australian ground forces from Singapore and conveyed his view that the result would be the "destruction of the credibility of Australia as a Five Power partner" and make "nonsense" of these arrangements that the countries had agreed on after the withdrawal of British bases. Australia, Tay went on, had to understand that Singapore "had for a very long time looked upon Australia (and through Australia to the United States and to Britain) as an element in [its] ultimate security". As a senior civil servant and one with experience on security issues, the message Tay conveyed was relayed to Canberra.

Another example of the ways Tay worked can be seen in the process of "Track II" diplomacy. In those years especially, and even into today, there was a rich and often influential involvement of experts and professors with officials and ex-officials and politicians. This supplemented what were often stilted formal meetings between the leaders and ministers with a buzz of exchanges and dialogues that were more practical and candid than purely academic discourse. In this period, such exchanges might be centred around the Institute of Southeast Asian Studies headed by the energetic and well-connected Kernial Sandhu, whom Tay knew.

One example of such interactions can be seen in the reports of the dialogues in that time. For instance, from 31 May to 3 June 1974, the international conference on Southeast Asian Security was organised. The participants included incumbent office-holders like Tan Sri Ghazali Shafie, the Malaysian Minister of Home Affairs, and the US Commander-in-chief of the Pacific, Admiral Noel Gayler, as well as former office-holders like the redoubtable Thanat Koman of Thailand, who had been Foreign Minister and continued to advise the Thai PM. Among the participants were three Singaporeans who were then academics but would later play wider roles in Singapore: Dr Lau Teik Soon of the Political Science Department of the then University of Singapore who would be a PAP MP for decades; Professor Chan Heng Chee, also then at the university's Political Science Department, later Singapore's Ambassador to the UN and for a long period in the USA; and Professor Tommy Koh, then the dean of the Faculty of Law and later Ambassador for Singapore to the UN, USA and at-large. As the then Permanent Secretary for Home Affairs, Tay joined in this meeting, as he would others when needed and time allowed. He saw value in the exchange of ideas, and the networks and informality created in the process.

Internal Security and Detentions

Tay's continuing voice and role regarding external security was on top of the additional and new responsibilities he had as the new Permanent Secretary of a new ministry with a focus on the nation's internal security. Even prior to this, as Director of Security and Intelligence in the MID years, Tay had known and kept a watch on the police in general and specifically on the use of preventive detention, a key tool for the internal security issues that were part of his mandate; there were complex interplays between external and internal dimensions of security, especially when operations were carried out on the political opposition and those thought to support Communism.

In 1966, when Tay was still the Director for Security and Intelligence, the government moved against members of the

Barisan Sosialis who had newly abandoned Parliament and detained them without trial. How did he think and act in this situation?

In the 1960s, although the Emergency had been officially ended, there continued to be considerable turbulence whether from leftists or racial and ethnic conflict. To Tay and his colleagues, preventive detention was an established practice and a necessary tool to be used, if and when a situation arose that required such action.

In the decades since, while the powers remain in effect, controversy has grown. From the 1970s, there may be more who question preventive detention in principle, as an exception to the general requirements to provide evidence and prove the allegations in a court of law. There are also criticisms about the length and conditions of detention. Notwithstanding a review of detentions every two years, there have been individuals who have remained in detention for decades. Controversies over the treatment of detainees have also been raised, as many were held in solitary confinement for long periods. These came to public attention in the 1970s when some detainees went on a hunger strike. Questions about the use of preventive detention only increased as the Emergency and other threats from the early decades of independence receded. On the other hand, there is a recognition of new threats – such as violence carried out by terrorist networks and radicalised individuals. These have led to an increased acceptance that such powers remain necessary, and detentions have generally been accepted by the public.

In the 1960s too, there were both reasons to accept the use of the powers of detention in the face of a widespread and often subterranean Communist United Front, and concern that, unless used scrupulously, it could stifle political opponents and critics. The Lim Yew Hock government had lost support because of the massive security crackdowns that it had signed off on. There was considerable controversy that still lingered about the 1963 Operation Coldstore when the Special Branch detained a large number of opposition party members and MPs, as well as left-wing unionists.

Against this background, the ISD operation of October 1966, when Tay was in charge of security and intelligence, bears some consideration. Some 23 members of the Barisan Sosialis were detained under the Internal Security Act.

After the 1963 Operation Coldstore, the party's new leader was Dr Lee Siew Choh, and he led the remaining MPs to leave Parliament to take up an "extra-parliamentary struggle" in the streets. By doing so, the Barisan MPs effectively abandoned Parliament. On 15 April 1966, two of the MPs – Chia Thye Poh and Koo Young – were arrested on the charge of sedition on the basis that an article they had authored alleged that the government was plotting to murder Lim Chin Siong while he was being held in preventive detention. In that same month, while speaking at a political party meeting in Malaysia, Chia called for an armed struggle to be taken up, drawing a parallel to events unfolding in Vietnam. Then, back in Singapore, Chia was part of a demonstration on 3 July to protest the Vietnam War, for which he was arrested with 19 others and charged with unlawful assembly. Found guilty, he chose to go to jail until the Barisan paid the fine for his release on 24 October. This came soon after the Barisan announced the resignation of all eight of its Members of Parliament.

Upon the en bloc resignation, Chia was quoted by *The Straits Times* as saying, "We cannot remain in Parliament because parliamentary democracy is dead. You can say we are now taking our struggle to the streets. We are going to strengthen our extra-parliamentary struggle. It takes various forms – street demonstrations, protest meetings, strikes." Chia was detained just days after.

The operations carried out at the Barisan office took place as he and others were planning a demonstration against the Vietnam War that was to coincide with the visit of then US President Lyndon Johnson to Malaysia. The Singapore government explained, at the time, that the Barisan's attempt to arouse a mass struggle outside of Parliament was prejudicial to the stability of Singapore.

This summary of events preceding the detention sets a

broader context. The words used by Chia and Dr Lee Siew Choh characterised the Barisan Sosialis not as a parliamentary party that would contest the next elections. Rather, they were setting out to instigate demonstrations, protests and strikes. This would be in tandem with various other organisations such as worker's unions and groups on the Left. The grievances, moreover, were not only national but regional, using the Vietnam War as a rallying cry, with the aim of triggering a struggle not just in Singapore but also in Malaysia.

Taking Chia and the Barisan Sosialis at their own words, an objective threat assessment of their actions and intentions would have tripped a number of critical concerns of that era. The emerging scenario was that the Barisan would seek to be the fulcrum for the continuing Communist networks, who were already shifting from guerrilla warfare to political and street action, as protests against the Vietnam War were gaining traction in the USA and the West. The promise of the Barisan taking up "extra-parliamentary" efforts would have considerably alarmed the security analysts, especially as this would seek to connect internal unrest with wider and regional issues. In the calculus of that tense Cold War era and its concerns, what the Barisan was pushing for presented a real risk, and one that needed to be addressed early on.

The approach of the 1966 detentions was more selective and surgical, as compared to the larger scale and broader sweep used in Operation Coldstore. In part, this was because the earlier operation had already detained many who were involved in these activities and networks. But also, with greater insight and intelligence networks, the government authorities were better able to parse the united front tactics and coalitions of different actors to assess the security threats. On the facts on the public record of that time, the factor that must have been in the calculus for Tay and others involved in the making of the decision in 1966 was security – not only the national security concerns but also a situation with critical external connections.

It was not a question of politics between rival parties. By the time of the 1966 detentions, the Barisan Sosialis was a spent force in conventional electoral politics and was not to last. Instead of regaining strength with the planned extra-parliamentary struggle, the party lost ground and seemed increasingly irrelevant. Signs of internal fracture emerged, with its leader Dr Lee Siew Choh facing criticism from Lim Chin Siong, still in detention. The decision of the Barisan to boycott the upcoming general elections was its death knell, but it was likely that, even if it had contested, it would not have revived its fortunes. Going into the 1970s, and despite the pull-out of British forces, the economy was improving with more jobs and the security situation was stabilising. Support for the PAP government grew in this period.

When the detentions were announced, there were no significant protests against the action (in contrast, the 1963 Operation Coldstore triggered protests and conflict at City Hall even some two months after the detentions). Questions about the 1966 detentions arose only years later, and were focused on an individual, the ex-Barisan MP, Chia Thye Poh.

Unlike other detainees, Chia refused to comply when the authorities sought to persuade him to sign a statement renouncing the use of violent methods to overthrow the government in order to secure his release. He was to explain in a 1989 interview that, "To renounce violence is to imply you advocated violence before. If I had signed that statement I would not have lived in peace." Indeed, throughout his detention, Chia declined to appear before the ISA advisory board to contest his detention, which was subject to review every two years. Consequently, Chia was to become one of the longest-serving detainees in the world, with many human rights campaigners rallying to his cause towards the end of the Cold War and afterwards.

The treatment of Lim Chin Siong was quite different. While Lim had been detained earlier, in the 1963 Operation Coldstore, critical changes in his situation occurred during Tay's tenure. By the late 1960s, relations between Lim and his fellow detainees had broken down. Lim had expressed a loss of faith in Communism and, after meeting PM Lee in July 1969, announced he would give up politics and leave for London to do further studies. Lim accordingly resigned from all posts he held in the Barisan, for which his former comrades heavily critcised him. In contrast, the evaluation of the ISD was that Lim was under severe mental strain and the government agencies were to assist him not only to move to London, but to ensure that he received medical attention – at government expense.

Another point of criticism was about the conditions of detention. This notwithstanding, the International Red Cross was allowed access to ensure that the conditions met basic international standards and that the facilities were the same as those used during British times. Those taken in were held in solitary confinement rather than being held in a group. These, and other measures, were intended to isolate each detainee and to add psychological pressure when they were questioned. These practices, like the detention facilities, were carried over from the British colonial period and were widely regarded in that era as more or less similar to those practised by the security agencies elsewhere and as not being especially cruel or controversial. Detainees who gave their undertakings were released. Some chose to leave Singapore and restart their lives elsewhere. A number have, after decades, issued their memoirs of these times, told from their perspectives.

In the 1970s, when he served as Permanent Secretary of the Ministry of Home Affairs, Tay was not directly in charge of the ISD. But, while having due regard for the views of the staff then in charge, he would have had oversight. There were no new large-scale internal security detentions in this period. However, there was controversy when detention laws were used against the media.

In 1971, *The Eastern Sun* newspaper was shut down. This was followed by actions against *The Singapore Herald*, another English-language daily run by former journalists from Reuters and *The Straits Times*. The editor of *The Herald* accused the government of "premeditated murder" of the newspaper which, he claimed, had done "nothing at all" to warrant the government actions. A third action against the media, also taken in 1971, was when the top four executives of the Chinese-language *Nanyang Siang Pau* were detained under the Internal Security Act. These three operations against the media drew considerable attention. While the Singapore government felt vindicated in establishing stability by these actions, critics saw the same acts as the start of oppressive censorship and control for political ends. Tay was in the USA for the Eisenhower Fellowship in this period.

In his absence, S R Nathan was appointed to take charge as Acting Permanent Secretary of MHA, and presumptively would have signed off on these operations, based on the evaluation of the then ISD Director. It is neither clear nor perhaps helpful to enter into conjecture if Tay might or might not have agreed.

During his tenure, there were issues relating to whether to release the detainees taken in and, if so, when and on what conditions. It was already the established practice to question the detainees and request them to sign off on statements that detailed their involvement as well as undertake to cease the activities for which they had been detained. Short of a court trial, this was seen as a way to clearly show the detentions were substantiated and admitted.

But a number of detainees had declined to sign off on such statements, and the length of their detention and treatment while detained were becoming more controversial. There was a hunger strike that arose in 1970-71 when the authorities tried to force the detainees to work. They maintained that as they were political detainees – and not criminal inmates – this was not allowable. In response, the authorities at the facilities force- fed the detainees, which some regarded as a breach of their rights. A number of the detainees at the Moon Crescent facility lodged complaints to the courts. In this period, Amnesty International raised complaints about the conditions of detention, alleging that medical care was inadequate. Some in the international community questioned the need for laws of preventive detention to continue altogether.

While these controversies arose from that time, the critics were largely from the West and most often from specialised human rights non-governmental organisations. In those years, the US government and those of Western allies might have voiced some criticism but mostly they gave priority to Cold War preoccupations – so long as there were no blatant and wide-spread abuses. Nor were there many critics or any mass protests within Singapore itself. It was really only from the 1990s that international questioning about Singapore grew, after the Berlin Wall fell and the Cold War ended.

In the period when Tay was Permanent Secretary, he was to leave these matters largely to the officers directly in charge, and they followed the procedures laid down previously by the British; the thinking was not to argue with what had been successful. The view of the political leaders was summed up by PM Lee, who would always pay close and personal attention to matters of security, in his book, *From Third World to First*: "We had to be as resolute (as the Communists) and unyielding in this contest of wills."

A Wider Home Team Agenda

The dangers from Communism were receding, together with its tactics of agitation among workers and the masses. Overall, politics in Singapore was cooling down, especially after the elections of 1968 when, following a boycott by the opposition, the PAP government had won all seats to usher in an absolute monopoly in Parliament that would last until 1981. Singapore was stabilising, compared to the situation around independence. Yet, risks of conflict remained, especially relating to race and religion, long-standing fault lines.

Beyond the question of detentions, there was much else to be done at Home Affairs and the timing was right from the 1970s. A broader agenda was gathering momentum – to discipline the diverse and even motley population into a real citizenry: nation-building. The brilliance of Lee Kuan Yew and the pioneer generation politicians was to understand that to maintain the political consensus and their support, they needed to build a cohesive society that could move forward into the future, and that it had to be a future that could best and perhaps only be articulated and implemented with them as government. From experience, PM Lee had stepped away from liberal notions of the use of law to emphasise stability and order, and this was reinforced in the 1970s.

The mandate of the MHA broadened to new concerns that were different in nature, more public-facing. One example of this was the war against drugs and efforts to stop gangs and trafficking circuits. Another involved the government's efforts against the "yellow culture" that some associated with hippies and unrest from the West. It was in this period that Singapore became a "fine" city, as the well-known joke went. There was much for the Home Affairs Ministry to do as part of this, and much to be done within the ministry during the time Tay was Permanent Secretary from 1971 to 1975.

To make Singaporeans over, the Police Force too had to be transformed. Fines could only do so much. The Force needed to be better able to maintain order and prevent problems. Much of this work was internal to the MHA and agencies under its supervision and not well-known to the public. But much as a machine is fine-tuned or overhauled, this was visible to insiders, things very much for a permanent secretary to take care of (even if it would be the minister to lead on the public announcements and engagement). Tay respected the professionals in the Force, just as he had the soldiers in the Armed Forces at MID. Many of the changes within the Force would be driven by the policemen themselves, and as Permanent Secretary, while supervising the Police Commissioner, he would always seek the collaboration of the officers to bring about those changes.

Tee Tua Ba told me that, when he was a junior officer around 1971, he was called to see Tay together with Tan Teck Khim, the Police Commissioner. This related to a suggestion to have front-line supervisors take charge of small groups of officers on the ground in the command divisions, so as to mentor and review them. In that small and private meeting, the Police Commissioner initially hesitated to endorse the idea and make changes but, Tee recalls, Tay was supportive of the idea.

As Permanent Secretary, Tay quickly acquired an in-depth

understanding of police management and operations and identified the problem areas. In late 1970, he launched a process to modernise the Force. Some of the changes included creating project teams to study various aspects of the Force and from this emerged innovations such as a Team Policing concept for patrols. He also would start a review of the terms and conditions of service. While this was called the Lee Soo Ann Committee after the respected university professor whom Tay had personally asked to chair it, Tay was strongly behind its recommendations.

At a Police Senior Officers' Seminar in 1971, Tay shared a certain intellectual framework to the process of change: "The Police Force, like any other institution in our society and indeed like society itself, is subject to continuity and change. This is a sort of dialectical process that continues if institutions are to remain relevant to their functions and roles in society. At one period of time, it may well be that consolidation or continuity will become the more appropriate process for a particular organisation. At other times… change would in fact become the appropriate process…".

In this work, Tay would never have minded that the real changes and initiatives he was undertaking were not publicly visible or even known outside of the circle of those who needed to know. In some ways, he was prepared for these tasks at Home Affairs since he had been a student. His Masters thesis had been an examination of the history of the Police Force during the British administration. It had, moreover, been a critical examination of whether it was fit for purpose. One of the issues was that the police needed to better reflect the make-up of the wider society so as to give the police a better chance of being accepted by the community itself, rather than being seen as an outside force designed only to punish at the behest of a distant government. This approach was to guide the development of the MHA following the early years of Singapore's independence.

While Tay was himself not Chinese-educated, he worked to recruit more people with such backgrounds, just as he had at the Special Branch and then at the ISD and SID. In this way, he reckoned the police would be better positioned to deal with the largely Chinese gangs and drug syndicates. Starting from the 1970s, Singapore stepped up efforts to deal with Chinese secret societies and syndicates. Their illegal activities in this period had grown to include unlicensed money lending and drug trafficking. The Criminal Investigation Department of the Police Force started the Secret Society Branch to monitor and stop the gangs. The effort largely depended on using the limits of the laws – primarily the Criminal Law Temporary Provisions Act (CLTPA). This law, in Section 55, gave powers of preventive detention, much as the Internal Security Act was used for political detention and suspected terrorists. Used on suspected gangsters, the tool was so critical to the police officers who were charged with the difficult challenge of taking on the gangs that some even dubbed them the Section 55 Unit.

It did not matter if some of these new rules might seem strange to the average citizen. One such rule that emerged in this period concerned the nunchaku, a martial arts weapon made up of two hard, wooden rods linked together by a chain, and made popular by Bruce Lee's movies. From 1972, it was deemed as an offensive weapon and was banned in Singapore, believed to be part of the crackdown of secret society members.

A similar approach was taken in the very public effort to combat "yellow culture". Stemming from the West and the social movements of 1968, this was regarded with suspicion by the politicians and conservative elements in Singapore. The most publicised rule related to men sporting long hair. The Singapore government began to strongly "discourage" male Singaporeans with long hair in 1970, and there were reports that groups of long-haired men were rounded up and questioned by the police. Dr Goh Keng Swee, the then Defence Minister, famously called rock and roll music a "menace" in 1973, citing its corrupting influences on the "mindless young", and a number of popular songs of the era were banned from the airwaves as they were seen to glorify drug use. Tay did not necessarily share these views. He was not a prude. But he knew social and cultural trends could create conditions of instability and contestation and, from his travels in the USA, could see first-hand what the era was unleashing, especially in relation to the Vietnam War.

Tay realised that more educated, experienced and trained manpower was critically needed in the ranks of the Force. While tough actions were needed against the gangs and hardened criminals, there had to be another array of approaches and tools for the police and security agencies. There was a growing ambit of rules and fines emerging from the government to try to instil discipline and order in the wider society. These would be resented and resisted, he reckoned, if they proved stultifying to too many or were administered harshly. Hence, he gave emphasis to reforming ways to recruit, recognise and reward officers and modernise the Force. As the Singapore government made and imposed more rules, there was a concomitant need to administer the rules fairly and realistically.

New focus was given to public education in combatting drugs. In October 1971, a new Central Narcotics Bureau was announced and then set up within the Home Affairs Ministry. While announced by the then-Minister Dr Wong Lin Ken, Tay is credited for coining its name together with the first director, John Hannam, whom he knew and picked for the appointment. The Central Narcotics Bureau (CNB) brought the different agencies with responsibilities for drug offences under one agency, and the CNB was better able to link up with similar national agencies in other countries as well as with international bodies fighting the cross-border movement of drugs. Beyond enforcement, plans were put in place to build a capacity to educate the public about the dangers of drug abuse. In 1973, the government introduced the Misuse of Drugs Act (MDA) to deal with drug traffickers, pushers and addicts. The enactment of the MDA was intended firstly to consolidate the provisions of the Dangerous Drugs Ordinance 1951 and Drugs (Prevention of Misuse) Act 1969 (DPMA), and secondly to more effectively deal with the worsening drug situation. Laws gave the police the power to detain drug users and traffickers without trial.

In this period, the Ministry of Home Affairs also reviewed laws that related to the treatment of criminals. In 1974, a 10-man Prisons Reorganisation Committee recommended a tougher line against criminals, repeat offenders and illegal immigrants. These and the segregation of hard core prisoners were among the recommendations accepted by the government. The committee, headed by Tay personally, also proposed that there would be allowance in some cases to permit community service in lieu of imprisonment for certain offences. Prison and remand facilities were expanded.

Improvements to the Police Force took place in 1972 after recommendations were made by a committee chaired again by Lee Soo Ann. Many officers were leaving, with com-plaints of low pay and poor working conditions. To help plug the gaps, full-time police national service was introduced from 1975 to provide additional manpower to guard important installations as well as to support the work of regular officers.

But, as Permanent Secretary, Tay sought a more permanent solution, and the report played a key role to recommend a pay revision and changes to the entry qualification of new recruits to the Force.

An overall assessment of his work was offered in the Police Force newsletter years later. This was that: "Officers both in the Force and in the Internal Security Department will remember Mr Tay as an administrator who could immediately reduce a complex problem to its bare essentials and evolve a strategy both simple and decisive to resolve the problem... He had an instinctive feel of the ground and his assessments of security situations was invariably proved by events to be correct."

Perm Sec

Beyond his focus on policing and security, Tay's role as a perm sec (as the role is truncated in civil-service talk, or "PS") was beginning to involve him in wider responsibilities – as was the case with other senior civil servants. As the 1970s began, the Singapore government had begun to look more closely at increasing efficiencies and its own revenues, in tandem with the start of a boom across almost all sectors and full employment. This led the government to allow and even encourage the formation of state-owned enterprises. Unlike most of the socialist efforts, however, those in Singapore were meant to be profitable and provide competitive services. The Ministry of Home Affairs too looked more closely at how this overall objective could be met within the scope of its work and agencies. It was at this juncture that Tay paved the way for at least two initiatives that would last. One was for the prison to develop services to meet the growing commercial demand in areas such as laundry, food, and business services like printing, and provide skills training to inmates. This would later grow into the Singapore Corporation of Rehabilitative Services (SCORE), the predecessor to the ongoing Yellow Ribbon enterprise.

The other was to spin off the provision of commercial security, much in demand for banks, goldsmiths and other businesses and larger facilities. There were three steps that Tay was quite pleased about when launching the statutory board in 1972. First, the new company would recruit largely from among many retired policemen since the retirement age for most was as low as 45, depending on their rank, and this could give those who retired with good records a second career. Secondly, in providing protective services, the guards from the Commercial and Industrial Security Company would have a monopoly to use firearms, and this was good for reducing the availability of such weapons in society as well as providing a great advantage over other companies not affiliated with the government. Lastly, and perhaps flippantly, he quite liked its acronym – CISCO. It echoed with the image of the gunslinging from the American cowboy West, the Cisco Kid, and was coincidentally a funky soul tune, recorded by War and released in 1972, that was popular enough in clubs of that time. Certainly, it was the thing that stuck in my mind when my father told me about this back when I was 12 or so.

But there was more to his involvement than the name. Tay

served as the Chairman of the CISCO Board and, as Permanent Secretary of the parent ministry, would have taken a strong hand in establishing its business in those early years. CISCO would be a money-spinner, and by late 1971, Tay announced plans for a new 10-storey HQ for its expansion.

As the statutory boards and state-owned enterprises grew, so did the role of the permanent secretaries in chairing and serving as directors. Some senior civil servants were appointed to many boards, especially those from the economic agencies. This was justified by the idea that this network of appointments ensured that these offshoots were kept within the control of their parent ministries and aligned to the broader policy goals. Tay did not accept so many appointments. But two he did accept and enjoy were both related to his previous work at the Harbour Board – for the Port of Singapore Authority (PSA) and the national shipping line, Neptune Orient Lines (NOL). Both appealed to Tay not only because of his past work but also in how they related to the security of Singapore; while commercial, the flow of trade into and out from Singapore was of wider security and strategic importance, and he always championed the need to keep a government hand on the ports and shipping. The thinking was that it might prove essential if ever a foreign power tried to blockade Singapore; this type of just-in-case scenario was part of the way Tay thought.

On both of these boards, he was one among the early supporters of the benefits of containerization, and made it a habit to visit ports during his work trips abroad, including those in Japan and the USA. He understood how critical it was that Singapore got ahead on the curve on that key change in the shipping industry. When it started, NOL had a poor reputation and lacked scale, and containerization was at that time a bold call to move it forward. Tay assisted NOL with the Far East Freight Conference (FEFC), at that time a powerful cartel controlled mainly by private and European carriers. The FEFC had the power to apportion loading rights to members and did so on a historical basis, which severely disadvantaged NOL and other national carriers that were newer and trying to grow. Tay, together with Eric Khoo who was NOL Executive Director, represented the Singapore shipping company at the London conference of FEFC. The upshot of the meeting was that NOL decided to walk away from the FEFC and the constraints imposed, to deal directly with local shippers. By the end of the 1970s, NOL had become something of a "brand name". Tay was on the NOL board when a young civil servant was recruited into the company and, in 1973, was selected to be its CEO – Goh Chok Tong. He supported the selection, although it was just four years after the 32-year-old Goh had joined the company. Tay was to keep in touch with Eric Khoo, who had lost out on the top job at NOL but moved on to join the PIL shipping line – also Singaporean but privately owned.

Besides PSA, NOL and CISCO, Tay was a director at National Iron & Steel, United Metal Plant Corporation, and Mitsubishi Shipyard. When he was a young civil servant, there had been little need for such engagements and there were in fact admonitions and warnings against relationships. Corruption was targeted by the PAP government, contrasting itself to the Lim Yew Hock administration, and civil servants were not only to avoid corruption but to be cautious and distant in any engagement with commercial entities. Although Tay's portfolio never involved economic policy-making, he grew to have an understanding and appreciation of the private sector; not just the government-linked companies and multinationals but also the indigenous Singaporean companies. Many of them did business in nearby countries and what they knew and did on a practical basis was useful input to Tay's reading of the region. His networks broadened.

A number of key working relationships and networks developed through the Pyramid Club. When the PAP first came to power, the main effort was to make a clear demarcation to keep politicians and civil servants separate from the business community and minimise the temptations of corruption. But the club, started by Dr Goh Keng Swee, was begun as an exception to that rule. It was necessary to foster exchange and informal networking among an elite. Not all politicians were invited to join, not even most Members of Parliament. Civil servants too were invited selectively, the private sector, in those days, even more so. Tay had been inducted early after his appointment into the Special Branch and MID. He would occasionally meet there informally. The caretaker would do a decent English-style breakfast and there could be discussions that were private, whether by the poolside or in one of the rooms of the large but less-than-pristine black-and-white bungalow that served as the clubhouse. Occasionally, in those days, PM Lee himself would come to swim. But Tay knew well enough to leave him alone as he did laps, unless it was the PM who summoned him over.

More often it would be a place to catch up with some of the other senior civil servants, exchanging perspectives and keeping others informed, given the broad compass of security. There were times when he would go with the children for a swim during the week, when there was no time to get to the beach.

Tay would often engage his civil service colleagues personally and outside the office. This was especially with those counterparts in ministries that were outside the usual ambit of security. One of these was Sim Kee Boon, whom he had met while serving in Commerce and Industry and got on with. They kept in touch as both progressed, even if Sim was deployed in infrastructure and economic ministries, quite different from Tay's remit. They both liked their food and would often go to a favourite coffee shop or else to try some new restaurant. Their families would also meet. Sim's son, Peter, recalls Tay coming over one afternoon and then going off with his father for a swim at the Chinese Swimming Club, with him in tow. There were evenings after work when the two senior civil servants would find time to play badminton.

Among the pioneer civil servants, there was every reason to maintain good ties, both professional and personal, and it was not unpleasant to do so. It was often more than networking. Amicable and long-term relationships resulted.

While the retirement age was only 55 in that era, many

of the pioneer cohort of senior civil servants would go on to serve long afterwards in different capacities. Some of these pioneers would continue service by chairing and guiding the development of key and new companies, as did Sim Kee Boon at Keppel. A few ventured into politics, like Howe Yoon Chong. S R Nathan, whom Tay had worked so closely with for so many years, would go on to be appointed to Singapore Press Holdings, which published the main newspapers, then serve as ambassador to key posts in Malaysia and the USA, before returning to start up a government think tank that focused on security, and then finally to stand for election as President of the Republic.

Others pioneer civil servants did not do so well or live as long. These included those who served in the MID in those early years with Tay. One was a former principal secretary to PM Lee, Pang Tee Pow, who was promoted to be the Permanent Secretary of Defence when the MID was split. He sadly succumbed to lung cancer in 1977. George Bogaars, the MID Permanent Secretary, continued on afterwards at the Ministry of Finance and the Ministry of Foreign Affairs. In mid-1975, Bogaars would step down from that post and be replaced as the overall Head of Civil Service by Howe Yoon Chong. When Bogaars reached retirement age, he was given the reins of a major company, Keppel Shipyards. But in 1980, he suffered a heart attack, the first of more attacks and strokes that, by 1985, incapacitated him.

For Tay, there had been just ten years from the time he left the port to lead the Special Branch in 1965 to the *Laju* Incident in 1974. The challenges he faced in this period were relentless. Few things, if any, were ever easy and nothing was without hardship and cost. The direction had mostly run straight, and he was making substantial contributions to the country and clear progress and recognition in the career he had chosen. The handling of the *Laju* Incident confirmed this and, in some eyes, had stepped up a level in recognition.

Soon after, however, Tay's fortunes would suffer a sharp turn and steep descent.

Chapter 8

ENDINGS

TAY STOOD at 5 foot 10 inches, as it was measured in those years. He was tall for his generation. He played sports intensively and looked fit, athletic, even when dressed for work in a suit and tie. More than a few contemporaries described Tay as looking very much the part of a spy chief. He was full of life, and lived it fully.

A Sudden and Inevitable Illness

But these appearances disguised much; he was not medically healthy. Even in his early 30s, his blood pressure was high. He was predisposed to hypertension, the doctors said, and, in those years, medicines to suppress its ill effects were not available. It did not help that his pace of work was intense and the hours long. The insecurities for the country were real and fully in his focus. They became very concrete and immediate when the SID operational personnel would be put into difficult and often tense situations. His travels for SID work were challenging and stressful. He had a bout of headaches of such intensity that the doctors conducted a battery of tests and kept him in hospital for an extended period for observation. It was said to be some kind of unspecified virus, and he was discharged and quickly returned to work. Indeed, even during the hospital stay, files from the office had been sent to him for decision. Routine work in this period was heavy and often urgent. So much of it, moreover, was wrapped in secrecy and the inherent tensions of knowing who to trust with how much knowledge, and what could be said and what should not: he had to make these decisions.

There were additional and specific incidents. In 1972, an Olympic Airways flight 472 coming from Sydney was thought to be hijacked. Based on a warning from the Australian Civil Aviation Authority, Singapore's police and Special Operations Unit were scrambled to be in place to surround the aircraft on the tarmac. It turned out to be a false alarm as the crew had accidentally activated the hijack alarm. But before that was revealed, the security agencies in Singapore had been mobilised in a situation that was live and at the highest level of alert. Tay had been central to the rapid response.

Another event was the killing of a senior Malaysian police officer in June 1974. Inspector General Abdul Rahman Hashim was assassinated in a resurging wave of violent attacks by the Communist Party of Malaya, and this was very real and proximate to Tay. There were reports and rumours that attempts would also be made in Singapore, targeting either Tay or the Police Commissioner at that time, Tan Teck Khim. In between these smaller incidents, there had been the *Laju* Incident. It was not a coincidence that, just short months after *Laju*, Tay suffered a heart attack.

Tay was working in his MHA office at Pearl's Hill when the heart attack struck. It was said that he collapsed across his desk, and was found by his secretary, Ruby. The Singapore General Hospital at Outram Road was not far away. Tay was rushed across, stabilised and diagnosed.

The prognosis was not good. There had been a major tear to his aorta. While this was patched up, the damage required further attention and repair. Moreover, the loss of blood flow to the heart during the attack had left a valve in his heart permanently damaged, and it would need to be replaced with an artificial valve. Major open-heart surgery was required, not a simpler bypass, and it could not be done in Singapore. At that time, the know-how and equipment for this kind of surgery was not widely available. There were really only two experts in the world who were capable: one in South Africa, and the other in the USA. The Singapore doctors recommended the latter: Dr Michael DeBakey based in Houston. DeBakey was already a world-famous cardiovascular surgeon who pioneered such now-common procedures as bypass surgery. In the process, he had helped turn the Baylor College of Medicine, where he was based, from a provincial school into one of America's leading and great medical institutions.

The government extended latitude in covering the considerable expense of ensuring Tay received the best possible medical care in the world. In September 1974, he was flown over to Houston for the operation.

The surgery would be difficult. To gain access to the heart, the ribcage would need to be sawn through, open by perhaps 10 inches or more. The heart would need to be stopped and, before that, the arteries and veins shifted to a heart-lung machine to temporarily take over the function of the heart and lungs. Where today there are procedures so that only small insertions to the heart are needed, back in the 1970s, the surgery was much more invasive, especially when the valve would need to be replaced. The valve had to be tested for blood flow. After that was done, and the heart stitched up, the patient's rib cage would be wired up, and finally the wounds sewn up. The operation would take 12 or more hours, a marathon that would increase not only the surgeon's risk of error but, even if all went well, take a heavy toll on the patient's system and increase the risk of infection. Surgical mortality for the procedure was high.

Tay got through. The surgery was, DeBakey judged, a success. Yet, the recuperation afterwards was prolonged and would bring new challenges. With the artificial valve in his heart, there would be medicines to thin his blood to prevent rejection. Tay would have to address the underlying hypertension with a regime of drugs, as well as a shift to a low-salt diet. His body wore the visible scars, with a neat but very obvious and long criss-cross of scars where they had wired and stitched back his rib cage. The heart valve replacement functioned well enough, but its every opening and closing could be heard audibly. For the rest of his life, there was never really a moment when the scars and the valve did not remind Tay what he had suffered and would never fully recover from.

He returned to Singapore in late 1974. Resuming his position as Permanent Secretary of MHA, he could feel the effect on his capacity for work. His stamina and physicality, which Tay had assumed to be limitless in the years before, were impacted. For the first months, he struggled through what used to be normal tasks and the doctors said his stamina would be notably impaired even into the middle-term. He needed more time to recuperate, this was clear.

The heart is a mysterious organ. It is a muscle, allied to arteries and veins – an organic pump with piping. It is in so much literature and many cultures, the locus of human emotions, even of love. Studies tells us now that after open-heart surgery – especially of the kind that Tay had endured – there are more than physical effects. Anxiety and depression are common psychological after-effects, as are the loss of appetite and ability to sleep. More than a few patients experience bouts of paranoia and sharp changes of character, even after the physical pain of the operate remits. Today, counselling and support groups are offered to patients, alongside the physical recuperation and the medicines. These were not available in those years.

After a short respite and physical check-up, Tay would have to cope and adjust whilst returning to work. Back at the MHA, it was evident that the intensity, pace and heavy workload offered no respite. At the end of 1974, Tay left MHA and was moved to the Ministry of Defence.

Boat People, End Games

Defence was a portfolio that he knew well and could have enjoyed. He retained the rank of permanent secretary but there was an incumbent at the Ministry – Pang Tee Pow, who had also been in the MID and was older – and Tay would be designated as 2nd Permanent Secretary. The government had exceptionally covered the cost of the operation in the USA, and this reassignment was a way of giving more time and some reduction in duties to allow him to recuperate. One key duty in this period grew from an issue that Tay had been involved with for more than a decade: the Vietnam War.

In 1975, with the collapse of Saigon, the war was ending in victory for the Communist north, and many concerns and strategic calculations flowed from this. It was an important and complex situation, with many implications for the US presence and the ability of the ASEAN countries, including Singapore, to survive as independent non-Communist states. There was a confluence of the different issues that Tay had been involved in for many years. The emerging situation occupied much time to consider the different possible scenarios and strategies that could be used in response. While the heart operation had slowed him physically, Tay would have been involved in these discussions of policy and positioning.

Additionally, beyond the strategic questions, there were practical impacts in which he would be involved. Some of this could be handled quietly, away from the public spotlight. For instance, there was a controversy involving a C-130A Hercules plane carrying some 56 people fleeing Saigon which landed in Paya Lebar Airport on 4 April 1975. There was sympathy to the situation, but something of a legal conundrum as the airplane technically belonged to the Vietnamese Air Force and, with the impending surrender, could be claimed by the government in Hanoi. There were, moreover, five other aircraft being serviced and refurbished in Singapore in much the same situation regarding their ownership.

The US were anxious to lay claim to its aircraft rather than seeing them claimed by Hanoi. But it recognised legal issues and Tay played a role in resolving the case for Singapore. In particular, his brief was to press for the Americans to accept all the Vietnamese on board the plane as refugees to enter the USA. This was to include another plane coming into Singapore on 29 April that was reported to be carrying 19 mechanics. This plan, as reported in *The Straits Times* on 5 May 1975, succeeded. Not only did the refugees find themselves a new home in the USA, so did the airplane. The C-130A Hercules, nicknamed *Saigon Lady*, was first at the Smithsonian Air and Space Museum, and later received a new lease of life at the National Warplane Museum in New York. It was a small story set in the much larger canvas of the swift collapse of Saigon and South Vietnam after some two decades of fighting. It was a relatively positive story for all parties, including Singapore.

Another emerging situation from the fall of Saigon was much larger, very public and less positive: the hundreds of thousands fleeing South Vietnam in boats and desperately seeking refuge abroad: the "boat people" crisis, as it came to be called.

Tay was again involved in 1975 when this crisis was just beginning to unfold. Over two decades up to 1995, about 800,000 refugees reached destinations outside Vietnam safely and were resettled in other countries. But in the same period, it is estimated that some 200,000 to 400,000 did not survive, succumbing to the dangers at sea of storms, overcrowded and unseaworthy boats, and pirates. In this passage, Hong Kong and the ASEAN countries were the first to receive the outflow of refugees, although many were eventually resettled in developed Western countries.

How would Singapore respond? Being a small nation with limited space, Singapore simply could not afford to accept the inflow. There were also security concerns that, among the numbers, some might be Communists disguised as refugees to enter Singapore illegally. From this calculation, Singapore became the first country to stop the boat people from landing on its coastlines.

The task of turning the boats away would involve the armed forces and the navy for surveillance and interception in what was dubbed Operation Thunderstorm. It was necessary to ensure coordination with the relevant domestic agencies and carry out this work with a degree of political sensitivity. While Singapore was not legally obliged to receive the refugees (neither it nor any of the ASEAN governments had accepted the United Nations Refugee Convention), Singapore did not want to appear brusque. Defence Minister Dr Goh was overall in charge. Tay was involved in the operation, working with Colonel James Aeria, Commander of the Navy, and, for the Police Coast Guard, Tee Tua Ba whom he had known from the *Laju* Incident. The key person to deal with the situation, as Tay duly credited, was the Director for Refugees – a young Wong Kan Seng, who was later to enter politics. It was Wong who was tasked to organise the resources and coordinate the efforts to supply food, water, fuel, and fix the boat engines if necessary, to keep the refugees moving on to their next destination. The young civil servant impressed Tay and the ministers in this work.

On 2 May 1975, the first wave of 300 refugees arrived in Singapore waters on board the vessel *Truong Hai*. A total of up to 8,355 refugees was believed to have entered Singapore waters during this period, from 2 to 14 May 1975. Amidst this, Tay had the unenviable task of explaining Singapore's actions to an often critical media. On behalf of the government, he announced on 4 May 1975 that provisions and fuel would be provided to the ships, 25 of which were at anchor off Singapore, with some 3,710 refugees on board. He explained why Singapore would not take in the refugees, and replied to accusations that authorities had impounded the vessels or diverted them away. As Defence Minister Dr Goh instructed, the officials were not to allow any of the Vietnamese on the boats to land in Singapore. Accordingly, Tay was to make the case that none of the refugees had expressed any keen interest to stay on in Singapore and chose instead to try to be admitted into countries like Australia and the USA.

There were letters from the refugees addressed to the Australian government, which had declared an "open door" policy to receive them, and other messages hoping that the Singapore government would provide humanitarian assistance to help during their "short stay in Singapore". In these letters, the refugees hoped for the USA to assist, and the Singapore authorities conveyed this to the US Embassy. This buttressed the explanation of the Singapore stance not to accept but also not to detain or harm the boat people, and instead to provide supplies and assistance.

The crisis escalated. By 1979, more than 50,000 refugees were arriving every month. In other Southeast Asian countries such as Thailand and Malaysia, incidents were reported that some refugee boats were not only denied entry but had even been dragged out into the open sea, with some capsizing. No less than the Prime Minister was then to explain the Singaporean position: "We are a small, weak and overpopulated country...". When some took the view that it was a hard-hearted policy, PM Lee added in his inimitable style: "You've got to grow calluses on your heart or you just bleed to death."

Did Tay have doubts about this policy? He could see the concerns in terms of security. Yet, the situation was different from other threats that he had analysed and acted against. Onboard the boats in 1975 were ordinary people running away from war, not terrorists like those who had seized the *Laju* ferry in 1974. Tay, having been a child during WWII, knew about the desperation of such circumstances. At a personal level, having just survived a severe heart attack and body-wrenching surgery, he might have been bemused by the image of the callused heart that the premier chose in his media remarks.

Tay had, in the course of his public service, learnt to prioritise the security of Singapore and to guard against sentimentality. Yet, especially after his near-death experience, he also wanted to believe that a basic humanity could endure and be squared with the priority of security.

For the boat people, the effects of the policy to provide them supplies and push them off were mixed. Some did make the journey to Australia and other countries that were willing to offer them refuge. But others were not fortunate and were lost at sea or preyed upon by pirates. The Singapore government only deviated from this policy in a very limited way and later: in 1978, a small refugee camp was set up in Hawkins Road. It was considered one of the better and more humane refugee camps in the region. Yet, this was meant to accommodate very few arrivals and then to clear them out as soon as practicable. From here, some would go on to the USA and other countries and make something there for themselves and, of these, there were those who returned to Singapore to acknowledge the help given.

There is no public record that Tay disagreed with the policy that he helped explain to the media in 1975. It would be mere conjecture to ask what he would have thought and argued for as the numbers of boat people climbed in the next years, and if he might have sought other approaches. For, Tay would not have to debate this issue with the premier and other policy-makers in the coming years as the situation worsened. He would no longer be at the Ministry. Dealing with the boat people and the aircraft coming in from Vietnam was at the closing stages of a conflict that Tay had been watching for decades. It was an endgame for which he was in many ways prepared and had expected. There was, however, another ending for which he was less well-prepared, and which was more personal.

At the end of 1975, Tay was assessed by a government medical board. The view reached was that his health was compromised, as was his ability to work. On this basis, he was to be retired.

He was not prepared for this. He realised his physical limits and no one was more frustrated than he that he could not do more. He was just beginning to accept the realism that, one year after the critical surgery, he still needed to work on recovery. He also knew that the time the government would give to him to recover would be finite. While a permanent secretary's appointment is meant to be permanent, a precondition is the medical fitness to carry out the duties of the job.

Although he had served the senior government leaders directly and reliably, he knew they were not given to sentiment. Indeed, honed by the urgency and do-or-die of those early years, they were tough taskmasters. It would be a hard road to manage his still considerable day-to-day work load and work on his recovery. But Tay was not a person to give up. He had faced many trials in his life and had come through and proven himself, and he was determined to do so again. Just as his WWII scar had become something he lived with and could even turn to advantage, he was working towards recovery from these new scars.

What might have been hoped for was to have more time. There could have been a redeployment to a less intense portfolio role, perhaps one that could tap into his knowledge of the region's politics and skills in providing his analysis, advice and recommendations. But the decision reached and announced was that from mid-1976, he would be retired from the civil service on medical grounds. This was barely 18 months since his return to service, and not three years from his handling of the *Laju* Incident in early 1974. He had served ably and his heart attack had been almost a direct outgrowth of the costs of that service. There was a kind letter from Dr Goh Keng Swee, the Defence Minister and DPM, appreciating his service to the country and clearly stating that the medical conditions had determined the government decision.

Still, the decision was a great shock; almost on par with the heart attack itself. Tay was just 43.

The media reported his retirement quite extensively. The *New Nation* report of 18 June 1976 covered most of his career, recounting not only the *Laju* Incident when "Mr Tay hit the limelight", but going back to his port days when the workers had tried to persuade PM Lee to allow him to stay on. His work at the SID and MHA was also written up, as was his Eisenhower Fellowship. The plaudits given were nice and when contacted by the newspaper, Tay quipped that, "I am on holiday and enjoying it."

This was not entirely true.

After the decision was reached that he would be retired, there was a holiday to Malaysia. He not only visited his brother in KL, which was quite normal, but extended the trip to Taiping, where he had lived as a child and had not been back frequently. Tay brought his wife and two children. The holiday visit to his home town went well enough. It was not only nostalgia that prompted the trip but a need for closure.

Since he had left that small town to come to Singapore for studies and upon graduating, joined the civil service, he had focused on work. It was urgent and gave him a sense of purpose that, if done right, what he did mattered. He did really not want to do anything else, and was not at all ready to give that up. When it was taken from him, and so early, he did not really know what else there was that he wanted to do. Like so many others in public service during the pioneering years, his sense of purpose and much of his identity was tied to what he did.

He was glad to be alive, and in future years would meet his surgeon in the USA, not only for a post-operation evaluation but also sentiment. The life he had known and its purpose was gone, and not by choice. He knew his Dante and, more than once, reflected on its famously dark opening lines. With a wane smile, somewhere between pathos and bathos, he might even recite them or sigh: "Ah me."

His was by no means a happy retirement. The professional turmoil spilled over into Tay's personal life. Years of disappointment were to come.

Too Quiet A Life

After leaving the civil service, Tay was given refuge in the University of Singapore's History Department. He had done his university degree in that subject but did not have a Masters, let alone a doctorate as was the usual requirement for teaching. But from 1976, he was appointed a Visiting Fellow. He found humour in this. No one knew from where precisely he was visiting but he was, to be sure, some kind of fellow.

At the History Department, he would share experiences and insights with graduate students into the recent history of the Emergency and Konfrontasi and, more broadly, the early years of Singapore. There was very little written about these events at that time. In teaching, he tapped into the years of first-hand knowledge and he would have had to structure these real-life experiences so that these could be conveyed academically, and to link the recent and contemporary events to longer arcs and patterns in Asian history. His knowledge, both first-hand and from a wider reading, was attested to by none other than Prime Minister Lee Kuan Yew, who had no doubt that he would have had a wealth of of interesting data relating to Singapore in this period. The PM had specifically named Tay when speaking to the media about the need for oral history.

He enjoyed reading, exchanging ideas and dialogue. This was somewhat like what he had done before in his 1970 lecture and in many other talks for SAFTI and other institutions. Teaching at the university could have been something Tay enjoyed. It should also have been a comfort that the History Department in those years was based at Bukit Timah. Tay had studied at the same campus, at the then University of Malaya. Just across the road and canal were the Dunearn Road Hostels – the first place he had ever stayed in Singapore after coming down from his family home in Malaysia. Things were familiar and even coming to something of a circle.

Perhaps if these developments had come later, after a full career and reaching the age of retirement, the situation might have satisfied him. But he was just 43, an age which should have otherwise been the apogee of his work and contributions in the public service. Despite his physical condition after the surgery, there remained an energy and desire in him to do more, and his mental acuity was undiminished. Tay did not settle into university life. He chaffed and grumbled.

The quality of the students was low, perhaps unfairly comparing the students to the bright and dedicated staff and colleagues he had directed in the ministries. Pay was poor. Upon retirement, there was some pension but the renumeration of civil servants in this period, even permanent secretaries, was low. Still, the pay in the university, especially for a Visiting Fellow, was even worse, and there were no perks. A permanent secretary of his grade was entitled to a car, a Mercedes, and a driver. Now he had to settle on a serviceable, sensible VW, and drove himself. More than this, there was a sense of mission and respect at the ministries, as well as a certain pomp, with sentries saluting and ceremonies where he would be a guest on the stage or even the guest-of-honour. When he was in office, he had not been especially enthralled by these ceremonial aspects of the position and often said he preferred to just run a meeting where real discussions were taken and decisions made. At the university, there was none of either pomp or clear decisions and policy-making, and he missed it all, and very much.

He did not mind being a Visitor; knew he could not stay on and did not want to. He would often explain his time at the department as "taking refuge" and, like the refugees he had seen on the boats, he knew it would be best to figure out a preferred, final destination and move on. But what would lie ahead, and what preparations could he make?

The Head of the History Department was Dr Wong Lin Ken – the same man who had once and briefly been Minister of Home Affairs when Tay was Permanent Secretary. Dr Wong must have played a role in reaching out to offer the arrangement to be a Visiting Fellow. Dr Wong had been a history lecturer before politics and it would have seemed natural that he would return after his tour as ambassador and minister. Yet, Dr Wong had found political life difficult and challenging, serving only two years before being dropped from the cabinet and Parliament, and remained unsettled, disconsolate. After he was found dead in 1983 at age 51, the coroner judged the cause to be suicide.

Tay, too, sensed the shadows gathering. He was determined to escape them. In this period, he would deal with personal challenges. Sonnie was estranged from Cecelia. The problems in their marriage that simmered for many years had boiled over during his illness and recovery. After the heart attack, he was so changed and so changeable that Cecelia wondered if it was the medications or the influence of a third party, even perhaps black magic. There is no need to dig up old gossip and stir up past turbulences after the passage of time and the passing of people, to respect privacy. But once his health improved, it was Tay's choice to move out from their home at One Tree Hill and live away from her and the family. He said it was to search for happiness. Certainly, he had much to cope with and adjust to: so much of his personal life had changed in this period in terms of his career, his health, energy and spirit, and in his personal and family life, and each of these areas complicated the other.

While teaching at the university, he rented a small apartment on West Coast Ridge. Some of his former colleagues from the ministries would reach out to him and keep in touch. He also found new circles. Sailing became one new pastime that he took up as his health recovered. He acquired a small catamaran and would spend time in Changi every weekend. This returned him to his old enjoyment of the sea and sun but in a quieter way than the motorboats and skiing of the past. He even made new acquaintances among some of the sailing club members who were convivial.

But there were evenings when he would be alone in that apartment, just eating an early and simple meal and then reading and mulling things over. Afterwards, one of the consolations was that there was an ample garden in front of the apartment block that looked down and across the sea, to the lights of the West coast and the islands beyond. These were industrial complexes but at night their lights cast a certain beauty. From here he could see Pulau Bukom and its refinery and some of the southern islands beyond, and perhaps he might have thought back to the events of the *Laju* Incident. Otherwise, he would have just laid back in his leather armchair, listening to classical music in the soft light or the dark, his eyes closed lightly so that if anyone were there, they might be unable to say if he was awake or had drifted off.

The slower pace of work at the university gave him time for rest and also for light exercise in his efforts to recover. He could feel his energy returning, even if slowly and never fully. He endured, adjusted and was not uncomfortable. He did enjoy the reading and knowledge. Yet, this was too quiet a life for his inclination.

In April 1978, there was a high-profile televised discussion with PM Lee Kuan Yew. Focused on bilingualism, this was one of the first national dialogues to revisit language policy in the education system and would push for an end to a system that had divided schools into English, Chinese, Malay and Tamil language streams. Lee was determined to push the reforms forward but knew they would be controversial. The move would be resisted by the Chinese-language teachers and the considerations could be more than professional. Their unions had been those cultivated by the Left wing in the 1960s and Chinese language and culture remained potential hot issues that could still trigger a broader reaction. There was need to prepare for broad acceptance and, if need be, give some room and comfort to those who emphasised the Chinese language, even as their schools were phased out. The first Speak Mandarin Campaign would be launched only in 1979, more than a year after this televised dialogue. After PM Lee had set the direction, Dr Goh was sent across to take charge of the Ministry of Education and bring a wave of changes in policy and personnel.

This was a notable dialogue by PM Lee, and Tay Seow Huah was specifically selected to chair the session. He was not an obvious choice to serve. He was not really bilingual; he could not speak any Mandarin and his dialects were rudimentary. While he did know about China and the Chinese-speaking community, these had been lessons from life and work, as well as coming from history and political studies that were written in English. Nor could Tay speak Malay very well. He conversed passably for everyday things and often used some Malay when interacting with counterparts from Malaysia. But he did not master this formally and had in the past struggled with the civil service examination on Malay that used to be required.

It was known how PM Lee would consider the smallest details for his public appearances, especially on occasions like this when he would be telecast with an audience and panelists, so no one imagined Tay had been chosen by accident or mistake. What likely qualified Tay for the role was the trust he had earned. He was also known to be well-spoken and yet concise. He could be relied upon to avoid missteps and instead to assist to guide the discussion if need be. In the end, this did not prove necessary. The Prime Minister was determined, and very much in command of the issues and the audience. Tay therefore had the wisdom not to intrude, and limited himself to steer the panelists, and to opening and closing the discussion.

In his closing as chairman for the discussion, Tay summarised key points the PM Lee had made: "[T]here is a limit to the language-learning competence of children and that, in fact, in Singapore what is being practised is a trilingual learning situation in the schools and at home, and that under the stresses of the trilingual learning situation, there is a very close limit of what can really be achieved." This pointed to the policies that Lee preferred as being absolutely necessary, responding to the needs of the families and future generations. In this way, Tay down played any suspicions that the aims were political and aimed at the Chinese-speaking community. He then closed by thanking PM Lee as speaker.

The archived transcript of the dialogue records the premier's response: "Thank you, because I think I am more indebted to you than you are to me." This, no doubt, was focused on this dialogue and the audience. But looking across to Tay, the pleasantry and acknowledgement from the PM could also have applied personally.

The dialogue was significant not only in terms of education policy. For Tay, being entrusted to chair the televised session was enough to signal that, even with his illness and early retirement, he was not forgotten and might be of some value and service; that he continued to enjoy a degree of trust from the Prime Minister. Although he pleaded to be self-conscious about being on television, the occasion raised his spirits. It had been one of the steps up from the darkness he had felt after being retired, and out of the quagmire of despondency that could easily have enveloped him. He would find a path out of that valley of shadows.

Out from the Vale of Shadows

Before much longer, he left the university History Department. He would head up the Singapore Manufacturers' Association (SMA) as Executive Director from July 1978. The SMA was then a leading business chamber that represented all the major private sector Singaporean manufacturers.

In the 1970s, the Singapore economy was growing exponentially but a lot of that growth was from multinationals and the government's own corporatised entities and companies. The private sector manufacturers were challenged to keep pace with the MNCs in terms of productivity, manufacturing standards, quality control, skills training and innovation. The SMA reckoned Tay could help increase its connections and credibility with the Singapore government, as well as to increase its relevance to the country's economic development. There was much to be done and, on his part, Tay welcomed the challenge.

His past government work had always focused on security and he was glad for the chance to be more involved in the commercial and economic aspects of Singapore's growth. He was prepared to roll his sleeves up to modernise and grow the secretariat and its capacity to represent and add value to the sector. He enjoyed engaging the companies who were members of the Association and learning more about conditions facing businesses in Singapore and the region.

After a dip in 1974-75, manufacturing was booming at 14 per cent in 1979, when Tay was the Executive Director. The sector contributed a significant 31 per cent of GDP. Productivity too was increasing; at 5.1 per cent, almost double the national average increase. This was a crucial turning point. Singapore was adjusting to the high-wage policy set by the government and had little choice but to move towards higher technology and higher value-added industries. The manufacturers supported the policy but expressed their concern that "every assistance be given to capable local companies with the potential to upgrade in order to preserve a fair measure of local manufacturing content, and stimulate the continuing development of local entrepreneurship". There were tax and financial incentives on offer from the govern-ment to selected companies. A dialogue was arranged for the executive committee to discuss the new policy with the Minister of Trade and Industry, Goh Chok Tong, whom Tay knew when Goh was the CEO of Neptune Orient Lines. This came after the National Wage Council's recommendations for higher wages, and the Skills Development Fund initiative.

The economy was really taking off and Tay could sense the trends from his work at the SMA. Regional linkages and Singapore's role as a hub were growing and the SMA would begin to assist their Singaporean membership establish a regional presence and grow the external wing of Singapore's economy.

By October 1979, Tay announced five overseas business missions for the SMA, including an initiative to look at opportunities in Sri Lanka. Representing the interests of the members also created opportunities to give inputs to government policy. He was asked to represent Singapore to speak in a series of high-profile seminars about the country and ASEAN, to be held across the US – in Los Angeles, Houston and New York. There was also an initiative discussed to try to bring together the many different business chambers in Singapore, including the SMA, into a larger federation to represent the apex for the whole business community. This set the context for Tay's involvement in these seminars and, indeed, the SMA.

Personally, Tay relished the chance as Executive Director to take charge of things again, to direct and manage people, and build up another institution. The terms offered were attractive; a welcome step up from the university and indeed above what he had received as permanent secretary. On top of the pay, a car and driver were provided. Things were improving for him in rebuilding his career, and it was important to him to find a purpose.

So it was, to a degree, with his personal life. He bought his own place. It was nothing grand; an apartment, and smaller than One Tree Hill, a two-bed room on the ground floor of an old but sturdy block, again just off Orchard Road. He furnished it in a modern way but with a few pieces that were more Malayan and traditional. He lived alone and did not entertain much at the flat. Entertainment and dining would be in restaurants. The SMA too had its share of engagements and evening events. There were some who kept him company – colleagues from work or from the Ministry. Now and again, he caught up for some *makan* with old friends like Edwin

Thumboo and Eric Alfred. He would go over to the East Coast to visit his sister, especially when his mother was down from KL where she now lived. One new set of acquaintances was those he had met sailing. Others were from the SMA office and its circles. As his health stabilised and energy was returning, his mood improved and his convivial and engaging nature returned. He widened his circles.

The turbulence with his wife was subsiding. There were things to be settled personally, and although these would not be easy, he felt more stable and was able to see the way that matters could be managed fairly for all. He was better reconciled to his circumstances, physically and emotionally; beyond the bare fact of survival, there were things for which he should be grateful. He not only felt more energetic and motivated, he also felt a little more settled and at peace. Work was not the same as it was in the government but it was satisfying enough.

After a dinner out, or just a meal of food that the driver got for him from a favourite stall, he would lay back in his leather-and-bamboo easy chair, put his feet up on the matching otto-man and read, or just shut his eyes in the near darkness of his small but tidy apartment – alone. For health reasons, there was no longer a pipe, or the unfiltered Camels that he used to puff almost non-stop. There was no jaunty Nat King Cole playing, or even the lighter classical pieces, but instead the slow and deep symphonies of Sibelius and Mahler. There were no noises from the children, in fact they could hardly be called children anymore; Joanne was at Liverpool University in the UK, and I was in junior college with my own social life of a teenager.

When Jo was back, we would go over. When she was away too, he would have me over to the flat for dinner. It was not easy when there was still tension between my parents. But he had always promised that he would be more present when we were grown and needed him more and he wanted to continue to be our father. This was a promise made not only to us but to himself. He knew what it meant to be raised without a father.

On the evenings that I would be there alone with him, we would sit together. If we could avoid contention, our talk would meander well enough. How was my tennis? He was chuffed to see me captain for my college and part of the junior Davis Cup team. How were my studies? He was a little happier that these had improved after I opted to study arts. How was my writing? He encouraged my poems but wondered if I should try stories. What was I reading? He would recommend and offer me books on history and politics. I was, in my teenage years, reading everything Fleming wrote and then Deighton and spy novels. I would exchange them with his books, and he would read, laughing at how unreal they were. Sometimes on such evenings, he talked half in jest about writing a spy novel of his own, fictionalised of course, with an impossibly skilled agent, but set in an Asia that was all very real. Often, he would hum along with the classical music and drift off into the quiet, his eyes closed so that I thought he was asleep. Then his eyes would open and he would say sorry that he slipped off, and call for the driver to take me home.

I do not know what my father saw when we were together in his apartment at the end of his day and our dinner, in those moments when his eyes closed. Perhaps it was where he was at that time, in that small, spare flat, content enough. But I sometimes think if he wouldn't be situating himself elsewhere, perhaps at the window of another house from the past.

From the house in Taiping, he might have looked out on all that was happening beyond the edges of town with some concern at the Emergency but also with a sense of adventure and a knowledge that his future would go out beyond the confines of that small, colonial world. From the bungalow at Raeburn Park, where we all lived when he was appointed to the Harbour Board, he could look down from the hill and see not just the port but also the main terminal for the railway; quite literally, the line that connected where he had come from to what he was working to protect and strengthen. From that black-and-white bungalow at Mount Pleasant he would have looked out at a canopy of green and sensed a quiet that disguised how busy and intense those years were. Before the house was taken back and demolished for the expressway, there had been another smaller change; the authorities had renamed the small road that led up to the house from Mount Pleasant Road, so that without moving house there was a new address. The name given was Jalan Mendaki, which translates to "the road climbs".

Indeed, his life had been a climb. Implicit in that climb is that the path must also descend, and come to an end. So much in his life would have told my father this.

Not long after he was settled into the SMA, talk started to circulate that Tay might be asked to return to public service, perhaps to be appointed as ambassador to one of the European capitals. There was no doubt that he had the background for such an appointment or something else. Although not as young or as strong as he was, his recovery was sufficient so he would be able to take on more active work again.

From his reading of the classics, he knew well that, in its last phase, the hero's journey is to come home and that the real battle is not waged with an external enemy but against one own's demons, to test personal strength and character. Five years from the heart attack, he could feel some part of himself returning, out from a vale of shadows where the heart attack and sharp change of circumstances had left him.

But then another shadow imposed itself.

To be Remembered

Headaches began. In his recovery from the heart attack, or even before, this was not unknown to him. Whether from the surgery or the underlying hypertension or the various side effects from the many medications he had to take, he was used to not feeling 100 per cent right, and still getting through. But these were not the same intense ones that he had suffered in the past, instead a kind of aching numbness in the neck and back of the head. Other symptoms came to attention. His usually clear speech would turn slightly slurred, especially when he was tired. He had problems swallowing and it was more than reflux or dysphagia. There were times when he was drinking water and it would go down the wrong way, or he might bite his tongue. None of these conditions, in itself, seemed too serious.

But a check-up was done, an MRI, and the diagnosis was not kind. In the image, there was the darkest shadow: what appeared to the doctors to be a tumour at the base of his brain. It was already sizeable and his symptoms suggested that it was growing. The situation would deteriorate further.

An operation was recommended which came with considerable risks. Even if the surgery was successful in removing the growth, there was a question of whether it was benign or cancerous. Removal carried many risks in itself, depending on how the tumour was linked to the brain. That area of the brain was responsible for breathing and the most basic movements. There was a chance of success. But the risk was that he would die in the process or that, even if he survived, he would no longer have the full function of his body or his mind. Among the possible outcomes of the operation, the one that Tay feared the most, was to survive as a cripple. Yet, he had no real choice. To Tay, it would be worse to do nothing and just wait while the situation worsened and took whatever remained of his life.

His doctor, Gopal Baratham, was then reputed to be a top brain surgeon in Singapore, having left the government hospitals for the private sector. But Baratham would not take on such a delicate operation himself. He, instead, recommended a doctor in London who was considered a leading authority. Arrangements were made for Tay to travel across and undergo the surgery. Tay informed his employers and some of his closer friends and former colleagues of the situation. He also had to tell his mother and siblings, and his children. But perhaps the most difficult conversations would be with his wife. It had been his decision to move out from the house and, coming on top of the shock of the heart attack, the relationship was raw. As time passed on, there was some calm on the surface but more out of exhaustion than resolution; many unresolved emotions remained and would be further stirred by this new development.

He put a stoic front on all of this. He packed up his bags. He even took care of small matters such as to leave behind the watch he treasured for safekeeping; it was a Rolex and had been a gift from colleagues at the SID when he left them. There were many who came to the Paya Lebar Airport to see him off and there were more than a few who shed tears. But not Tay. He walked through the doors, and he turned after immigration was cleared, stood tall and found it possible to smile as he waved goodbye.

When he arrived, he went to meet the surgeon for a pre-operation consultation and deal with the paperwork for permissions and payments. The surgery was scheduled for Tuesday, 15 September 1980. In the days before, he made time to meet some of those he knew well in London, including his old university friend, Chan Ki Mun. A number of his siblings were also there. There was his youngest sister, Peggy, and her husband, the Scottish missionary, Peter Ferry. His youngest brother David had been travelling in Europe and had a home in London, so he was there too. As was his daughter, Joanne, who had just completed her university degree and begun the slog of becoming a chartered accountant.

There was time to head out in search of good Chinese food in East London, not too far from the hospital, for meals with this daughter, siblings and friend. But the mood of these meetings was sombre. There was a suggestion that he could put off the surgery but he remained resolved, resolute to move ahead quickly and with equanimity.

The surgery did not go well. This is what my sister Joanne wrote about this time, many decades after, when I was writing this book.

"My brother told me today that he could not write about our father's death. It occurred to me that if I don't, there would be no record of how he left us, other than what the newspapers reported.

"My father's operation was scheduled for Tuesday, 15 September 1980. I last saw him for dinner on Sunday 13. Uncle Ki Mun and I picked him up from the London Hospital and we drove to the Isle of Dogs looking for Chinese food. I recall we ate *char siew* and rice, and the two of them remarked it was good because the pork had enough fat.

"The next day, I was working somewhere in High Holborn, which was close enough to visit my father straight after I finished. But for some reason, I chose to go back to the house I was renting up in High Barnet, north of the city, and after that, I just didn't have the energy to trek back down, all the way. Not to see my father for what I now know would have been the last time: it's my everlasting regret.

"Instead, we spoke on the phone. As a private ward patient, he was in his own room with a phone. His youngest brother, my uncle David, and youngest sister, Aunt Peggy, were there with him. I could hear them in the background when we spoke and he assured me that he was all right, asked me to get a good rest, and that he would see me tomorrow.

"After work the next day, I went straight over to the hospital. I was directed to the Intensive Care Unit, and when I saw Dad, he was stretched out on the bed, hooked up to various monitors, and still unconscious. I stood by his side for a while, as a few nurses flitted around tending to the machines. One of them called out, 'Mr Tay! Wake up!', and repeated that every few minutes. I thought it was the after-effects of the GA.

"After a while, I was joined by Uncle David, and we waited a little longer. Then a nurse came over and asked us to accompany her to meet the surgeon – whose name I have forgotten.

"We sat down in his office and I noticed he didn't look me or my uncle in the eye. He explained that the diagnosis had been mistaken. My father had not had a brain tumour after all. I can still recall the disbelief on his face when he told us that he had instead found a large aneurysm in the brain stem, packed with so many clots that it had presented as a solid object in the scans done back in Singapore and also in London.

"About halfway through his explanation, some part of me realised he was saying that my father would not regain consciousness, not recover, would die. I began crying soundlessly.

"My uncle and I went back to the ICU. Dad was there, looking as I had seen him so many times – sound asleep. But this time, from all the surgeon said, his eyes would not suddenly open. He would not sit up and ask, as he did so many countless times, 'Who wants to go…?'"

Afterwards, my sister called Singapore to tell my mother and me that he had gone into a coma and the situation did not look good and that they would wait for me to come over. I was then in National Service and special arrangements had to be made for my release for travel overseas, and for a new passport with a visa for entry into the UK. This was all expedited; while he had retired, he was still remembered and many lent sympathy and assistance beyond the normal channels.

I arrived at Heathrow Airport on 18 September. I felt stunned in several ways. First and primarily by the news. My father had said that the operation was serious and there were risks. But he had not dwelt on the possibility of death and few of us thought it could come to that; even so close to the end, he seemed so full of life. Secondly, were my own circumstances. At 19, this was my first time to travel so far and on my own. I had not been expecting this, no one really had, and I was pulled out of NS and just put on the plane without much more being told to me. Even the autumnal cold surprised me, and things that seemed simple like clearing immigration and getting into the crowded arrival hall, where it was not my sister but her then boyfriend, Derek, who was there to receive me and take me directly to the hospital. There were more shocks when we got there.

My father was not only unconscious as I had been told. He was on a life-support system. I was ushered in to see him for a few minutes, and there met with my sister. Then, in a quiet small room in that hospital, we met the surgeon and he spoke to me to explain what had happened, about the clusters of many aneurysms instead of a brain tumour. The blood clots in the walls around that part of the brain weakened the wall and could have burst at any time, whether with or without the operation, and trigger massive bleeding that would likely have led at the minimum to stroke and paralysis or else to death. The surgeon said they had done the best that could be done in the circumstances to clear up what they could of all they had found. But he could not look my sister or me in the eye.

When they closed up after, the signs were not good. The brain was showing no signs of life and there was nothing to be done. Should the life support system be shut off, the body might go on for a while or longer, but recovery was ruled out. They had waited for me to arrive to tell me. My sister and I would have to be the ones to make the final decision. On 19 September, my father's condition deteriorated further, and we sat by his bedside as the vital numbers monitored on the machine slipped lower and lower. He was gone.

Then came so many more things that were happening and needed to be done, with the morgue and the paperwork and deciding about arrangements for his return to Singapore. There was tension amongst the family members in London who were coping with the emotions as well as all the details. There was talk of his mother flying out and while this did not happen, some of his siblings thought it best that they should be in charge and decide matters, instead of us, his children, who were only young adults.

Moreover, he had died on a Friday and with the weekend, some things were delayed, including the official death certificate required for almost all of the other arrangements. In that pause, my sister and I moped around the small house that she shared and decided that we should go out to the parks and see a bit of London since it was my first time and there was nothing else that could be done. It was surreal to wander through the city streets and leafy parks amidst all that had happened, as if everything was somehow normal. I wondered if people could see the situation and the emotions on my face, or else if we were floating around like ghosts pretending to be fully alive still. I especially remember going to see a movie, *All That Jazz*. The plot develops to see the main actor face death and go through the stages of denial, rage, despair and finally acceptance, I could not decide if I felt like running out of the cinema or just sitting on, in the dark, laughing.

There was a ceremony in London attended by all the family members there, followed by a cremation in Golders Green.

Afterwards we – his children – returned to Singapore, bearing his ashes, and a memorial was arranged.

First, a wake held at his elder sister's home, and then, on 4 October 1980, a memorial service at a church nearby. There was some controversy about the arrangements. His wife, Cecelia, our mother, was going through a strange mix of emotions, with shock, anger and still remnants of love, as well as genuine concerns about what would happen next to her and the children without Sonnie. Since they had been estranged, she was uncertain about how best to conduct herself. So when his sister, supported by the siblings and of course their mother, pushed to make all the arrangements and even to host the wake at their home, rather than One Tree Hill, she did not want to fight. His mother and his siblings mourned him very publicly. His wife turned up every night and put a brave face to things, doing what she needed to, best as she could. So did we children, exhausted and empty after London. These differences and details do not matter now.

The way a man dies does not say much about how he lived, and the ceremonies for his death do not matter compared to what marked his life. Instead, from the fragments of memory from that time, larger pictures could be formed.

At the wake and the church, there were so many visitors who came that neither his widow nor we, his children, recognised by face or name. There were those who had been at the airport when he left. There were those he had kept up with and those who had not seen him for many years, even decades. There were some dignitaries and senior civil service colleagues, and there were some who said they had been workers at the port those many years back. There were tears among many. The church was full and the service was reported in some detail by the newspapers.

Edwin Thumboo delivered an eulogy and read a poem that he had composed for him, "The Return", with the assertion that "we live beyond the body's season". Thumboo eulogised the friend he lost: "… Seow Huah invariably gave more than he received. If he knew you needed help, he would help without ostentation, without fuss so that the help did not leave you feeling you were obliged…. For someone whose work would have brought him into contact with the whole range of human behaviour and misbehaviour, instances of ingratitude, of viciousness, of a lack of principles, it is remarkable that he, in his own life, would maintain an attitude that was remarkably Christian… not in the orthodox sense but he always had a profound feeling of the diety presiding over all.

"He had his share of human frailty… but that was so much outweighed by his goodness…. He had a just, strong spirit."

There was brief mention about what he had done in his public service before his retirement. There were so many more untold stories in the memories of those who came to pay their respects and to say farewell. But the overall conclusion was that he was a man who had not only contributed to the country as a whole but who made an impression on many he had encountered in his life. As for us, his family, and for me his son, I do not know how we managed in those days, but I suppose we did.

This was from *The Straits Times* report of 21 September 1980, "Tay dies after operation in London":

"… former top civil servant, 47, died in a London hospital on Friday night after a major operation to remove a brain tumour. He leaves behind his wife, Cecelia, 47, a teacher, daughter Joanne, 22, and son Simon, 19. Former Permanent Secretary to the Defence and Home Affairs ministers and director of the Security and Intelligence Department, Mr Tay went into a coma and died at 9.21pm on Friday. His two children were by his bedside until the last moment. Mrs Tay yesterday said he would be cremated in London on Friday and the family is finalising plans to fly back his ashes."

The Sunday Times of 5 October reported on his memorial service: "It was drizzling when 350 people gathered yesterday afternoon… for a memorial service to Mr Tay Seow Huah, 47…. Yesterday afternoon Mr Fred Sabapathy the former Deputy Controller of the Immigration Department led the simple hour-long service with prayers and hymns. Professor Edwin

Thumboo, head of the English and Literature Department at the National University of Singapore, read a very moving eulogy and a poem he had written for the late Mr Tay.

"The Minister for Defence, Mr Howe Yoon Chong, was present for a brief moment. Other VIPs included top civil servants like Mr Sim Kee Boon, head of the civil service; Mr George Bogaars, permanent secretary of the Finance ministry, and professors from the university.

"After the benediction, with the congregation standing, heads respectfully bowed, Joanne Tay stepped forward to receive the casket containing her father's ashes. Her mother's face was a pale expressionless mask. Her brother Simon stood stiffly at attention, a tiny muscle flickering in his jaw. As the family slowly filed out of the church with the casket, the sun suddenly came out."

When he died, Tay Seow Huah was 47: a civil servant and spy chief who had contributed in the pioneer years of Singapore. My father.

A Memoir

It was really only years after that I could look back more clearly and speak about my father, in life and in death, let alone to write about him.

The first time was a poem written in memoriam, combining some images of my father with the cold of England where he died, and of Hampstead Heath, where I went on a long walk days after. The poem mourned, but said little directly about him. Sometime after, when I began writing stories, there was more. The stories in *Stand Alone*, published in 1991, drew on my childhood with stories that touched on the history of the Tays – including a grandfather killed by Japanese – and my memories of the days when the "Mexicans" were guests in our home and my father would have Jaffa orange juice at breakfast. In between, when I was an active president at the university students union, some of his friends would call my mother with some concern about what my father might have thought of my statements and activities. But otherwise, in those years, becoming an adult, finding a job and a place in the world, I went my own way; never hiding who my father was, but not having to say it or have it matter too much.

In 2002, the Internal Security Department (ISD) started a heritage centre to assist the public to better understand threats to the country's security. They asked me and my family for some photographs and memorabilia of my father from the days he was at the Special Branch and Director for Security and Intelligence. We found what we could and, for those who are invited to visit the centre, they are on display together with write-ups on the earlier period of the Special Branch. There is also a prominent exhibition focused on the *Laju* Incident. When I visited the centre in preparation for this book, I learnt that it will move to a new location, with new exhibits. It is unclear whether the new exhibitions will carry over the current focus (or indeed where the new centre will be housed).

In 2015, the 50th anniversary of the founding of the Security and Intelligence Division (SID) was marked. A commemorative book was planned for the occasion. As my father was the founding Director for Security and Intelligence, I was approached to write an essay about him. I agreed and asked if they might make available archival information and help me to touch base with his contemporaries and those who served with him, all of whom had retired. They later reverted with complimentary recollections about my father as a person and a boss but little else. In fact, they asked me for photographs of my father that might have been taken at work.

For a moment, I was incredulous that they had few, maybe none. Then I realised that the SID had such a culture of confidentiality that they were not the kind of institution that would have a staff photographer on hand at their events, no matter how innocent. I remember going to staff functions, family days, outings on the weekends that combined some work visit to a facility and yet on which we, as children, were permitted to tag along. There were memories, images in my head, but perhaps nothing on record. Then, for an even shorter moment, I speculated that this might indeed be some kind of trap; that we were in possession of sensitive materials. I laughed off that reaction and asked my sister, who is much better than I am at remembering, to go through what there might be.

There are a number of albums left by my parents. Pictures they took – on camera and then to process into photos – and then put into large albums with thick paper alternating with thin separations so that the pictures would not stick together. All that effort. Today, with everyone snapping selfies and wefies and pix of just anything on their phones, such albums and the care given to the photographs within will be seen as a rare curatorial function, and it might be assumed that every picture so selected and preserved must have some special meaning. Not all do. Some of the photographs uncovered were sent across.

One is of Tay Seow Huah at his desk, a grand wooden example of the mid-1960s. There are four phones on the desk and two pipes propped up. He looks across at the photographer, and there is a file in front of him. From this and the neat, short-sleeved white shirt and dark narrow tie, it seems an official photograph. It is the desk from which he served as Director of the Special Branch. There is also a photograph of a government security pass issued to him with his photograph and the serial number 0001. I guess, but cannot ascertain, it was an SID pass; at the time it was issued he was serving as its inaugural Director, and the number might attest to that.

Then there are photographs of him mostly abroad and often with Bogaars. The images are clear enough and yet each presents a mystery of context. In one, there is Tay with Bogaars and a naval officer in front of a large sign that says, "Corregidor Lighthouse Station". This is a historic and strategic location off the Philippines, near the entrance of a bay, at a converging point of two lines of approach for vessels from the South China Sea into Manila. But what are two senior MID officials doing in the Philippines?

In another, Tay is in a conference room behind two men who are seated at a position designated for Thailand. This must have been some meeting of a regional group, perhaps an early ASEAN meeting, when the Singapore delegation and

Tay would have been next to Thailand by alphabetical order. The next photograph has Tay being introduced to a dignitary who looks like the Thai monarch. But the dignitary is young and smiling broadly, and even shaking Tay's hand. It is hard to imagine the late King doing that. But this was in the 1960s and a younger king at that time might have acted much less formally and taken on Western customs in receiving foreign visitors; he had, after all, been educated in the West as a child and composed jazz music. Perhaps it is him. But again, there is little more, not even a firm date.

There are several more of Bogaars and Tay receiving or being received by foreigners, some in uniform and others in suits and ties. There are some of Tay with an SID colleague and, I speculate, from the complexion and uniforms of the others, that they are in Taiwan, visiting a military base. It might have been in the late 1960s or early 1970s; by 1975, Singapore would openly establish Operation Starlight to conduct military exercises in Taiwan.

There are some things I know and remember and more I can find out. There are things that can be guessed at, deduced as best guesses even if it is seldom as simple as one plus one. But there are secrets, things to be withheld, both for the state's reasons and familial, personal. There are also matters that are unknowable because of time and because people are mysteries at some level, and often in more ways than we might guess. That applies not only to this small number of photographs but so many of the memories and even of the facts on record: enigmas.

Yet, it is possible to write some things about these enigmas, based on memory and record and what others say, as well as building with what might be deduced, conjectured and imagined. This is the essay I wrote for the SID in 2015, on its anniversary, for a book that they never showed me. (It was a limited edition, restricted circulation only.)

My Father's Secret Life

"My late father led a life that was secret from our family and me, and doubly so. When he served as Director of the Security and Intelligence Division from 1966 to 1970, I was only a child, and even when he passed away in 1980, I was just 19. More, the work he did was inherently secretive – as were many tasks he undertook in his positions in government both before and after.

"He could not tell me much of his work and, even if he did, I would not have really understood – at that time back then. There are limits to how a child sees a parent. Yet, the sense of his work often set the mood for many childhood experiences for me and my sister, Joanne.

"The day I registered in Primary One, the teacher opened the official class register and asked us all, one by one, what our parents did. 'Civil servant', the six-year-old me replied, as my father instructed. 'Boy', the teacher said sternly, 'you must tell me what he actually does. Even I am a civil servant.'

"The next day, after consulting my father, I came back and told the teacher 'Senior Civil Servant'. I was scolded soundly. On the third day, however, the teacher did not call me up at all. She had been told not to ask, my father explained casually.

"On his desk in the upper floor of the old government black-and-white off Mount Pleasant Road where we lived in those years, there was another marker of my father's secret life. A telephone rested on top of a special metal box with a switch.

"'Don't touch it,' I was told and, as a young boy, this seemed an invitation to do precisely the opposite. I remember calling a school friend and then, in mid-conversation, flicking the switch to scramble his voice just for the fun of it. Ordinary things were made special.

"Special things were, conversely, made quite ordinary. In that same house, at more than one dinner, I remember foreign guests. There were 'Mexicans' who spoke no Spanish. There were also English guests whom, my father said vaguely, had been his hosts in London.

"These dinners included wives and, for those who had family here, their children. The events were convivial, sociable and often with something to drink. A number of his colleagues would be present too, including Mr S R Nathan and the late

Mr George Boggars. I grew up calling these men, 'Uncle'.

"My father did not draw hard lines between work and leisure, office and home. When there were no guests, he would often withdraw after our family dinner to the study. There, he would smoke his pipe or else his unfiltered Camels, and thumb through files marked with a coloured slash and the words 'Top Secret'.

"Some of his colleagues have generously said that at work my late father was usually calm, unhurried and prepared to smile and encourage them. I am told that my father would sometimes interject and take over conversation with staff when he felt that the officer was wasting time and correct the views he thought wrong. We saw those sides of him too.

"Despite all the things he had to do, he would try to find time for us to talk, question and debate after dinner about anything and everything or play card games. On some weekends, he would drive his family up to Changi Beach, or to parts of Johor to camp along a river.

"But on other evenings after work, my father was too tired. Sometimes his mood would be darker and even terse, impatient. Quite often, we children, Joanne and I, would be told to be quiet, when he was afflicted by pounding, unrelenting headaches.

"My father always gave his best to his work and enjoyed it fully.

"I remember once going to the Istana with the car and driver, immediately after my school ended, to fetch my father from a meeting. I was slightly awed to be waved through the gates without fuss. When my father got into the car, he beamed. He confided that he just convinced the Prime Minister to his point of view and adjust a decision.

"He may have hid the toll of the long hours and pressure from others but the strains were apparent to us. For many years, he suffered from high blood pressure – even before his major heart attack in 1974. This happened shortly after the false alarm over the Olympic Airways hijack, the killing of his Malaysian counterpart along a busy road, and the response to the *Laju* Incident, which he oversaw and coordinated.

"He acculturated us with concerns far beyond anything school taught us. I was a child who knew that the Domino Theory was not a game played with tiles. I grew up with a sense of anxiety about events in the region, about Vietnam and also Indonesia.

"About Malaysia, where my father was born and where his brothers and many friends still lived, there was ambivalence. It came up in small ways when we drove up country on family visits. The coffee shop meals and banter between him and his brothers about whether Singapore or KL was doing better was always undercut with remarks about the politics, race and religion.

"My father also felt that the policies of the USA would be pivotal for the region. He relished the Eisenhower Fellowship he took up soon after leaving SID to spend an extended period in that country. He returned with many books about American history and thinking.

"Until today, some of his books line my shelves, including Greek classics and Chinese poems in translation. There are also books of that period like *The Battle for Merger* by then Prime Minister Lee Kuan Yew, and Dr Goh Keng Swee's *Socialism That Works*. After his death, I read through many of these, as if looking for his footsteps along an intellectual path.

"Fifty years after he was tasked to set up and serve as the first Director of the SID, my father left memories and also his example. He taught me to treasure knowledge and the need for a questioning mind. He showed me how it can be a mission to give of your best to serve Singapore, even at personal cost.

"His death at the age of 47 left gaps and mysteries too. There are some black-and-white photographs of him in Taiwan and also Bangkok in a suit, among other men in suits or military uniform at formal receptions and in meetings.

"There is also his watch, a Rolex that, on the back, is simply engraved 'To Mr Tay Seow Huah'. There was once a date engraved too – but that was inadvertently erased when the watch was serviced and polished.

"My father told me that it had been a personal gift from his SID colleagues when he left for his next posting. It was a watch my father cherished and used to the end of his days and wished me to keep for posterity.

"I do."

Chapter 9

CODA: CONVERSATIONS, MEMORY & IMAGINATION

IN 2022, as I was completing this manuscript, a book entitled *The Last Fools* was published about eight of the pioneer generation of civil servants. They were described as "immortals" who had left a lasting mark on Singapore. Tay Seow Huah was not amongst those featured. This is understandable.

Tay did not live long (as the others did), dying at 47 in 1980 and being retired out from the civil service on medical grounds even earlier. There were only some 10 years from the time of his appointment as Director Special Branch to his last position as Permanent Secretary. Additionally, most contributions of those featured in the book are marked in the public record and often via visible infrastructure, whereas much of Tay's work was by nature secretive, then and still today. The *Laju* Incident was exceptional, in the public domain and splashed across headlines. The rest remains in files that have yet to be declassified and perhaps will never be.

In the event, this book is not posited on Tay Seow Huah being any kind of "immortal". He was very much human and his mortality evidenced by his early death. I hope I have not pretended otherwise, even as his child. I have written this book because he is my father and as a way of trying to understand him better, from the perspective of adulthood and the distance of many decades. My additional hope is that what is offered can serve as an example of what one member of the pioneer generation did, in public service and personal life, and add to the ideas that motivated the many more whose stories have not been written. This is despite challenges in remembering and retelling what happened in this period and how he contributed – even as we must recognise how enigmas remain.

Conversations

I always enjoyed talking with my father. When I was young, I felt that there was nothing he didn't know. That is common enough for children but that continued when I was in my teens and until the end. He was broadly read, full of insights and details and, mixed into serious points, he was humorous. Even when I had studied something quite thoroughly at school or as an interest, like poetry, he would know something I didn't or explain it in a way that made me think, "Aha!" He could sometimes be intellectually intimidating, even cocky. But, for Joanne and me and for his family and friends, there was a warmth in him that stopped short of arrogance. There was nothing I felt we could not discuss, whether politics or religion, or relatives and others. He would not only be willing to edify me and also, more unusual for a parent, was quite unafraid that I might disagree with him.

This last part presents three conversations with my father – Dad as my sister and I would call him. These conversations are imagined, fictional; not factual, history.

However, some of the things said are from memory, or gleaned from quotations and reports he wrote, and the settings are places he did dine at. My father is represented as real as I can write him. He is 47 and about to leave for London for a major operation. He knows that the surgery carries considerable risk that could, if successful, ensure a long life or else end it. He has noticed a slurring of his speech and slippages in his basic functions; he bites his tongue and has to be careful when sipping water so that it does not accidentally get into the wind passages and make him cough violently. My father is months away from his death.

He is dining with me, his son. In these conversations, I too am 47. When I was that age, in 2009, I was in New York. After some ten years of public service – as a Nominated Member of

Parliament in the Singapore Parliament and then as Chairman of a statutory board – I took up a year-long Fellowship to write *Asia Alone,* about the changing relationship between Asia and the USA. These are facts of my life. Obviously, I was never 47 years old at the time my father was; our encounters framed here are fictional. This may seem odd or even outrageous, given that the earlier parts of the book are based on facts and may be approached as a biography and memoir (subject to the codicils I have already stated). There are reasons for this.

Much relates to the timing of my father's death. In 1980, when my father died, he was 47. I was 19. Singapore had come through its turbulent start and had done well in its first real boom of the 1970s. So much has happened in the years since. There would be a long spell of high growth in the years to come, interrupted only by collapse of the Pan-El corporation. Then the economy would again boom for a near-decade until the 1997-98 Asian Crisis. Emerging with a V-shaped recovery, Singapore would grow strongly. There would again be crises triggered by external events – SARS in 2003 and the Global Financial Crisis of 2007-2008 (not to mention the Covid-19 pandemic, which is beyond the time of this imagined conversation). In each of these events, the country has been more resilient than in the past, with capabilities and reserves that go far beyond what was available in the 1960s and 1970s. The city skyline would grow and grow again, as would the infrastructure – icons like Changi Airport, and daily conveniences like the MRT which might today be taken for granted, and the financial system were yet to be built. While Singapore was stable internally and growing, there were events of quite profound political significance in the world: not least the collapse of the Berlin Wall in late 1989 and of the Soviet Union that quickly followed; the 9/11 attack on the USA and the global war on terrorism waged afterwards, including the invasion of Iraq; and the rise of China's power and an increasing rivalry with the USA. I grew up in these decades.

My father did not live to see these times and events, or to know me as an adult. When a person dies early, there are effects that ripple for those left behind in the world. In my father's case, he was prepared for the possible outcome that he would die in that operation. But none of us were. There was a strong sense of shock. There were also many things left unresolved, for while he was mentally prepared, there were other preparations left undone – practical things like a will providing for his surviving family – and even more so with relationships. He had tried to say goodbye but his going had been abrupt. It felt as if the main character in a TV series was abruptly written out, with lines of plot and dialogue left hanging. Yes, the world and his country would move on, and his friends and family too. However, Tay Seow Huah did not. He would always be 47 years old.

There would have been so many changes and shifts to the view of the world he had developed, and yet there would also have been discernible echoes and lessons from the past. To try to imagine what Dad would say to these events and developments: that is the first reason for these conversations. I hope that, by this method, some things may be said that help a reader bridge from that distant era when my father was alive to the present, that there are thoughts of a pioneer that might speak to the present.

Moreover, I do not think my father would have minded this experiment. He always read literature, and listed it as one of his pursuits in *Who's Who* biographies. Moreover, he knew I was writing and encouraged me to do so. In creating these fictional discussions, I have sought to take the reality of my father as written in the earlier parts of this book and project his character and essence. I have drawn on a report that he wrote at the end of his time in the USA on the Eisenhower Fellowship – using his own words, almost verbatim. I hope what is written will not break reality, even if it bends.

Conversations imagined here will be, well, conversational. They try to avoid long one-sided diatribes and soliloquies. Conversations will, by nature, wander, especially those over dinner. But there are central questions in each. The first is about world events and our region; issues that were part of my father's work and of mine. How well is Singapore prepared to ensure security and prosperity in a changing world? The second conversation is about Singapore and the changes the decades have wrought to the country and to some of his closest colleagues. What has changed and how have our nation and people progressed? Our third and final conversation is about family, the people and contexts that link us. How shall we then live?

While these conversations are imagined, there were similar conversations while he was alive. In the years before his retirement from the government, when I was still young and he was often pressed for time because of work, there were evenings when we would go out for a drive in whichever open-top sports car he had at the moment. We would not talk very much and what words we said might be carried away on the wind but, after each drive, I would feel closer to him. In the last years, when he was retired out from the government and before his death, I was in my middle to late teens and we would sit down together more often. But these were not always easy conversations. His health and frustrations, and all that had happened, wore on him. His estrangement from my mother, and departure from our home at One Tree Hill, weighed on us both. As a teenager, I could be moody and I often felt he did not understand me. On my part, I did not always feel, at the end of the conversation, that I understood him better.

My father had always said that when I was older, he would play a larger role with me, and we would spend more time together. He made every effort to keep true to this. He would make time almost every week without fail for us to have dinner together. It would usually be just the two of us. These conversations from those evenings from 1976 through to 1980 will be a point from which to jump into the imagined conversations here. I wish that I could revisit those conversations with perspectives I have gained as I grew into adulthood, after his death; still a son but no longer a child, a man who has lived through the same stages of life; trying to speak of him as I would a contemporary.

So this is how our conversation would begin:

"It's been many years. I almost didn't recognise you."

"Oh, you haven't changed at all. It's really good to see you."

Top of the World

How well is Singapore prepared to ensure its security and prosperity in a changing world?

The Four Seasons in New York, at the top of the iconic Seagram Building, is one of the most famous restaurants in the world. Or so it was. Established in 1959 and running for almost six decades, it was a pioneering fine-dining restaurant that was always more than the food. With its soaring, 22-foot-tall glass windows and views above the city, its Grill room was a place for the power makers of the city as well as out-of-towners to hold a power lunch whether to discuss business, politics or the entertainment world, or all three. It pulled in the right crowd of the affluent and influential, the celebrities as well as those who had corner offices in the corridors of power. The restaurant provided a most elegant setting with elements of art and design from iconic names van de Rohe and Philip Johnson (architects of the building), and artists like Joan Miro and Picasso.

Tay Seow Huah dined here in 1971 when he was on his Eisenhower Fellowship, as a special treat with his wife. They also drank well, selecting one of the best Californian wines which were just starting to be noticed for quality. This evening, when he walks in, I am again struck by how tall he is. For a while after his operation, he had the habit of holding his chest in a little – natural enough given the stitches from the procedure. But tonight he stands straight and seems almost as he was before. The change in posture is a good sign. So are his clothes. He is wearing a light-blue blazer by a French designer, and it sits well on his broad shoulders. He does not have a tie but a silk cravat, with a splash of colour, to keep his throat warm in the autumnal weather. He never followed fashion but was unafraid to dress up for the occasion. The same man who would wear a sarong when relaxing at home or a dark suit for formal receptions and white short sleeves and tie in the office would also be turned out sharply for a special dinner in a special restaurant.

He sits down in the plush booth seat and smiles, at ease and putting me at ease. He recommends a lobster bisque and steak and I am content to follow – we are in America after all. He asks for the wine list and then asks the sommelier his opinion about whether to choose the Ridge Monte Bello or something from Heitz. We talk about America both in terms of what is happening within the country and what it could mean for our region and Singapore. When he visited the USA on his Eisenhower Fellowship, protests against the Vietnam War were intensifying, even after Johnson's decision not to seek a second term.

"You could see the ferment in this country, and get a sense of things happening – momentous events, historic change. The attitude towards the war changed from weariness to revulsion."

"Have you read Thomas Wolfe?" he asks. "He wrote: 'I will go up and down the country, and back and forth across the country on the great trains that thunder over America. I will go out West where States are square.'"

I have tried to read Wolfe but he has fallen out of literary fashion.

"I like that quote," he continues. "The Americans are so open, it is remarkable. This is responsible for the great adventures and explorations of human endeavour that make the country great. It is compelling that so many Americans attempt to come to terms with themselves, their problems and their society."

"What happens next in America?" I ask, although I already know.

"Among the professional and business circles you can detect a somewhat wishful belief that the radical youth movement would sooner or later be absorbed into the existing order of things. But they don't get the sentiment of the youth and black Americans. Values are being rejected, history and national myths are being questioned. These movements seem – to me at least – to have the greatest long-term significance in the development of American society. "

"So the Americans will withdraw from our region because of domestic politics?"

"They have no choice but to withdraw. But the way they withdraw could afford reasonable prospects for the region to remain viable."

I tell him about my own Eisenhower Fellowship in 2002, when the country was about to invade Iraq, which would, together with Afghanistan, turn out to be another decade-long and exhausting overseas commitment. He listens too about the Global Financial Crisis, and some of the points from my 2009 book, *Asia Alone*, about the prospect of a dangerous divide between the USA and our region, and the rivalry with China already growing in the wake of the GFC.

My dad can be good at listening, just as he was at work with colleagues. He pauses, and takes a bite of the steak, followed by careful and thorough chewing, and then a sip of the red wine. He avoids talking while chewing or drinking these days; with the brainstem condition, the automatic reflexes to close off the windpipe when eating are slowed and sometimes the liquid or bits of food go down the wrong way, and badly. He deliberates and has to be patient. So must I. Anyway, there is no hurry on this occasion.

"Continue to engage the US," he offers. "Remember that when we started during the Vietnam War, we were still building up our SAF and there was not much to offer to the US then. The gap was so big between their capacity and capabilities and ours. When PM offered them the bases after the Brits went, it was worth a try but really pie-in-the-sky. The Americans already had Thailand and the Philippines who were ready and able to host their bases and they didn't need that from us. What did the PM have when he walked into the White House to meet Nixon, when the relationship really started? It was ideas and words. That's about all."

He clears his throat, with an ah-hem that is throaty, audible and habitual. The Anglo-American world was his choice not only when the British were preparing to withdraw, but when he declined the invitation back in Taiping to back the

Communists. But his was not a naïve attitude towards the USA; he was always conscious that the way they saw our region and the world was not the same as we did, and could turn on other factors and often domestic concerns. Singapore would have to build up our own capacities not only in military but in intelligence and diplomacy, and with other ties to a range of countries, outside of the great powers. This was the world in which I was brought up.

What about China? There are elements who have felt closer to China than either he or I have. He does not have to say this.

"We will have to watch China. We always have but now in new ways." He says slowly and quite softly, in a way that makes me lean forward to listen. "Watch what the US does after the isolation of the Great Proletarian Cultural Revolution, the re-emergence of China offering to conduct its external policy which would cut across US commitments to Taiwan. There is a general acceptance that the former policy of total commitment to Taiwan and total containment of mainland China is bankrupt. What will the new policy be, and to what extent are the interests of countries in Southeast Asia involved?

"When the visceral memory of the Communist movement eases in our region, there will be new ways of dealing with China." He supported the relationship that was growing after the visit that Deng Xiao Ping made to Singapore in 1978, and points out that this reciprocated an earlier visit that Lee Kuan Yew and Singaporean officials had made in 1976. "Just like the US and Nixon did in 1972, we need to revisit China policy.

"The problem will come not when China needs our help and we can find opportunity there because we are ahead. When China has grown strong, and they will, it will be different. For us, they will also have influence in other ways – ethnic ties, culture, business – new forms of the united front tactics we have experienced."

Our talk strays to talk about the US and American life. He remembers being on a farm owned by an American he met as part of his official programme, and how spontaneously the invitation was made for him to spend the weekend at their country farm. They had picked apples. He had enjoyed that time, so genteel and different from the wartime farm he had known. Decades later, that same American who hosted him was to come to Singapore on a biomedical conference and, through a Singaporean at the conference, make contact with me. There is now a faded photo of my father in a V-neck sweater, with sunglasses on under a bright sky, holding a single, huge and shiny apple on that farm, and grinning so broadly.

"There is an appeal in the way they live, in the democracy the Americans have developed. But we cannot just copy them. We need to see how it is different from what they had before, and how they changed what was the way in Europe."

Our conversation meanders to the wine. This is another thing that the Americans do well, and in their own way. We drink a toast. I ask him about the photos of him travelling across the region, sometimes with Bogaars and other times with men I cannot name. He remembers each of them and tells me what he was doing there, working behind the scenes and without too much publicity and ceremony. The trips were hard work, but eye-opening and essential. He tells me that he is surprised that the photos are available. I ask about a plaque that used to be in his study and is now in my university office. It is a large thing of heavy wood and brassy metal, from the Philippine Constabulary in appreciation to Tay Seow Huah for "valuable cooperation". It is dated June 1974, and is signed off by the chief of the constabulary, Major General Fidelis V Ramos.

"Ah, Eddie. Some of us joke that he should be called Fast Eddie (like the character in the classic movie *The Hustler*, which he liked). I wonder how he ended up." He is unsurprised that Ramos became a key player when the tide turned against Marcos, who was his cousin and whom he had served, and then eventually President. Very capable and very political, he remembers of his counterpart, and very good at hiding that.

I tell him that I once hosted Ramos at the think tank I chair and he remembered the occasion when that plaque was given. "He would. But he didn't tell you why they gave us the plaque did he?" We laugh. He tells me more stories about generals in Indonesia and Thailand he met, not just in an office or at a reception, but in border towns and small roadside coffee shops. I have spent years watching the politics in the region too, but in the decades after – and I do not recognise most of the names. People who were in key circles can fade over time, just like newspaper columns and headlines do. He thinks one day he will write a spy story; fiction, of course.

"It was important that I went to every single country in our region before my time in the USA. To see things for myself. Otherwise, you just read – in English – and see things through the authors' eyes."

"But your library is full of books that colonialists wrote about the tropics. Or from Western observers who came later."

"You have to understand power and the perspective of the powerful, and it was the West who had power – who still have. But once we do understand, then we have to find our own way, you see. Get beyond orientalism in understanding ourselves. Understand history and race but to be modern, to look ahead and move forward."

It is time for dessert and he suggests crepes done at the table. He jokes about how when I was a kid, I used to always choose chocolate ice cream with chocolate sauce, and then ask for additional sauce.

It is he who then turns to talk about the refugees, the boat people from Vietnam. He asks if it is true that I had questioned during a public seminar the very policies that he had explained in 1975. Yes, I say, but it was almost a decade later, when the worst of the situation had ebbed, and Singapore was more stable and secure. The talk was at the university. I was a student and believed that surely, we as a people could do more, especially the pioneer generation like him who suffered WWII. His lips purse, thinking. It is not wrong to question a policy when conditions change. But it is not wise to do so at a public forum. You never know who is listening, not for the ideas but only to note who is saying what. In his own time in university, there had been students who had spoken up so eloquently and passionately about causes, and little good came of it.

We talk about the end of the Cold War, and what it meant for the region. I tell him about the visits I made from 1995 to 1999 to Vietnam, Cambodia, Laos and Myanmar, all the countries that were closed in his time. He nods and tells me about a trip to Moscow when it was so cold he returned with an *ushanka* hat in charcoal grey. No one bet on a peaceful resolution to the Cold War but all of them worked towards such a hope. "I never accepted the Domino Theory as fate; I mean, these are scenarios not determined outcomes. It could have happened, but by engaging the USA and using that time for our own progress, to stabilise. There was so much that the people wanted, and needed, were hungry for. Not so different from us. We could put down ideological cudgels, beat swords into plough shares."

When they serve the dessert, he rubs his palms and purses his lips so the tip of his tongue is visible. To think he was once a hungry boy at the side of a street during the end-years of the war, and now was dining at the best restaurant in the most powerful country in the world.

"You aren't going to ask me secrets?"

"Would you answer if I did?"

"Maybe." He smiles broadly. "But even if he knows, a son may do best to keep his father's secrets."

Makan

What has changed and how have our nation and people progressed?

He always loved a good curry and we would go regularly to Banana Leaf Apolo where Mr Chellappan, the owner, would be sitting behind the cashier, with a photograph of Lee Kuan Yew proudly displayed on the wall behind him. The banana leaf is set out in front of us, and the server comes around with the rice and complimentary vegetable dishes. He rattles off the order – just about everything, especially the mutton curry but not the giant prawns which are not worth the money. He asks if they have a small fish head and, when they say no, he just asks for a small plate of the fish curry (without any fish) to be added to some of the fried fish roe, if they had it.

Tonight, my father is looking relaxed, wearing a short-sleeved shirt and casual light-grey trousers. He managed to get home before we came out. After a shower and without applying hair cream, a heavy lock of his hair, wavy when longer, is touching the severe straight black frame of his glasses. He gets up to wash his hands thoroughly and with a lot of soap and water at the sink on one side of the restaurant. I do the same. We are going to use our hands to eat.

"What if I were to tell you that some students these days don't eat Indian food, except for Roti Prata?"

"Not surprised. It's very different from Chinese food. Just as most Indians are different from most Chinese, and most Chinese don't really mix around so well. But they eat spicy?"

"Yes, chilli is the national condition."

"Good."

When we head back to the table, tray-loads of small melamine plates of dishes are brought and laid out between us. It looks too much for two but, with big helpings of rice and lime juice or, for him, a cold Tiger, we always do our best to finish whatever is before us. He has told me before about the origins of Fish Head Curry. The one at Banana Leaf Apolo was, to his taste, good but not his favourite. However, on balance, the other dishes were good and it was air-conditioned, so that's why he took me there. But more than just being a foodie, he told the story as one about the fusion and opportunity of Singapore, if the racial differences could be managed and the energy of change could bring positive dynamics.

We talk about culture in Singapore, how it has changed. From his time in the USA, the cultural revolution struck him strongly while, in the 1970s, Singapore put into place regulations against long hair and Western "yellow culture". It was a high political signature of that era. I update him on the cultural wars in the USA and how some aspects have rippled into Singapore. In his time, the links to the West were far fewer and confined to a small proportion of people. The changes since – in globalisation, in the Internet and social media, and the everyday nature of flying to the other side of the world – are hard to imagine. Have I read Mead and Geertz, he asks, and I think he is surprised that I have. Mead's ideas can be applied to Singapore. He was, I knew, about to launch into a long paragraph of exposition; he was always sharing ideas with us, even when we were children and so much of it seemed above our heads.

"So you know the idea of figuration? The first stage is when the grandson accepts that his life and his society will not be in many ways different from that of his grandfather's, and that's not possible today. The second stage, which she calls co-figurative, is when there is distinct change but still incorporates most of the attitudes and values transmitted from the father's generation. 'Pre-figurative' is the third stage: where change is brought about by continuous adjustments to ever rapidly increasing developments. Experience and previous cultural processes of dealing with change are no longer regarded as adequate. Authority is seriously attacked and questioned, and existing institutional values are turned over. No one can stop change, and no one should deny the need. But there is a question of pace, of adjustment."

"So you made a very different life from your father's, and I have to figure out my own?"

"All your generation and those coming after."

We are quiet for a while, just enjoying the food and passing the plates between us, with a few comments of what he or I like. He pauses to take a sip of the Tiger beer, which has left a ring of condensation on the table. I am aware of the continuing tick from his heart valve as it opens and closes.

"The situation on independence and into the 1970s was fraught. There were challenges on many fronts, and we had little capacity, insufficient resources, and if things really went bad, no reserve, no assurance that we would not end up in a downward spiral. Look at Sri Lanka. I don't think anyone needs to apologise for what we did in the 1960s and the early 1970s. Even students and social activity groups were not innocent, they were part of a wider network – sometimes unknowingly manipulated. We did what we needed to do."

I tell him I was involved in student politics in the mid-1980s, leading the university students in a public petition against the graduate mother policy that PM Lee proposed. He reminds me about the actions against the student union leaders a decade before me.

"Did any of my old colleagues call you?"

"Should they have?"

"If students protest peacefully on an issue and keep to the campus, that should be allowed. When students take their activities outside campus and join hands with diverse groups, especially workers, that's different. You see, people get used to seeing patterns, and these ways of seeing impose themselves on how we look at connections, motivations. You are looking for something and sometimes you see things that may or may not be really there."

"You are trying to tell me something."

"Perhaps I am. But it could sound in my own head too much like a *mea culpa*. I would not intend that."

"So...?"

"Maybe we can just enjoy the meal and time together?"

"We don't have to agree on everything."

"We are family."

We talk about his family. How his siblings have aged and what their children have done, as far as I know. They are dispersed across the world, in the UK, Australia and even Italy and Thailand, and of course in Malaysia. He frowns from concern and asks more details, and I tell him it is mainly Joanne who has kept up with them, sent them birthday greetings or attended funerals and sent condolences. I cut off contact with them after he had gone. When his mother, my grandmother, died, they called me out of the blue to ask me to head the funeral procession as the eldest son of her eldest son. I had declined. He frowns and looks down. He tells me how when Joanne was studying in the UK, she would keep in touch regularly with her aerogrammes and neat handwriting. She was at the time seeing a British lad and he was not at all sure if he approved, afraid that she would never return. He looks up again when I tell him that, in more recent years, I have called on the uncles and met some of my cousins in KL. I also keep in touch with my cousins, the Wees from my mother's side, with whom we had shared a house decades ago, children I had grown up with. There is an approving nod, and I realise that at this late age, it matters that he might approve of what I do.

We talk about his colleagues who had been closer, those I grew up calling "uncle". That is for many a common social habit but, in our house, I was encouraged generally to call them by their surname, unless they were closer friends (similarly, he preferred that when my friends visited and met him, they might call him Mr Tay). I do not talk about the past, but rather about what happened to them since last he heard. What happened to George Bogaars saddens him. Not just the strokes that he suffered but before that, when he was in service but sidelined. How Nathan went on to chair Singapore Press Holdings brings a wry smile. His appointment as ambassador and then President does not surprise him. He is pleased that each of them made the effort to meet me after I entered university and was active in the students' union. "What did they say about government?"

When I visited Uncle George, he was living in a small apartment in the city. He had long retired from the civil service, and had stepped down as Chairman of Keppel Corporation. He advised me against joining the civil service. It was not the same as the early years, Bogaars said firmly, even if his voice was weaker after his heart attacks. There was no need and there was little appreciation of the sacrifices. My father nods. He asks me if I know any other children from his peers in that early batch of senior civil servants and perm secs who entered the civil service. I can think of politicians who are children of politicians, but struggle to name one in the civil service from the permanent secretaries of the pioneer generation.

I would interact with Ambassador (as he was then) Nathan fairly often, especially when he started up the Institute of Defence and Strategic Studies for the government and I was a young chairman of the Singapore Institute of International

Affairs. We would meet in various Track II meetings and were the two government nominees to an expert and eminent persons group for the region, discussing the peace and security of the region, and sometimes he would, for a moment, refer to me as Sonnie. But I tell my father about the first time he reached out to me.

"It was when he was Chairman of Singapore Press Holdings. After I had been in the news about the students' union petition against the government scheme to give privileges to graduate mothers."

"He invited you over to meet? He was decent about things?"

"Yes, very. He gave me a photo from the newspaper of me shaking hands with the government minister when the student delegation handed over our petition."

"Good. And good thing it was a petition – you didn't organise a mass sit-in or a protest march."

"No, some wanted that. But, no."

"Good."

Another time was when S R Nathan was Ambassador in the US and I was finishing my Masters there and went to DC. He invited me to stay with him, and we had dinner together. There had been a controversy back in Singapore when an author had spoken up to critique the new PM Goh Chok Tong in a way that was taken to be too personal. My father remembered Mr Goh from the NOL days and thought well of him.

"Ambassador Nathan told me he knew I would want to comment on politics when I got back."

"He didn't try to stop you."

"No, just warned me about the limits. To watch what might be allowed and accepted."

"He was always very careful."

"When I was appointed Nominated Member of Parliament for the second time, he was President, and presided at the swearing-in at the Istana."

"Sorry I missed that."

I now mention the book prize that we created in 2000. The Tay Seow Huah Prize for the best Masters thesis at the

S Rajaratnam School of International and Security Studies, part of the Nanyang Technological University. It was endowed by Joanne and me, with Nathan, who also arranged to personally give out the prize that first year. He was then President. My father finds irony in this.

He talks about his choice to stay on in Singapor rather than return to Malaya, and what has happened since. By 1980, Singapore was ahead but many thought it was a matter of time before Malaysia would catch up and overtake us. Dr Mahathir was yet to become Prime Minister but, as DPM, had already combined Thatcherite changes with the *bumiputra* New Economic Policy to give Malays a stronger hand and larger share of business and profits. As PM, he made some bold steps and, for a while, it was Malaysia that seemed on the rise. But after the Asian Crisis of 1997 and the split with Anwar, the antagonism increased and the talk of KL competing with Singapore faded.

"Choosing Singapore, well it wasn't really much of a choice. The events just happened so fast, and then there was so much to be done."

"Remember how you and your brothers would always debate about which country was doing better?"

"What's happened since is just tragic. And the Chinese?"

"Your brothers are still there. But many of my friends are ex-Malaysians..."

"Refugees from a slow-motion ethnic cleansing."

" ... like you."

He guffaws.

Have I ever thought of migrating? I tell him I once did, when a number of the activists I knew from the students' union were swept up in the 1987 Operation Spectrum. But I didn't and then work swept me up. Later, I even helped start the Singapore International Foundation, which had been adopted by the second-generation government leaders of the Next Lap and, then 10 years on, was in Parliament.

I ask him if he ever thought of that, entering Parliament and politics. A contemporary of his among the civil service permanent secretaries, Howe Yoon Chong, had after retiring from the civil service. Elected in 1979, Mr Howe served as Minister for Defence and then Health before stepping down in 1984.

"They once asked me to consider."

"Why didn't you accept?"

"As a permanent secretary there's already a lot you can do, and you get it done behind the scenes. Politics is not easy and it's not for everyone. Look what happened to Yoon Chong. When you live and especially when you live long enough, there are going to be many twists and not all are going to end happily."

Supper at Home
How shall we then live?

"Are you still grieving?"

"I guess I am, in my own way. I regret there wasn't more time to know you better."

"I do too."

"Explain."

"I am no storyteller. You are and you know the story."

"I am not asking for a story. Tell me the truth."

"Ha. What is truth? There are, sometimes, things that are not the truth, and yet are still true."

He is relaxing after dinner at home, lying back in an easy chair with his feet up. It is an interesting piece, with khaki leather around a bamboo structure, stained a dark brown. A bit Western but tropical, and yet not colonial. He is dressed in a white linen short-sleeved shirt, casual and cool with cassock-coloured pants, something like what a priest or else Nehru would wear. He has taken off his glasses and, as he leans back, a lock of his wavy hair tumbles over his forehead.

"What are facts, especially after so many decades?

I nod and he carries on: "You write fiction, right? What if I told you that not every Konfrontasi bombing was real? That out of all those bombings that history books tell us went off some may have been planted and detonated without harm to anyone so that our operatives inside Indonesia would not be fingered? Or what if I told you not every Communist detained was more than a misguided idealist who was too stubborn to confess?"

We discuss fiction. He encouraged my writing from the start, asking Edwin Thumboo to read and assess them. In 1980, *Prism*, a slim collection of poems that a teenaged me had written and Thumboo had vetted, was issued, which my father arranged to be published. In 2009 came my novel, *City of Small Blessings*. In the latter, there is an old man who grew up during the harsh war years and contributed to the country, to retire and then emigrate but then to return, only to find that so much had changed that he was lost. There is also a son, who studied abroad and stayed on to work, only to return when things went badly with his father. Both were dedicated to him.

"It's not an easy read."

"Don't think you meant it to be."

"You have to sort things out, when you are in the middle of things, living things."

"Hmm, yes. 'Life is very short and anxious for those who forget the past, neglect the present, and fear the future.' Is he meant to be me, the old man?"

"You were never that old."

"Is the son, you?"

"I never went abroad to study or to work."

"You did the torture scene well."

"Thank you."

"Reminds me of the time I had to go down and see your teacher in school."

"Oh yes, when I got the F for English composition."

"Well, first he marked it as an A. Then the bugger scribbled, 'You are sadist', and changed the mark."

"So you went down to tell him that such tortures do happen."

"Haha. That, and worse. Look at Pol Pot."

"My teacher was terrified."

"Deservedly." We both laugh.

Then I have to ask: "Did we?"

"No, never. But if you say that, in questioning, we use psychological methods, you would not be far wrong."

It has been a pleasant evening. He had earlier wanted me to go up to dinner with his family, at his sister's, but I hadn't wanted to. He then called the day before to say that he wouldn't go up to that dinner, and so I changed plans. We ate just at his place. He had cooked steak for us – a good cut of meat that he then doused in thick soya sauce and Maggi garlic chilli sauce as a marinade, and threw on a hot pan. There were Birds Eye peas from a packet in the freezer, and a cabbage that he bought thinking it was iceberg lettuce. He had never really cooked, never really lived alone. But the cabbage was remedied by also being thrown on the pan and singed, and the whole meal was just fine for me. He was relaxed and our talk meandered.

Some of it was about his family. He mentioned some of the things that were parts of stories told and retold at the dining table when I was young, and when one or another relative would visit. Yet, even in these old tales, there were snippets, nuances that are newer. But tonight we talk less about his family and days back in Taiping and more about ours, and in Singapore. We talk about the long days we would spend at Changi Point under the tall Casuarina trees, and how Joanne and I would squeal and protest when we stepped on the prickly cones, with her picking a way gingerly around them while I ran right through, yelling as if my lungs would burst. My mother, his Cecelia, would be there, sitting on a mat on the sand, with her cat-eye sunglasses. We do not talk much or even directly about her. But I have to ask.

"You said somewhere, when someone asked about your work in security and the risks, that this is a quality that our wives have – they don't nag? They allow us to pursue our ambitions without holding us back."

"Yes."

"But mum used to nag me all the time. When I got into student union politics and then later when I was in Parliament. When I was travelling across the region, when I went up to

Pakistan after 9/11, or in Bangkok when there were street protests against Singapore and they burnt effigies of our PM, and when they had a coup."

"Ah yes, well… I did say it. But it doesn't mean it always was the case. Sometimes we just say what we hope would be true."

I laugh. "Mind you, I miss it now she is gone. It was her way of caring, I think."

"Yes. It was."

I do not tell him how Cecelia struggled in the years after he left, as if she had been in a dialogue and argument about all that mattered and he had just walked away, wordlessly, the points left hanging in the air. Grief and anger took her to a place that she had no idea existed until she had arrived. What I do tell him is how she learnt to cook in the later years. Where she had been a poor cook when he lived with us, she was then able to turn out Nasi Lemak meals that were so good that not only Joanne and I craved for them but so did our friends who had tried it. She coped. She put the cudgels down slowly, and took up the Bible, and was to find her own peace. He would not have had to worry about her.

We talk about how Changi Point gave way to the airport. There was a poem in *Prism* about that construction. I came back to Changi and the theme of change in a later poem: "Nothing is as it was. Nothing as it will be."

"Things do change so fast, agreed. But be careful about nostalgia."

"Odd thing for a historian to say."

"It's good to remember. The danger is when nostalgia clouds the memory in a glow, a patina, that the past were better times, that maybe we used to be better people."

"They weren't? You weren't?"

"Well," he smiles. "Maybe in some ways. Certainly it was simpler, clearer what had to be done. But none of us were nostalgic ourselves. We were trying to be modern. Much more concerned about the future than the past, and doing what we could to make that future eventuate."

"We have to move forward, and we have to let go of the past."

"For a long time, I would think of your grandfather, my father. I hardly knew him before he was taken. I don't know where he's buried. I don't know what he would make of the decisions I made."

"Yes."

He pauses.

"Then I realised so long as I was trying to keep him alive like that, I could not really decide things for myself. If we are to live ourselves, as we want and need, there comes a point at which we must let go, relinquish the dead."

"Let them become the photograph on the table."

Now it is he who nods and says, "Yes".

"You don't have to do what you think I wanted for you. Live your own life."

I will, I say to myself. Yet, beyond 1980 there is to be no future for him. How should we talk about the past, the ending?

When we returned and a memorial service was organised, there was some debate about whether a church service was appropriate. It had been a public decision for him to leave the church in Taiping and, in all those years after, he had never gone back. In London, however, something had happened; at least, according to his sister, Peggy. She had been at his bedside in the hospital that last evening before the operation, with Uncle David, his youngest brother, and her husband, Peter Ferry the Scottish missionary. From that evening, his sister was convinced that he had found peace no matter what the outcome. They had prayed for him that evening.

But she was to recount this only many years after his funeral. Some five or six years after my father's death, Aunt Peggy was at another family funeral in Singapore, at which any number of prayers and hymns were sung. My sister, Joanne, dutifully attended the proceedings, and she had looked and felt downcast at the outpouring about the blessings of dying in faith. Afterwards, our Aunt had told this story to her in consolation, assurance. Joanne, regularly attending church since her teens, was happy, relieved.

It was to be more years before my sister told this to me. It was a surprise to me, but not an unpleasant one. By the time I write this, there is no way to verify this. My Aunt Peggy and her husband have both been in and out of hospital and may not remember this. My Uncle David, who was also there, had a condition that affects his memory, and passed on in the year I was finishing this book. Perhaps what my Aunt remembers of my father that evening so long ago was real. Or perhaps it was what they hoped for. These are matters, after all, of faith.

In this conversation on a late evening after dinner, in his apartment shortly before he would go to his operation, we cannot raise this and the conversation must acknowledge the risk but at the same time be circumspect about possible death and what comes thereafter. We talk about his motto.

Magni Nominis Umbra was the motto he had adopted as his own. He appropriated it from his school in Taiping that he entered as a charity case and emerged as a top student and a sportsman. It was always taken that the translation was: "In the Shadow of His Greatness." In the context of a Christian upbringing, it might mean the humility of a servant, that we human beings are in the shadow of the greatness of God. At the end, together with his name, a photo and the dates of life and death, the motto was chiseled into the slab of marble that sealed the niche with his ashes in 1980.

Decades after, the government closed the Mount Vernon columbarium and required families to remove the ashes and remains interred there. Joanne arranged for my father's ashes to be moved to a private memorial chamber in a church and placed alongside the ashes of Cecelia Cheong Keong Hin. We informed his siblings. By then, his mother and elder sister had died, but his two younger brothers, Jack and David, despite their being in their late 70s, made the journey down from KL. Opening up the niche at Mount Vernon, the memorial slab with the motto had to be broken, then the ashes transferred from the old wooden casket from that cremation in England into a new metal urn. When I did that, my hands were grey and dusty from the ash from the marble and what remained of my father. The slab from the niche was now in three fragments, from which the words could still be read: *Magni Nominis Umbra.*

In the shadow of His greatness. What did this mean, really?

Knowing that we are all in the shadow of God's magnificence has wisdom. Other interpretations, bereft of the link to the Christian faith, are also possible. The motto can mean the shadow of a great name: one whose early greatness has been attenuated by circumstances.

Might it signify the first steps Sonnie made to recover from the impacts of WWII and the killing of his father, and the entry into a school and then finding a path out from that small town and its colonial world? In that journey, it could signify the pressure that you are in the shadow of great expectations. In the context of a pioneer and a civil servant, could it alternatively signify that his efforts are in the shadow of the grand endeavour to build up a state and assist its political masters? This is especially when decades pass, and the telling of history conceals almost as much as it uncovers and the names of so many pioneers who contributed are forgotten, left behind in the shadows of a few great names. A final way of using the phrase is to signify someone whose potential achievements have been attenuated, less than what is could have been because of some circumstance, such as a heart attack and an early death.

I cannot decide which is correct or more appropriate. I do not say this to him during our conversation. I am not worried of his reaction; he would just smile. But it is not the right way to close off a fine evening, let alone a life that was too brief. My father, who had learnt Latin and adopted the motto in the first place, might have known and, I suspect, would have laughed.

"I should have liked to have written a letter. Something you and Joanne could keep and maybe one day give to the children I hope you each have."

"Don't worry about such things."

"Maybe later. Right now, I think I better let you go. I am not sure how things will go for me. Not sure when we might meet again, if it will be possible and if so how and where."

"Of course, we can. There won't hardly be a day when either I or your daughter will not think of you."

"Then I suppose I won't really be gone."

He pauses and I reluctantly rise to go.

"Do you remember the big old house? The one at Mount Pleasant?"

"Yes of course, I grew up there. It's gone, demolished for the expressway. But it is still the place I dream of, when I dream of home."

"Well, next time you think of me and want to talk, we can meet there."

CHRONOLOGY OF KEY EVENTS

23 April 1933   Tay Seow Huah was born in Penang to Tay Hooi Eng, a civil servant, and Mdm Goon Goot Meng; the second child and eldest son, and known in the family as Sonnie. Tay senior is posted to work in different colonial posts and the family follow, ending up in Taiping.

1942   The Japanese overwhelm the British and occupy Malaya. Tay senior is accused of helping the British and taken from the family house in Nibong Tebal. He never returns. Sonnie is 9 years old and there are six other children. The widow Tay returns to Penang to seek assistance and shelter from her family.

1944   Leaving Penang, the Tays attempt to run a farm. Within months, the widow and and most of the family give up and return. Sonnie and one brother stay on with an uncle. The experience is one of hardship, hunger and severe illness. He recovers but is scarred.

1945   At the end of the Japanese Occupation, the Tays move again to Taiping. These are hard times, and they are taken in by the church. Soon after, the widow secures a job with the colonial administration and things settle. He joins King Edward VII School and becomes one of the best students in both studies and sports. The school motto *Magni Nominus Umbra* will later be adopted as his personal motto.

1949-50   Sonnie transfers to St Michael's Institution, a mission school in Ipoh, to prepare his Form 6 and university entrance. He also studies Latin to prepare for medical school.

He completes his School Certificate, emerging as a top student in the state of Perak to win a scholarship.

1951   He is admitted to the University of Malaya, based in Singapore, and enrols in the medical faculty. Just weeks after, he shifts to the Faculty of Arts. He stays at Dunearn Road Hostels and makes many friends there. He meets Miss Cheong Keong Hin, known as Cecelia, a Singaporean student at the Teachers' Training College, and they court.

1954   He graduates with a BA. However, he is not admitted to do his Honours as he had hoped. He returns to Malaya and teaches at a school in Port Dickson and briefly considers joining the armed forces. He climbs Gunung Tahan, the highest mountain in peninsular Malaya. He decides to return to Singapore and enrols for his Honours in History.

1956   He graduates with Honours and joins the civil service, as part of the administrative service. He begins work as Assistant Commissioner for Labour, arbitrating disputes between workers and employers.

1957   Sonnie marries Cecelia. They move into their first home together, a rented house on Kampong Java Road. He sends funds to support his family and his brother studying abroad, and the young couple struggle.

Aug 1957   He is posted to the Harbour Board where he is assigned to look at the situation and welfare of the port workers.

1958   His first child, Joanne Tay Siok Wan, is born. The family move to another rented house, in Katong, which they share with Cecelia's sister and her husband.

1959   The People's Action Party (PAP) wins elections and form the government. Shortly after, they administer a pay cut for all the civil servants. With the monetary obligations to his family, the young couple struggle.

1960   Tay is posted to the Ministry of Finance and its Division of Commerce & Industry. He sees how the PAP led by Lee Kuan Yew begins to split from the Left and pro-Communists.

1961   His second child, Simon Tay Seong Chee, is born

1963   Tay is appointed Acting Staff Manager at the Port of Singapore Authority. The family move to government housing, at Raeburn Park near the port. His work is to deal with workers and unions, to negotiate their terms and conditions and develop schemes for job improvement and productivity. Underlying this are the strains with the Left-leaning unions.

1965   On behalf of the government and port authority, Tay negotiates improvements to pay and conditions for the workers, and this eases tensions with the workers and unions. When he leaves the job, the 11,000-strong union for port workers appeals to PM Lee for him to stay. They cite him as being: "greatly responsible for the betterment of the port workers and also for the friendly and harmonious relations that have existed hitherto between the union and the PSA for the last two years."

1965   He is appointed Director of the Special Branch, a key agency for security from the colonial administration in dealing with the Emergency Communist insurgency. He is the first Singaporean director appointed after Separation and the country's independence. Tay is also involved in the wider work of urgently building up Singapore's defence capability and military with advice from "Mexicans".

Feb 1966   He reorganises the Special Branch to establish the Security and Intelligence Division, separate from the Internal Security Department. Both are under the Ministry of Interior and Defence and Tay serves as the first Director for Security and Intelligence, considering both external and internal challenges.

1966 Operations are undertaken to detain former Barisan Sosialis MPs under the Internal Security Act. This is after they abandon Parliament to take the struggle to the streets, and some organise protests against the Vietnam War.

1967 Tay receives a prestigious National Day Award, the Meritorious Service Award. His citation reads: "He brought to this completely new job a critical and enquiring mind, a robust outlook in tough situations. These together with great application enabled the internal intelligence of the Government to anticipate and meet with sensitiveness and effectiveness the many new problems independence brought to the security field."

1970-71 While retaining his position as Director for Security and Intelligence, he is appointed Acting Permanent Secretary. The MID is split into two ministries, separating Defence and Home Affairs. He receives the prestigious Eisenhower Fellowship in the USA, which lasts six months. Upon his return, Tay resumes his position as Permanent Secretary at the Ministry of Home Affairs.

September 1972 At the Ministry of Home Affairs, he drives efforts to strengthen and modernise the Police Force and to establish CISCO. He continues to be involved in external security matters, especially to engage the USA. He accompanies PM Lee to a series of Commonwealth meetings and trips.

31 January 1974 Terrorists attack and bomb the Shell oil refinery on Pulau Bukom. In trying to escape, they hijack the *Laju* ferry but are surrounded by boats from the Marine Police and other Singapore agencies. Tay directs the government operations to deal with the situation and also briefs the media on the situation each day.

8 February 1974 The Singapore government offers safe conduct out from the country to the attackers, who ask the

Japanese government to provide a plane for them to go to the Middle East. There are eight intense days of negotiations, in which Tay plays a key role, with the attackers and with other governments, especially Japan. After the Japanese Embassy in Kuwait is attacked and captured, the Japanese accede to the attackers' demands. They are released and escorted to Kuwait.

Mid-1974 Tay suffers a massive heart attack while at work in his office. He is stabilised and is sent to Houston, USA for open-heart surgery.

Dec 1974 He returns and slowly resumes work. He leaves the Ministry of Home Affairs in December 1974 and is posted to the Ministry of Defence as Permanent Secretary.

June 1975 With the Vietnam War ending, Tay is involved in operations to deal with the swelling crisis from the outflow of people by air and sea and to explain Singapore's policies.

June 1976 After a medical review, he is retired from the civil service at age 42. He joins the University of Singapore as Visiting Fellow to teach at the History Department.

6 April 1978 He is selected to chair a high-profile discussion with Lee Kuan Yew on TV, focusing on bilingualism, a controversial and new policy.

1979 He is appointed Executive Director of the Singapore Manufacturers' Association. The sector is growing strongly in Singapore and expanding in the region, and the Association is the leading chamber for Singaporean manufacturers and businesses. There is talk that Tay may return to public service.

1980 Tay is diagnosed with a brainstem tumour and leaves for surgery in London. The surgery uncovers instead a mass of aneurysms.

19 September 1980 He dies in London without regaining consciousness from the operation. After a funeral and cremation in England, a memorial service is held in Singapore. Tay was 47.

SELECTED BIBLIOGRAPHY

This book is not an academic work and footnotes have not been used. Acknowledgement is, however, made to books referred to, especially when they have been quoted. Further, there are books that were owned by Tay Seow Huah and lined his bookshelves. There are also unpublished reports and archives that he wrote or for which he was interviewed. A selection of these sources is set out briefly below.

Specific Sources and Books

An Unexpected Journey: Path to the Presidency, S R Nathan and Timothy Auger (Singapore: Editions Didier Millet, 2011). The memoir was of specific reference for Chapter 1 on the *Laju* Incident, and Chapter 4 on Tay and Nathan as civil servants during the early years of the PAP government.

Malaya Upside Down, Chin Kee Onn (Malaysia: Federal Publications, 1976). Containing information about Malaya during WW2 and the Japanese Occupation, it was used for Chapter 2. Tay's copy was purchased in 1977 and has his signature.

Not for Circulation: The George E. Bogaars Story, Bertha Henson (Singapore: NUS Press, 2021) was referred to for chapters 4 and 5. Bogaars was an exceptional man and a most distinguished pioneer civil servant. The author is glad to see this book written about the person who preceded Tay at the Special Branch and is thought to have recommended him for the post. Henson suggests that Bogaars and Tay were "family friends". They were friends but had met in the course of work.

Standing Tall: The Goh Chok Tong Years, Peh Shing Huei (Singapore: World Scientific, 2021) was specifically referred to for Chapter 1, contrasting then PM Goh's response to a later terrorist hijacking.

The Jungle is Neutral, F Spencer Chapman (London: Chatto & Windus, 1949) was a book that Tay read more than once and regarded as a classic reference for jungle trekking and survival. He always kept a copy on his shelves – the last being a 1973 Corgi edition. It was a reference for chapters 2 and 6.

The Last Fools: The Eight Immortals of Lee Kuan Yew, Peh Shing Huei (ed.) (Singapore: Nutgraf Books, 2022) was referred to for Chapter 5, about George Bogaars, and in Chapter 9 more generally.

Towards Tomorrow: Essays on Development and Social Transformation in Singapore, (Singapore: NTUC, 1973). Specific reference for Chapter 4 was made from the chapter by then PSA chairman, Howe Yoon Chong, "The Port of Singapore". The book was dedicated to Lee Kuan Yew on his 50th birthday. Tay's copy was sent with compliments from the Director and Staff, Internal Security Department, dated 19 September 1973.

War of the Running Dogs: 1948-1960, Noel Barber (London: Fontana, 1971) was of reference for Chapter 2. Tay's copy is marked, in sections, with notes disagreeing with some assessments by Barber.

Why Am I Here? Overcoming Hardships of Local Seafarers, S R Nathan; Bernard T G Tan; Wee Seo Lay (eds.) (Singapore: Centre for Maritime Studies, National University of Singapore, 2010). Specific reference is made to this book in Chapter 4. The book is dedicated by S R Nathan, "To the memory of Tay Seow Huah, a buddy who stood by me and shared the unpredictable stresses and strains I faced at work during those times". The author's copy was presented by then President Nathan at the book launch to Mrs Tay Seow Huah, the author's mother.

Primary Materials

Declassified Materials referred to in Chapter 7 are cited from Ang Cheng Guan's article (*see* General Sources) and include: (1) "Ambassador Bell meets with PM Lee", 3 Apr 1966, RG 59, Box 2651, POL 2-1; and (2) "Memorandum of conversation: George Bogaars, the permanent secretary, Ministry of Interior and Defence; Tay Seow Huah, Director; John B Dexter Deputy Chief of Mission American Embassy Singapore, 12 Jan 1968, Singapore 1-256 Enclosure No 2, RG 79, Box 1622, 7-Singapore.

Edwin Thumboo, eulogy delivered at Tay's memorial service, 1980, was a reference for Chapter 6 and referred to in Chapter 8.

Police Life magazine, an internal magazine of the force, Volume 4 No 6 of 1980, carried an obituary tribute to Tay and was referred to for Chapter 1 and Chapter 8.

Tay Seow Huah, interviews by the Oral History Unit, recorded in the year before his death, were specifically referenced for Chapter 4.

Tay Seow Huah, Eisenhower Fellowships confidential trip report, 1971 is referred to in chapters 5 and 9. For Chapter 9, sections of Tay's observations are used in the constructed conversation, verbatim.

Tay Seow Huah, "War and Peace in S.E.A: A Singapore Perspective", *Singapore Herald*, 25 Aug 1970. Adapted from a speech Tay gave for the Ministry of Education, it was referred to for Chapter 5.

This Singapore, Ilsa Sharp (ed.) (Singapore: Times Publishing, 1975), a magazine published to mark the tenth anniversary of Singapore's independence. Tay's interview in the publication was referred to in chapters 6 and 9.

Newspaper Reports
For Chapter 1, the author referred to the extensive coverage of the *Laju* Incident in *The Straits Times,* as well as *The Japan Times* and *The New York Times.*

These include: from *The Straits Times* (all in 1974), (1) "Safe Passage for Bukom Bombers", 1 Feb; (2) "Boatman attacked, Then Scrambled to Plant Explosives", Feb 1; (3) "Three Men who had to deal with the Bukom Bombers", 12 Feb; (4) "So I thought I was marked for death: Freed hostage", 2 Feb; (5) "We were not pushed overboard", 2 Feb; (5) "JAL: We Won't Send Pick-up Plane", 2 Feb; (6) "Hijackers: Three Moves by Govt", 4 Feb; (7) "No Pushover", 9 Feb.

From *The Japan Times*: (1) "Singapore-related Raid Items Seized by Police", 3 Feb; (2) "PLFP, Red Army Strike Again", 8 Feb; (3) "Opinions from Abroad", 12 Feb;

From *The New York Times*: "Terrorists in Singapore Menace Refinery Then Take 5 Hostages", 1 Feb.

Additionally, the transcripts of the briefings conducted each night by Tay to reporters from the newspapers were of reference.

In 2024, two articles were published in *The Straits Times* on or just before the 50th anniversary of the Laju Incident: (1) "The Laju Incident: A Reminder about Security and Palestine Issue" (by the author), 29 Jan, and (2) "Risking his life to save hostages", 31 Jan.

For Chapter 4, the author referred to the coverage on port disputes with unions and in the arbitration in *The Straits*

Times. These include from 1963: (1) "Lee Meets Harbour Staff Leaders", 14 June; (2) "Port Men to Vote on Strike", 21 July; (3) "PM Lee Announces Cancellation of Harbour Staff Union", 23 July; (4) "Ong's Strong Blast at SATU", 27 July. From 1964: (5) "Registrar gives nod to SHBSA", 16 Jan; (6) "SHB End Contract Labour Use", 26 Mar. From 1965: (7) "Annual Wage Bill Would increase to $38 million", 30 Apr; (8) "Port peace plea", 21 Feb; (9) "Petulant Officials of the Authority", 27 Apr; (10) "Workers Claims Total $17 Million", 25 Aug; (11) "Let Mr Tay stay, unions plea to Prime Minister: Port Chief to Head Special Branch", 3 Sept.

For Chapter 8, the author referred to: (1) "Aid for Refugee Ships", *The Straits Times*, 5 May 1975; (2) "The dockers' best friend calls it a day", *New Nation*, 18 June 1976; (3) "Tay to teach post-war history at varsity", *The Straits Times*, 20 Jan 1977; (4) "Tay is tipped to be SMA Executive director", *The Straits Times*, 29 June 1978; (5) "SMA Plans 5 missions next year", *The Business Times*, 5 Oct 1979; (6) "US-ASEAN seminars early next month", *The Straits Times*, 16 Oct 1979; (7) "Tay dies after operation in London", *The Straits Times*, 21 Sept 1980; (8) "350 pay last respects to Tay at memorial service", *The Sunday Times*, 5 Oct 1980;

General Sources
Beating the Odds Together: 50 Years of Singapore-Israel Ties, Mattia Tomba (ed.) (Singapore: World Scientific, 2020) was referred to for Chapter 5, especially the contribution by Peter Ho, former Permanent Secretary of Defence and Head of Civil Service, entitled, "A Mexican Fandango with a Poisonous Shrimp".

Defending the Lion City, Tim Huxley (London: Allen & Unwin, 2001) referred to in Chapter 4, reviewing the early years of the SAF, which includes a brief history of the Security and Intelligence Division.

From Third World To First: The Singapore Story, 1965-2000,
Lee Kuan Yew (Singapore: Marshall Cavendish Editions,
2000) was referred to for chapters 4 and 7.

Indonesia in ASEAN: Foreign Policy and Regionlism, Dewi
Fortuna Anwar (Singapore: ISEAS Publishing, 2000) was
referred to for Chapter 5.

*Malaya's Secret Police 1945-60: The Role of the Special Branch
in the Malayan Emergency,* Leon Comber (Singapore: ISEAS
Publishing, 2008) was referred to for chapters 4 and 5.

One Hundred Years' History of the Chinese in Singapore, Song
Ong Siang (1984: Oxford University Press, first published in
1902 by John Murray). Specific reference is made in Chapter
3 about the Cheong family, from p.189-190.

*Original Sin? Revising the Revisionist Critique of the 1963
Operation Coldstore in Singapore,* Kumar Ramakrishna
(Singapore: ISEAS Publishing, 2015) was of general reference
in Chapter 5, regarding Operation Coldstore and recent
controversies.

Shades of Grey: A Political Memoir of Modern Indonesia, Jusuf
Wanandi (Singapore: Equinox Publishing, 2012) was referred
to for Chapter 5.

"Singapore and the Vietnam War", Ang Cheng Guan, in
Journal of Southeast Asian Studies (National University of
Singapore & Cambridge University Press, 2009) was referred
to for chapters 5 and 8. In Chapter 7, declassified memoranda
from the Australian and US governments were citied from
Ang's academic article. The same historian's book, *Southeast
Asia's Cold War,* was generally referred to for chapters 5, 7 and 8.

Singapore: The Unexpected Nation, Edwin Lee (Singapore: ISEAS Publishing, 2008) was referred to for chapters 3 and 4.

Spymaster, Martin Pearce (London: Corgi Books, 2016). This biography of the British spy chief Maurice Oldfield, written by his nephew, was referred to for Chapter 5.

The Communist Party of Malaya: The Inside Story, Aloysius Chan (Malaysia: Vinpress, 1994) was of general reference in Chapters 2 to 5. Chan was previously Deputy Director (Operations) of the Malaysian Special Branch. The author's copy is a gift from S R Nathan, soon after the publication of the book.

The Prophetic and the Political: Selected speeches and writings of S. Rajaratnam, Chan Heng Chee and Obaid ul Haq (eds.) (Singapore: Graham Brash, 1987) was referred to for Chapter 7 for the early years of the Ministry of Foreign Affairs, speeches by Minister Rajaratnam, and his assessment of those who shaped the early foreign policy.

The Tiger and the Trojan Horse, Dennis Bloodworth (Singapore: Times Books International, 1986) was referred to for Chapter 4.